W9-CCS-323

ANCESTORS AND RELATIVES

ANCESTORS AND RELATIVES

Genealogy, Identity, and Community

Eviatar Zerubavel

OXFORD
UNIVERSITY PRESS

OXFORD
UNIVERSITY PRESS

Oxford University Press, Inc., publishes works that further
Oxford University's objective of excellence
in research, scholarship, and education.

Oxford New York
Auckland   Cape Town   Dar es Salaam   Hong Kong   Karachi
Kuala Lumpur   Madrid   Melbourne   Mexico City   Nairobi
New Delhi   Shanghai   Taipei   Toronto

With offices in
Argentina   Austria   Brazil   Chile   Czech   Republic France   Greece
Guatemala   Hungary   Italy   Japan   Poland   Portugal   Singapore
South Korea   Switzerland   Thailand   Turkey   Ukraine   Vietnam

Published by Oxford University Press, Inc.
198 Madison Avenue, New York, New York 10016

www.oup.com

Oxford is a registered trademark of Oxford University Press

Library of Congress Cataloging-in-Publication Data
Zerubavel, Eviatar.
Ancestors and relatives : genealogy, identity, and community / Eviatar Zerubavel.
p.   cm.
Includes bibliographical references and index.
ISBN 978-0-19-977395-4 (cloth : alk. paper) 1. Genealogy—Social aspects.
2. Genealogy—Psychological aspects. 3. Genealogy—Political aspects.
4. Families. 5. Kinship. 6. Heredity. I. Title.
CS14.Z47   2011
929′.1—dc22   2011005663

1 3 5 7 9 8 6 4 2

Printed in the United States of America
on acid-free paper

To Yael, Noga, and Noam—
the relatives I have actually chosen

Attai begot Nathan, and Nathan begot Zabad; and Zabad begot Ephlal, and Ephlal begot Obed; and Obed begot Jehu, and Jehu begot Azariah; and Azariah begot Helez, and Helez begot Eleasah; and Eleasah begot Sisamai, and Sisamai begot Shallum; and Shallum begot Jekamiah, and Jekamiah begot Elishama.

—I Chronicles 2:36–41

All living creatures are cousins.

—Richard Dawkins, *The Ancestor's Tale*, 13

CONTENTS

Preface   *xi*

1. The Genealogical Imagination   3
2. Ancestry and Descent   15
    Lineage   16
    Pedigree   23
    Origins   26
3. Co-Descent   31
    Kinship   31
    Community and Identity   46
4. Nature and Culture   53
    Blood   53
    Nature or Culture?   59
    The Rules of Genealogical Lineation   65
    The Rules of Genealogical Delineation   71
5. The Politics of Descent   77
    Stretching   78

Cutting and Pasting 80
Clipping 82
Braiding 84
Lumping 86
Marginalizing 95
Splitting 97
Pruning 101
6. The Genealogy of the Future 105
Genealogical Engineering 105
Integration 106
Segregation 109
Extinction 113
7. The Future of Genealogy 115

Notes 133
Bibliography 183
Author Index 213
Subject Index 221

PREFACE

My fascination with genealogy goes back more than fifty years to the time when, as a ten-year-old boy, I loved reconstructing ancient dynasties. Years later, as a sociologist, I became professionally interested in both time and cognition, the combination of which ultimately led me to write a book, *Time Maps*, about the way we organize the past in our mind. The part of that project that most intrigued me was the chapter "Ancestry and Descent," and four years after completing that book, I indeed found myself gravitating back to that chapter, focusing this time on the way we organize our visions of relatedness. Finally, in June 2007, I started writing *Ancestors and Relatives*.

Several people—family, friends, and colleagues—were kind enough to read early drafts of the manuscript and offer me valuable comments and suggestions. I am particularly grateful in this regard to Yael Zerubavel, Noam Zerubavel, Asia Friedman, Tom DeGloma, Dan Ryan, Catherine Lee, Kathy Gerson, Ruth Simpson, Debby Carr, James Cook, Neha Gondal, Sarah Richardson, Stephen Rutter, Hannah Kwon, John Martin, Ethel Brooks, Phaedra Daipha, and Chris Nippert-Eng. I have also benefited greatly from discussing my ideas with Noga Zerubavel, Arlie Hochschild, Paul DiMaggio, Mara Loveman, Nadia Abu El-Haj, Robin Wagner-Pacifici, Wayne Brekhus, Rachel Brekhus, Kristen Springer, Marlie Wasserman, Jenna Howard, Paul McLean, Viviana Zelizer, Ira Cohen, Allan Horwitz, Cynthia Epstein, Lynn Chancer, Shelley Germana, Katherine Verdery, Alondra Nelson, and Hana Wirth-Nesher. Finally, I wish to thank Ilanit Palmon for her kind help with the graphics.

In the spirit of the book, I dedicate it to my lifetime companion Yael and my children Noga and Noam, the relatives I have actually chosen.

Eviatar Zerubavel
East Brunswick, New Jersey
January 2011

ANCESTORS AND RELATIVES

[1]

THE GENEALOGICAL IMAGINATION

*[R]elationships to ancestors and kin have been the key relationships in
the social structure; they have been the pivots on which most interaction,
most claims and obligations, most loyalties and sentiments, tur[n].*
—Robin Fox, *Kinship and Marriage*, 13

Why do we consider Barack Obama a black man with a white mother
rather than a white man with a black father? What are the implications of knowing, as we now do, that chimpanzees are genetically
closer to humans than they are to gorillas? Why did the Nazis believe
that unions between Germans and Jews would produce Jews rather
than Germans? Are sixth cousins still family?

By the same token, why is it considered more prestigious to be
a tenth-generation than a second-generation American? Why have
white segregationists always found sex between black men and white
women more threatening than between white men and black women?
Why do we tend to exaggerate our differences from the Neanderthals? Why do many people find the proverb "Mules are always boasting that their ancestors were horses" funny? Why do both ethnic
majorities and minorities often oppose intermarriage?

In order to even address, let alone answer, such questions, we
must first examine our unmistakably social visions of genealogical

relatedness. What we need, in other words, is a sociological understanding of ancestry and descent.

As evident from the wide popularity of the television series *Who Do You Think You Are?*[1] and the dozens of websites (such as Ancestry. com, Family Tree DNA, and FamilySearch)[2] and software programs[3] designed to help people construct their family trees and discover hitherto unknown ancestors and relatives, we certainly have a tremendous fascination with genealogy. Every day thousands of "root seekers"[4] comb libraries, cemeteries, and the Internet in an effort to quench their seemingly insatiable "thirst for tracing lineages."[5] Genealogy may indeed be "the second most popular American hobby after gardening and the second most visited category of Web sites after pornography."[6]

Such deep obsession with ancestry ("progonoplexia")[7] is by no means a distinctly modern fad. Indeed, it goes back thousands of years to Hesiod's *Theogony* and the Bible.[8] Nor is it a peculiarly Western phenomenon, as evident from various forms of ancestor worship all over the world. Traditionally aristocratic, however, it is nevertheless becoming increasingly democratized.[9] Over the past several decades, the range of Americans exhibiting interest in genealogy, for example, has clearly expanded "from those claiming descent from the Mayflower or from Southern aristocrats, to include the descendants of African slaves and immigrants."[10]

Our current fascination with genealogy has also been getting a tremendous boost from the growing popularity of genetic ancestry testing. Not only does genetics enhance our awareness of hereditary disease risk[11] as well as the ability to reconstruct national histories[12] and establish paternity, it has also prompted the rise of recreational genomics. Dozens of companies now offer genetic ancestry tests[13] that allow us to measure our genealogical proximity to distant relatives, define ourselves ethnoracially in terms of fractional, seemingly precise amounts of Europeanness, Africanness, and Asianness,[14] as well as trace the Paleolithic ancestor or ancestress from whom we supposedly descend.[15] Indeed, genetics can now essentially "demolish or affirm a family's most cherished beliefs and stories with just a bit of saliva and a cotton swab."[16]

As manifested in identity labels such as "an Italian American" or "a Kennedy," despite the modern meritocratic rise of the self-made individual, who we are still depends at least partly on whom we descend from. Thus, throughout the Muslim world, for example, descendants of the Prophet still bear the honorific title *sayyid* or *sharif*.[17] By the same token, in the United States, a so-called Indian blood quantum formally indicating a person's degree of Indianness in terms of a fractional amount of Native American ancestry still constitutes the official basis for federal recognition as an "Indian" as well as the main criterion of membership in particular Native American tribal nations.[18] This is the context within which a person is officially defined as being "seven thirty-seconds Cherokee, two thirty-seconds Kiowa, and two thirty-seconds Choctaw,"[19] and words like *pureblood*, *mixed-blood*, *full-blood*, and *half-breed* are still commonly used as nounlike identifying labels.

Furthermore, our ancestral background affects not only how others see us but even how we experience ourselves. Indeed, knowing who our ancestors were is fundamental to our sense of who we are.[20] Consider, for example, the way PBS describes its four-part television mini-series *African American Lives 2*:

> Henry Louis Gates, Jr. returns as series host to guide notable African Americans on a search for their ancestry. Genealogical investigations and DNA analysis help Maya Angelou, Don Cheadle, Morgan Freeman, Peter Gomes, Linda Johnson Rice, Tom Joyner, Jackie Joyner-Kersee, Chris Rock and Tina Turner discover where they come from *and who they are*.[21]

Indeed, after undergoing a genetic test to learn more about his African ancestry, a deeply moved Don Cheadle tells Gates: "You start feeling more grounded when you can reach back and go . . . 'This is who I am all the way back.'"[22]

By the same token, given the long history of human migrations, we often feel nostalgic about the long-lost time "when place, identity, culture and ancestry coincided."[23] "Standing on the land that ancestors knew" can thus

> produc[e] a sense of genealogical connection that is sometimes explained . . . as an inexpressible sense of spiritual affinity, and often experienced bodily in "shivers down the spine" and "goosebumps." . . . [It] is often imagined as a shared physical experience that links ancestors to their descendants across time.[24]

That explains diasporas' attachment to their ancestral homelands, as manifested in African Americans' special feelings toward Africa,[25] Jews' deep historical ties to the land of Israel, and the "homecoming" journeys (that is, genealogical or "roots" tourism) of Americans, Canadians, and Australians of Irish and Scottish descent to Ireland and Scotland.[26]

Cheadle's comment about feeling more grounded, of course, also underscores the tragic plight of most American descendants of African slaves, who know so little about their ancestral past.[27] When trying to trace their ancestors, they usually hit a "genealogical brick wall," as their African ancestral lines "[run] into dead ends in that mysteriously dark mausoleum called slavery."[28] No wonder so many African Americans opt to undergo genetic ancestry testing.[29]

Their predicament also resembles that of children of anonymous sperm donors, who have no genealogical context within which to "make sense of themselves."[30] People who experience such "genealogical void"[31] often have serious identity problems,[32] since "our psychological integrity depends very much upon . . . the extent to which we feel linked to our genealogical roots."[33]

Like having no navel, the very embodiment of our genealogical embeddedness,[34] lacking a sense of ancestry is tantamount to being "cast out upon [a] sea of kinless oblivion."[35] That explains why striking a person's name from his or her family's genealogical records used to be one of the most dreaded punishments in China.[36] It also explains the identity crisis often prompted by the realization that one was actually adopted, and the quest of many adoptees to find their "real" parents. Being cut off from their ancestral past, they often experience genealogical "bewilderment" and deprivation[37] leading to the deep sense of existential vacuum captured in the following testimonies:

> I don't feel I know who I am. . . . [T]he fact that you don't know who you are stays with you for life. . . . I still feel I have no identity. I don't think anybody can appreciate it when they have not experienced this vacuum.[38]

> I stand before the mirror and ask, "Who am I?"[39]

As exemplified by a book actually subtitled *A Quest for Wholeness* that portrays children who have been separated from their "natural clan" as having a major part of their identity missing,[40] no wonder adoptees are sometimes considered somehow incomplete.

Yet even children who were not adopted sometimes wonder if they may have been switched mistakenly with someone else at birth, very much like children of anonymous sperm donors who fantasize that their father is a celebrity[41] or people who insist against all evidence that there must be "some Jewish blood" running in their family.[42] Many African Americans likewise fantasize about having "some Indian blood" in their veins, as famously evidenced by Zora Neale Hurston's quip about being "the only Negro in the United States whose grandfather . . . was *not* an Indian chief."[43] As historian

Claudio Saunt explains, "If you are a slave or an African American living in Jim Crow America, who wouldn't want to be associated with someone like Crazy Horse or Geronimo?"[44] And comedian Chris Rock, implicitly invoking the widespread rape of African slaves by their white owners, adds: "It's easier to say 'We got a little Indian in us' than say 'We got raped a few times' . . . It sounds much better. Goes down a lot smoother."[45] It is the tremendous psychological appeal of such "genealogical fantasies" that has arguably made Hans Christian Andersen's little children's story "The Ugly Duckling" such a classic.[46]

New revelations about our ancestors' identity may even change the way we see ourselves.[47] (Such revelations, claims Sarah Jessica Parker, "changed everything about who I thought I was. Everything.")[48] And while they often entail some pleasant surprises,[49] they may also lead to great disappointments, as did the genetic ancestry test that ended Oprah Winfrey's fantasy about her Zulu origins.[50] Some geneticists, in fact, even recommend that persons undergoing such testing be provided with access to identity counseling.[51]

Such "genealogical epiphanies"[52] also affect the way we experience newly revealed "genealogical others." Particularly disorienting in this regard are newly revealed parents and offspring, as so evocatively captured, for example, by Sophocles in *Oedipus the King* and Marcel Pagnol in *Manon of the Springs*. But as one is reminded by the song "Shame and Scandal in the Family," which includes lines such as "You can't marry this girl. I have to say no. This girl is your sister, but your mama don't know" (later rebutted, however, with "Your daddy ain't your daddy, but your daddy don't know"),[53] so, for that matter, are newly revealed siblings. After all, we are genealogically connected not only to our parents and grandparents but also to our siblings and cousins. In fact, the very same ties that connect us to our ancestors also connect us to our relatives, with whom we share them, and the extent to which we are related to those "relatives" is indeed a function of our mutual distance from the common ancestors from whom we co-descend. The more recent those ancestors, the "closer" we are.

Theorizing relatedness in genealogical terms need not be confined, however, strictly to human ties. After all, as Charles Darwin first realized, the entire natural system is actually "founded on descent" and is thereby "genealogical in its arrangement."[54] Genealogical connectedness is, in fact, "the linchpin of evolution," which is "first and foremost a genealogical process."[55]

Indeed, long before we even knew about organic evolution (or about genetics, for that matter), we were already envisioning our genealogical ties to our ancestors as well as relatives in terms of blood, thereby making them seem more natural. As a result, we also tend to regard the essentially genealogical communities that are based on them (families, ethnic groups) as natural, organically delineated communities.

Yet nature is only one component of our genealogical landscape. Culture, too, plays a critical role in the way we theorize as well as measure genealogical relatedness. Not only is the unmistakably social logic of reckoning such relatedness quite distinct from the biological reality it supposedly reflects, it often overrides it, as when certain ancestors obviously count more than others in the way we determine kinship and ethnicity. Relatedness, therefore, is not a biological given but a social construct.

Indeed, it is socially constructed in accordance with certain sociocognitive[56] conventions that affect the way we trace our ancestors, identify our relatives, and delineate the genealogical communities to which we then believe we actually belong. Such conventions are based on particular norms (and are therefore part of specific traditions) of remembering, forgetting, and classifying people as well as other organisms. The major role such conventions, norms, and traditions play in the way we construct genealogies thus calls for a sociology, rather than just a biology, of genealogical relatedness.

Tracing descent, for example, involves certain norms of selective remembrance[57] tacitly embodied in the social conventions underlying the way we spin the threads connecting members of successive generations in our minds—norms that therefore tell us which of our numerous foreparents we actually ought to remember and which ones we can essentially forget. Ancestral ties are thus products of particular social traditions of reckoning genealogical relatedness that basically determine whom we come to regard as our ancestors. Similar social conventions, norms, and traditions of classifying people and other organisms likewise determine whom we come to consider our relatives, thereby also playing a major role in delineating the genealogical communities to which we believe that we organically belong.

Not only are genealogies more than mere reflections of nature, they are also more than mere records of history. Rather than simply passively documenting who our ancestors were, they are the narratives we construct to actually *make* them our ancestors.

As such, they often entail deliberate manipulations as well as actual distortions of the historical realities they supposedly document. By selectively highlighting certain ancestors (and therefore also our ties to other individuals or groups presumably descending from them) while ignoring, downplaying, or even outright suppressing others, for example, we tactically expand and collapse genealogies to accommodate personal as well as collective strategic agendas of inclusion and exclusion. The way we construct genealogies thus tells us as much about the present as it does about the past.

In fact, though usually seen as a retrospective attempt to reconstruct the past, genealogy also plays a major role in our efforts to prospectively shape the future. In the same way that the memory of their common ancestors helps make their co-descendants feel related to one another, the very prospect of sharing common descendants can actually transform even members of hitherto totally separate, unrelated genealogical communities into in-laws. Preventing such a future, however, can also be (and indeed often is) genealogically engineered through segregative policies specifically designed to produce ethnoracially pure communities.

This book is an attempt to uncover the normally taken-for-granted and therefore mostly ignored cognitive underpinnings of genealogy by examining the way we—experts as well as laypersons—envision ancestry, descent, and other forms of relatedness. Strongly believing, as did Charles Horton Cooley, that "the imaginations which people have of one another are the solid facts of society" and that "to interpret [them] must be a chief aim of sociology,"[58] I thus set out to explore here "the genealogical imagination."[59]

Peculiarly human (no other animals have "second cousins once removed"[60] or are aware of having had great-great-great-grandparents), it is such imagination that enables us to envision "ancestors" as well as "relatives." Exploring it will thus reveal the logic by which we actually select from all the individuals from whom we biologically descend the ones we come to remember as our ancestors, and from all our contemporaries to whom we are biologically related the ones we consider our relatives. Examining our personal as well as collective genealogical visions will likewise reveal the unmistakably social manner in which we construct families, nations, races, and other essentially imagined[61] communities in our minds.

My main goal throughout the book is to uncover the general (that is, transcultural as well as transhistorical) principles underlying the way we envision genealogical relatedness. Since the wider the range of the evidence on which one draws, the more generalizable the patterns it reveals, I try to maximize the variety of the specific cultural and historical contexts in which I examine my evidence, thereby drawing on as many such contexts as possible. At the same time, however, I try to detach those general principles from the specific contexts in which I happen to identify them, thus deliberately downplaying the singularity of the various cultural and historical configurations I examine and emphasizing their underlying commonality.[62]

For the same reason, I also try throughout the book to maintain a purposeful indifference to scale, consciously disregarding the particular levels of social aggregation at which those principles happen to manifest themselves.[63] Although conventionally considered distinct from one another, families, ethno-nations, and species are actually all based on the genealogical principle of co-descent. The ties we envision connecting cousins, fellow Norwegians, and penguins, for example, are thus strikingly similar, and the very same logic underlies both family and evolutionary trees. We are essentially dealing here with one and the same principle of genealogical connectivity evidently manifesting itself at many different levels of social aggregation.

The striking similarities among those manifestations, however, have thus far eluded scholarly attention, as evident from the total unawareness that the very same schematic diagram used by an anthropologist to depict lineage segmentation in China, for example, has quite independently also been used by both linguists and molecular biologists to respectively portray the divergence of English from Dutch and humans from chimpanzees.[64] The modern academic compartmentalization of knowledge has evidently kept them from realizing that they were actually all looking at different manifestations of the genealogical principle of co-descent.

To overcome this problem, I deliberately disregard throughout the book the boundaries conventionally separating different disciplinary "fields" and "literatures" from one another and often impeding intellectual cross-fertilization[65] in a conscious effort to highlight the remarkably similar ties we envision connecting us to our siblings, fellow co-ethnics, as well as zebras and baboons. Drawing on work done by sociologists, anthropologists, molecular biologists, geographers, taxonomists, literary scholars, psychologists, linguists, zoologists, philosophers, political scientists, legal scholars, paleontologists, historians, and geneticists, I thus offer an integrated, transdisciplinary perspective on (and therefore hopefully also a more comprehensive understanding of) the world of genealogy.

[2]

ANCESTRY AND DESCENT

Now Jesus ... was the son, so it was thought, of Joseph, the son of Heli, the son of Matthat, the son of Levi, the son of Melki, the son of Jannai, the son of Joseph, the son of Mattathias, the son of Amos, the son of Nahum, the son of Esli, the son of Naggai, the son of Maath, the son of Mattathias, the son of Semein, the son of Josech, the son of Joda, the son of Joanan, the son of Rhesa, the son of Zerubbabel, the son of Shealtiel, the son of Neri, the son of Melki, the son of Addi, the son of Cosam, the son of Elmadam, the son of Er, the son of Joshua, the son of Eliezer, the son of Jorim, the son of Matthat, the son of Levi, the son of Simeon, the son of Judah, the son of Joseph, the son of Jonam, the son of Eliakim, the son of Melea, the son of Menna, the son of Mattatha, the son of Nathan, the son of David, the son of Jesse, the son of Obed, the son of Boaz, the son of Salmon, the son of Nahshon, the son of Amminadab, the son of Ram, the son of Hezron, the son of Perez, the son of Judah, the son of Jacob, the son of Isaac, the son of Abraham, the son of Terah, the son of Nahor, the son of Serug, the son of Reu, the son of Peleg, the son of Eber, the son of Shelah, the son of Cainan, the son of Arphaxad, the son of Shem, the son of Noah, the son of Lamech, the son of Methuselah, the son of Enoch, the son of Jared, the son of Mahalalel, the son of Kenan, the son of Enosh, the son of Seth, the son of Adam, the son of God.

—Luke 3:23–38

To understand how the genealogical imagination works, one first needs to realize that our phenomenal world is socially inhabited not only by our contemporaries but also by our predecessors, who remain present in our minds long after they die.[1] Their symbolic immortality[2] is evident from their ubiquitous presence on banknotes, stamps, and public monuments[3] as well as in the names of streets (Paris's Victor Hugo), airports (Venice's Marco Polo), cities (Washington), and even entire countries (Bolivia).

Of particular genealogical significance, however, are those predecessors whom we also consider our "ancestors." What sets them apart from the others is the notion that we somehow personally "descend" from them.

What exactly are these notions of ancestry and descent? And how do we actually connect ancestors and their descendants in our minds?

LINEAGE

The most elemental ancestral relations are parenthood and filiation, the complementary pair of envisioned social ties that connect parents (mothers, fathers) and their children (sons, daughters) in our minds (such as the parental-filial tie between Robert and Peter in Figure 2.1). Our entire notions of ancestry and descent are but extensions of these elemental ties.

Yet it is the concept (and thus the idea) of grandparenthood that enables us to mentally transcend such strictly dyadic as well as direct forms of ancestry and descent, and also gives ancestry its distinctly human character. Whereas sea turtles, for instance, are not even aware that they have parents, humans are usually aware of not only their parents but also their grandparents.

Such "deeper"[4] ancestral awareness, however, presupposes our ability to perceive those individuals not only as our parents' parents

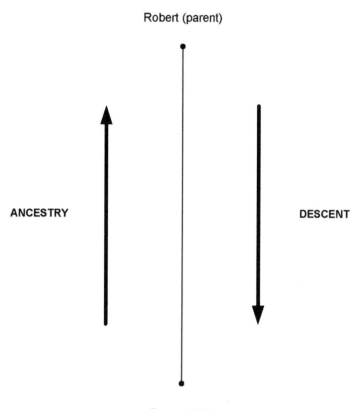

Figure 2.1. Ancestry and Descent.

but also as *our* grandparents, thereby effectively re-envisioning such inherently indirect ancestral ties as direct ones. With a concept like "grandmother," the two parental-filial ties between Margaret and Robert and between Robert and Peter, for example, can thus be mentally compounded into a single, seemingly direct grandparental-grandfilial tie between Margaret and Peter (see Figure 2.2). Rather than experience Margaret only indirectly as "Dad's mother," Peter

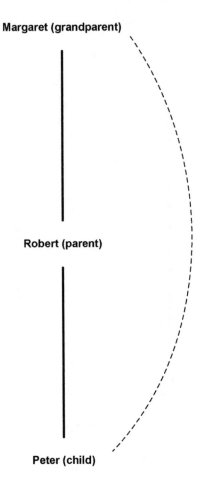

Figure 2.2. Grandparenthood.

can therefore also experience her directly as "Grandma." In addition to the inherently direct ancestral ties between parents and their children, the concept of grandparenthood thus allows us to also envision seemingly direct ancestral ties among members of nonsuccessive generations.

Grandparenthood is an inherently expandable concept. As such, we can extend it even further back and thereby also envision great-grandparents, great-great-grandparents, great-great-great-grandparents, and so on. Furthermore, since the invention of language, our genealogical memory need no longer be confined to, and can therefore also transcend, our personal, firsthand experience of ancestors.[5] Unlike any other animal, we can thus be aware of not only our parents, grandparents, and occasionally great-grandparents who are still alive, but also distant ancestors who had already died long before we were born.

Together, ancestors and their descendants form a "lineage," a dynastic mental structure that, despite its multipersonal makeup, we also envision as a single entity with a single identity.[6] Like the baton successively carried by members of relay teams, the common surname often shared by its members exemplifies our effort to project an aura of genealogical continuity and thereby enhance its perceived unity.[7] We sometimes also try to project such aura by assigning successive members of a lineage the same first name followed by the title *Jr.*[8] or the numerical suffix *III* (or, as in the case of the Rockefellers, even *IV*). Each of those members is thus essentially envisioned as

> the personification of all his forebears and of all his descendants yet unborn. He exists by virtue of his ancestors, and his descendants exist only through him. . . . In short, the individual alive now is the manifestation of his whole Continuum of Descent. His existence as an individual is . . . insignificant beside his existence as the representative of the whole.[9]

The perceived unity of the lineage also explains the tremendous pressure often experienced by its members to preserve the memory of their ancestors as well as to produce future descendants, on the combined existence of which this entire "continuum of descent" ultimately depends. After all, every single one of one's ancestors was effectively indispensable to one's own existence, since one would not have even been born without each and every one of them:

> The absence of any one of the millions of ancestors a man has had would have broken the completeness of the succession and rendered his individual existence impossible. . . . A remote ancestor may be represented by a single drop of blood in the body of his descendant, but its presence is necessary.[10]

By the same token, if any member of a lineage "dies without heir, the whole continuum of ancestors and unborn descendants dies with him."[11]

Various visual metaphors—a river, a thread, a rope[12]—represent various attempts to capture our vision of the lineage as a single continuous entity. A lineage, writes anthropologist Hugh Baker, resembles

> a rope which began somewhere back in the remote past, and which stretches on to the infinite future. The rope at any one time may be thicker or thinner according to the number of strands (families) or fibres (male individuals) which exist, but so long as one fibre remains the rope is there.[13]

Yet as explicitly evidenced by such common expressions as *ancestral line, line of descent, line of succession, line of inheritance,* and *bloodline,* the most common visual metaphor we use to portray our idea of lineage is that of a line. Given the linear manner in which we conventionally represent the flow of time,[14] the line is indeed a perfect metaphor for portraying our vision of the lineage. As a succession of points in space, it perfectly captures the way we envision the latter as a series of successions in time.[15] Even the ancient Romans already used lines to represent the envisioned connectedness of the various ancestors featured in their family trees.[16]

Given their inherently multigenerational makeup, however, we also envision lineages as chains made up of several distinct yet interconnected links.[17] Indeed, the ties among their members very much resemble the ties among members of acquaintance chains,[18] including those between friends of friends or even friends of friends of friends. Effectively constituting diachronic acquaintance chains, lineages thus offer their members a sense of vicarious participation in history "through" their various ancestors.[19] By proxy, they can thus figuratively touch the past.[20]

Membership in lineages thus promotes an almost interpersonal sense of the past. In other words, it promotes a way of experiencing even distant historical events quasi-autobiographically.[21] As geneticist Bryan Sykes describes such experience:

> Until I started this work I always thought of my ancestors . . . as [a] collection of dead people with no solid connection to me. . . . It was interesting enough to read about what "the Cro-Magnons" got up to all those years ago—but nothing much to do with me. But once I had realized, through the genetics, that one of my ancestors was actually there, taking part, it was no longer merely interesting—it is overwhelming.[22]

Such essentially genealogical experience of history presupposes our use of generations as standard units of measuring time. Thus, for example, we usually measure historical distances between members of a given lineage in terms of the number of "degrees of historical separation" (that is, generations) separating them from each other. We likewise measure our distance from various points in history in terms of the number of generations separating us from them, as when we say that the domestication of animals began about four hundred generations ago, or that anatomically modern humans first appeared about five thousand generations ago.[23]

Measuring historical distances in terms of degrees of historical separation rather than years makes them seem considerably shorter, as Stanley Milgram's "small world," famously popularized by John Guare's play *Six Degrees of Separation* and the trivia game "Six Degrees of Kevin Bacon,"[24] takes the form of a "short history." I remember as a child reading Avraham Shalom Friedberg's *Memories of the House of David*,[25] a Micheneresque attempt to portray Jewish history in such dynastic terms, and being thrilled by the idea of being historically situated less than "a hundred-and-fifty persons away" from Jacob, Moses, and David.[26]

The fewer the links constituting the ancestral chain (and the more direct, therefore, each of its members' "contact" with the past), the shorter the historical distance it spans feels to them—a considerable experiential distortion further exaggerated by the fact that intergenerational contact is not confined only to adjacent links in the chain (that is, to members of successive generations). As Don Cheadle explains to Gates:

> My great-grandmother lived to be one hundred and seven years old. . . . And I spent time with her, so that was a real link to the past. I mean, she was just a stone's throw-away from slavery. Just this close—you know? People go "Oh, come on, slavery, it's back then." But it wasn't that far back. I had a personal relationship with somebody who was a generation away from it.[27]

By the same token, it is quite possible that my own great-grandmother, who was born in Russia in 1876 and with whom I talked many times, may have heard from *her* great-grandmother a firsthand account of Napoleon's invasion of Russia in 1812, thereby literally situating me historically just "two conversations away" from a contemporary of

Napoleon (as well as of Beethoven and John Adams, who were both still alive then). In fact, I know someone whose grandfather told her that as a young boy, he once met a ninety-year-old woman who had been married in her youth to a (much older) former valet of King Louis XV of France!

Yet it is not just the number of links in our ancestral chain and the extent to which nonadjacent ones interact with one another that distort our experience of historical distances, but also the actual length of each of those links. The longer it is, the fewer the points of intergenerational contact necessary, and therefore also the shorter the distance spanned by the chain feels. After all, the fact that I may be historically situated only "two conversations away" from a contemporary of John Adams, who was born in 1735, is also a result of the fact that Adams was actually ninety, and my great-grandmother eighty-seven, when they died.

Longer links in ancestral chains also imply fewer necessary intergenerational transitions, and therefore also greater genealogical continuity. Indeed, since men can still father children even when they reach old age, reckoning descent exclusively through the father's line (that is, patrilineally) helps detach the concept "generation" from the far more restrictive biological constraints inherently implied in attaching it to women's reproductive spans,[28] thus involving fewer intergenerational transitions and thereby enhancing continuity within lineages.

PEDIGREE

As exemplified by the traditional practice of formally assigning people patronymics (such as the middle component of the name *Dmitry Anatolyevich Medvedev*, which in Russian literally means "Anatoly Medvedev's son Dmitry"), one of the most important forms of social identity is being someone's descendant. Indeed, around the world, many surnames, one of our major identity tags, have actually evolved from patronymics. Common surnominal prefixes such as the Irish *Fitz-* (as in Fitzgerald, or "Gerald's son"), the Hebrew *Ben-* (as in Ben-David, or "David's son"), the Scottish *Mc-* (as in McManus, or "Magnus's son"), and the Arabic *ibn* (as in ibn Saud, or "Saud's son") are all vestiges of a time when people derived much of their identity from that of their parents. So, for that matter, are common surnominal suffixes such as the Armenian *-ian* (as in Petrosian, or "Petros's son"), the Romanian *-escu* (as in Constantinescu, or "Constantin's son"), the Greek *-ides* (as in Christides, or "Christos's son"), the Spanish *-ez* (as in Rodriguez, or "Rodrigo's son"), the Turkish *-oğlu* (as in Muradoğlu, or "Murad's son"), the Polish *-wicz* (as in Tomaszewicz, or "Tomasz's son"), the Persian *-zadeh* (as in Mehdizadeh, or "Mehdi's son"), the Danish *-sen* (as in Nielsen, or "Niels's son"), and the Georgian *-dze* (as in Alexidze, or "Alexi's son"). Indeed, in Iceland (where a name like Björk Guðmundsdóttir literally means "Guðmundur's daughter Björk"), surnames actually *are* nothing but patronymics.

Ancestry and descent play a critical role in the way we structure the intergenerational transmission of both material[29] and symbolic forms of capital. We thus inherit not only our ancestors' property but also their social status and reputation.

Indeed, one of the main functions of genealogies is to solidify, let alone enhance, our social standing.[30] As part of our traditionalist reverence for the past, we draw on our ancestors as principal sources of "genealogical capital" socially bestowed on us by the very fact that we figuratively descend from them, in a top-down manner reflecting the traditionalist belief that lineages degenerate the farther one moves away from their founding ancestors.[31] Such retrograde vision is iconically embodied in the way we actually visualize the flow of genealogical time,[32] as manifested in the downward orientation of the lines conventionally representing descent on our genealogical charts.

As so explicitly exemplified by hereditary organizations such as the General Society of Mayflower Descendants and the Daughters of the American Revolution,[33] let alone the Indonesian "genealogical passports" documenting the ancestral histories of descendants of the Prophet Mohammed,[34] we basically use pedigrees to establish descendants' genealogical credentials and therefore legitimacy. That explains Matthew's and Luke's efforts to produce genealogies effectively portraying Jesus as a descendant of David (and thus as the long-awaited Messiah)[35] as well as attempts made by die-hard monarchists to stubbornly preserve royal lines of pretenders to long-gone thrones. It also explains the considerable efforts made by rulers throughout history to produce politically compelling narratives of descent[36] as well as rebuke the ones sometimes made by their enemies to challenge their claimed genealogical credentials.[37]

But deriving one's identity from those of one's ancestors is a double-edged sword. The targeting of innocent children in tribal blood feuds shows that we inherit not only our ancestors' assets but also the liabilities associated with being their descendants. Only a "guilt by genealogical association" kind of reasoning can explain the social stigma still attached today, for example, to "contaminative" descent from the British convicts who settled Australia two centuries ago.[38]

The eighteen-generation fictional ancestral chain symbolically linking Jews' traditional archenemies Amalek and Haman[39] constitutes a classic example of a "negative pedigree." The actual logic underlying such pedigrees is explicitly articulated in God's vow to punish not only sinners but also their children and "children's children, unto the third and unto the fourth generation."[40] The same logic, ironically, was later also used by the Spanish Inquisition to promote its vision of intergenerationally transmitted moral stains during its infamous campaign to rid Spain of permanently "stained" lineages of suspected crypto-Jews.[41]

ORIGINS

As exemplified by the following twenty-three-generation biblical genealogy, the lineages we manage to construct in our minds can be quite deep:

> Heman the singer, the son of Joel, the son of Samuel; the son of Elkanah, the son of Jeroham, the son of Eliel, the son of Toah; the son of Zuph, the son of Elkanah, the son of Mahath, the son of Amasai; the son of Elkanah, the son of Joel, the son of Azariah, the son of Zephaniah; the son of Tahath, the son of Assir, the son of Ebiasaph, the son of Korah; the son of Izhar, the son of Kohath, the son of Levi, the son of Israel.[42]

In fact, in Iceland, some lineages are actually traced back to the ninth century,[43] yet even they dwarf in comparison to the seventy-seven-generation pedigree of Jesus according to Luke[44] or the 2,500-year-deep lineages envisioned by people who claim to be the seventy-seventh descendants of Confucius.[45]

As a matter of fact, by having developed the inherently expandable concept of grandparenthood, we have also indefinitely expanded the concept "ancestor" to include not only parents and grandparents but also great-grandparents, great-great-grandparents, great-great-great-grandparents, and so on ad infinitum.[46] By continually compounding the elemental ancestral tie of parenthood, we can thus effectively envision "as long and complicated [ancestral links] as we wish."[47] Indeed, there is actually nothing stopping us from tracing our descent back to ancestors who lived thousands and even millions of generations ago.[48] Our genealogical memory, in other words, is, at least in theory, essentially boundless.

Yet the actual extent of how deep we now think it can reach would have been practically inconceivable only two centuries ago. As late as the 1850s, even scholars, essentially basing their calculations on the Bible, viewed the entire human history as less than six thousand years (that is, only a couple of hundred generations) long. Even the great eighteenth-century natural historian Georges Buffon, who did venture to reckon the age of the earth and even animal history in much longer terms than those allowed by the Scriptures,[49] evidently stopped short of extending his groundbreaking chronological claims to human history as well.[50] Our extreme recency compared to all other animals, argues paleoanthropologist Donald Grayson, clearly helped underscore human distinctness:

> [T]he appearance of humankind on earth represented a distinct break with the rest of the animal kingdom, a special event in earth history. . . . [T]he more recent people were, the more discontinuous their arrival would seem and the less they would have in common with other animals.[51]

It was our increasingly evident ethnoracial physical diversity that first led eighteenth-century scholars such as Benoît de Maillet and Voltaire to doubt whether a couple of hundred generations of human history actually allowed enough time to explain it.[52] Yet it was ultimately archaeology that "revolutionized the concept of [our] past and created for [us] a previously unbelievable antiquity,"[53] thus igniting one of the most important intellectual revolutions of the modern age.[54]

Throughout the early nineteenth century, various findings of human bones and stone implements in the same geological strata with remains of extinct mammals, first reported in the 1770s, prompted many speculations about the possible contemporaneity of ancient humans and prehistoric animals, leading archaeologist Jacques Boucher de Perthes to actually date the beginning of human history hundreds of thousands of years ago.[55] Such evidence, however, clearly challenged Scriptural chronology and was therefore explained away or ignored[56] until 1859, when even the preeminent geologist Charles Lyell felt compelled to admit that humans were "old enough to have co-existed . . . with the Siberian mammoth"[57]—an implicit critique of biblical chronology that he developed more fully four years later in *The Geological Evidences of the Antiquity of Man*.[58] Such a hitherto blasphemous "deep historical"[59] vision was soon also embraced by the great comparative anatomist Thomas Huxley:

> Where, then, must we look for primaeval Man? Was the oldest *Homo sapiens* Pliocene or Miocene, or yet more ancient? In still older strata do the fossilized bones of . . . a Man more pithecoid than any yet known await the researches of some unborn paleontologist? Time will show. But, in the meanwhile . . . we must extend by long epochs the most liberal estimate that has yet been made of the antiquity of Man.[60]

Such a "radical change of outlook" on our origins[61] effectively expanded our genealogical horizons far beyond the couple of hundred generations traditionally allowed by Scriptural chronology. Such "revolution in ethnological time," notes historian Thomas Trautmann, has involved nothing less than the practical collapse

> of the short chronology for human history based on the biblical narrative, a chronology in which the whole of human history had been crowded into the space of a few thousand years. . . . What replaced it was an ethnological time that extended human

history indefinitely backward, for tens or hundreds of thousands of years, or more. Very suddenly the bottom dropped out of history and its beginnings disappeared into an abyss of time.[62]

In fact, with the exception of fundamentalist creationists who have yet to give up their much shorter biblical view of human history,[63] we now trace our ancestors back to primitive microorganisms that lived more than three billion years ago.[64] But before we could do that, another major intellectual paradigm shift had to occur first, namely the realization that we are actually genealogically connected not only to thousands of generations of earlier human beings, but also to millions of generations of even earlier nonhuman organisms!

Although scholars had long accepted the philosophical principles of plenitude, continuity, and linear gradation implied in the neo-Platonist concept of "the Great Chain of Being,"[65] only two centuries ago did they first envision our connectedness to nonhuman organisms in the form of an actual historical[66] (and therefore also genealogical) sequence. Only then, in other words, did we first envision ourselves as part of an interspecific (and therefore historically even deeper) lineage.

The idea that species can, over time, undergo transmutation and evolve into other species was first contemplated in the eighteenth century by Buffon and later also by Bernard Lacépède and Jean-Claude Delamétherie.[67] Yet by specifically highlighting the gradual (that is, intergenerational) nature of such transformations,[68] it was the great botanist and zoologist Jean-Baptiste Lamarck who deserves the credit for our modern realization that different species are nevertheless genealogically connected.

In his 1809 book *Zoological Philosophy*, Lamarck explicitly laid out his revolutionary vision of phyletic series of species literally transmuting into one another. "After a long succession of generations," he proposed, "individuals originally belonging to one species" may thus be "transformed into new species."[69] Then, implicitly envisioning in great detail human evolution specifically, he famously added:

> [I]f some race of quadrumanous animals . . . were to lose . . . the habit of climbing trees and grasping the branches with its feet in the same way as with its hands . . . and if the individuals of this race were forced for a series of generations to use their feet only for walking, and to give up using their hands like feet . . . these quadrumanous animals would at length be transformed into bimanous. . . . Furthermore, if [they] were impelled by the desire to command a large and distant view, and hence endeavoured to stand upright, and continually adopted that habit from generation to generation . . . their feet would gradually acquire a shape suitable for supporting them in an erect attitude.[70]

As the first person ever to have had the "courage to include man in the evolutionary stream,"[71] Lamarck thus sowed the first seeds of the modern vision of our inherent genealogical embeddedness in the rest of nature.

[3]

CO-DESCENT

Two blood relatives are "related" by the fact that they share in some degree the stuff of a particular heredity. . . . Their kinship consists in this common possession [and depends] on the fact that each has some of the heredity that the other has and both got theirs from a single source.
—David Schneider, *American Kinship,* 24

Being genealogically related, however, involves not only lineal ties to our ancestors but also collateral ties to our relatives.[1] Yet the very same ties that connect us to our ancestors actually also connect us to our relatives.

KINSHIP

Thus far we have basically been trying to peek through a rather narrow crack in the curtain at the social drama surrounding genealogical relatedness. As a result, we have actually managed to see only a very narrow section of the proverbial stage on which it unfolds. It is now time to open the curtain all the way and get a full view of this stage.

We have thus far discussed ancestry and descent only in terms of the crude biblical "begat model"[2] whereby "Attai begot Nathan, and Nathan begot Zabad; and Zabad begot Ephlal," and so on.[3] While ideal for establishing royal dynasties,[4] however, such a narrow view of relatedness might implicitly suggest that each of the members of a lineage is an only child, which is often not the case. The genealogical landscape thus far portrayed here is therefore inherently incomplete, since it presupposes a one-dimensional "genealogical tunnel vision"[5] that cannot possibly ever capture the multidimensional nature of relatedness.

The contrast between the essentially one-dimensional mental structure depicted in Figure 2.2 and the two-dimensional one portrayed in Figure 3.1 is striking. As quite evident from the latter, the ancestral (parental, filial, grandparental, and grandfilial) ties between Margaret, Robert, and Peter depicted in Figure 2.2 are actually part of a wider network of genealogical ties which that figure practically ignores. In a somewhat similar vein, note also the essentially multilinear[6] nature of human evolution. Our current status as the only extant human species, after all, is a relatively recent historical anomaly, since we were actually sharing this planet with various other human species that coexisted alongside us as recently as eighteen thousand years ago.[7]

While unilinear genealogical narratives such as the one portrayed in Figure 2.2 certainly capture the "vertical" (that is, lineal) ties between grandparents (Margaret), parents (Robert), and children (Peter), they cannot possibly capture the "horizontal" (that is, collateral) ties between siblings (Karen, Robert, Nancy, and Philip) or cousins (Richard, Peter, Susan, and Henry) or, for that matter, the "diagonal"[8] ones between uncles (Robert) and their nephews (Richard, Henry) or nieces (Susan). (Note, however, that the horizontality implied in Figure 3.1 is graphically exaggerated, since both siblings and cousins are only roughly "contemporaries." Richard, for example,

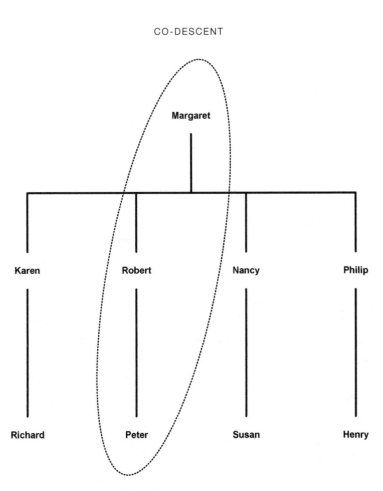

Figure 3.1. Lineal and Collateral Ties.

may in fact be much closer in age to his uncle Philip, who is conventionally placed in a different generation, than to his own younger brother Henry.) Thus, while metaphors such as the line and the chain clearly help us visualize dynastic lineages, they cannot really offer us a full, multidimensional view of genealogical relatedness. We therefore need another metaphor that can accommodate multilinear genealogical narratives and thereby help us visualize more than just ancestral ties.

An ideal choice for such a metaphor, the tree indeed constitutes the most common form of visualizing genealogical ties.[9] Using the tree metaphor implies a multidimensional view of genealogical systems that have depth as well as breadth. As such, the family tree (or its more abstract modern offspring, the genealogical chart) helps us visualize both lineal and collateral ties. It thus represents a virtual family reunion.

Yet the tree's effectiveness as a genealogical metaphor also stems from the fact that it evokes a vivid image of a trunk that represents the idea of a common origin. Arborescent imagery thus helps us visualize a particular form of relatedness essentially based on the notion of "co-descent."

Social solidarity presupposes a certain sense of commonality,[10] and one of the most elemental forms of social commonality is the image of two or more individuals jointly descending from a common ancestor. As we can see in Figure 3.2, the ties connecting Peter and Henry to their grandmother Margaret indirectly also connect them to each other as cousins.[11] We are thus genealogically connected to others not only as ancestors and descendants but also as "co-descendants."[12]

It is basically common ancestors, therefore, that provide the sense of kinship. Like the keystone of an arch that helps lock all its other parts in place, they are the social cement holding their descendants together long after they die. If they are ever forgotten, those descendants might no longer feel related to one another! Ancestor worship,[13] in short, thus helps foster the relations not only between the living and the dead but also among the living:

> If we think of descent as a tree with the founding ancestor as the trunk . . . we can also visualise the disastrous effect on that tree when the trunk died—the branches would all fall apart as there was nothing left to hold them together. If the tree were to be kept

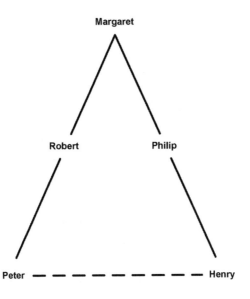

Figure 3.2. Co-Descent.

whole, a way of preserving the trunk had to be found: and this in effect is what ancestor worship did, it preserved the founding ancestor without whom there was no connection between the various lines of his descendants.[14]

The most elemental social tie based on co-descent is sibling-hood, genealogically connecting individuals descending from the same parent (in the case of half-siblings) or parents. It also consti-tutes the foundational template on which virtually any other collat-eral genealogical tie is modeled. In the same way that all forms of ancestry (such as both grandparenthood and great-great-great-great-grandparenthood) are but extensions of parenthood, all forms of co-descent are ultimately extensions of siblinghood.

As evident from the fact that the word for "cousin" is actually derived in various languages (such as Russian, Tamil, Hawaiian, and

Japanese) from the word for "brother" or "sister,"[15] that is certainly true of cousinhood. Whereas siblings are individuals who descend from the same parents, cousins are nonsiblings who descend from the same grandparents. By the same token, second cousins are individuals who do not share their parents or grandparents yet who do share their great-grandparents, whereas third cousins are individuals who do not share their parents, grandparents, or even great-grandparents yet who nevertheless do share their great-great-grandparents. (By compounding the extensions of both parenthood and siblinghood, we likewise construct even more complex forms of genealogical relatedness, such as when one regards one's grandmother's second cousin as one's own second cousin, twice removed.)

As evident from the fact that both the Latin (*propinquus*) and Hebrew (*qarov*) words for "relative" derive from the word for "near," we usually reckon degrees of kinship in terms of genealogical distance.[16] The difference between a sister and a second cousin is thus a matter of proximity, as the former is perceived as closer to oneself than the latter. The conventional distinction we make between "close" and "distant" relatives perfectly captures such genealogical topology, as did the medieval tree-like consanguinity tables designed by the Church to prevent incestual transgressions by marrying "too close" relatives.[17]

In the same way that we measure vertical genealogical distances in terms of the number of generations separating ancestors from their descendants, we also measure horizontal ones in terms of the number of generations separating co-descendants from their most recent common ancestor.[18] The distance between me and my second cousin is therefore three "degrees of genealogical separation" because we need to go back three generations to reach our most recent common ancestor (our great-grandmother).

The reason that the distance between me and my second cousin is exactly the same as the distance separating me from my great-grandmother is that, although the two represent altogether different dimensions of genealogical systems,[19] they are nevertheless highly interdependent. (Indeed, it is our distinctly human ability to envision grandparents, great-grandparents, and great-great-grandparents that actually allows us to also envision cousins, second cousins, and third cousins! While many other organisms have distinctive visual markings, auditory calls, or odors that allow kin recognition,[20] none of them can envision great-great-grandparents and therefore also third cousins.) Genealogies, after all, are two-dimensional mental structures whose breadth is directly proportional to their depth.[21] As we can see in Figure 3.3, genealogical distances between co-descendants are therefore a function of the ancestral depth of their relationship as measured in terms of the number of generations separating them from their most recent common ancestor. The more recent their common ancestor, the genealogically "closer" they are. We thus consider B closer to A than C because she shares with him a more recent common ancestor than he does with C.

The genealogical distance between co-descendants progressively increases with each reproductive step away from their common ancestor. As we can see in Figure 3.4, sisters are considered closer relatives than second cousins because we need to go back only one generation (to our parents) rather than three (to our great-grandparents) in order to reach the most recent common ancestor we share.

Using ascending numbers ("second cousin," "third cousin," "fourth cousin," and so on), we can effectively extend our notion of cousinhood to apply to virtually anybody with whom we share a common ancestor. Although our actual ability to identify our relatives clearly fades the further back we go in search of such ancestors (so that we rarely know, for example, who our third, let alone sixth, cousins are),[22] at least in theory we can identify more distant relatives as we trace our descent back to more distant ancestors.[23]

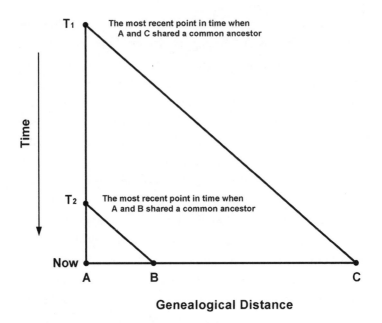

Figure 3.3. Genealogical Distance.

Indeed, since, as we have seen, there is practically nothing stopping us from tracing our descent back to ancestors who lived thousands and even millions of generations ago, we can actually extend our notion of cousinhood indefinitely.[24] In other words, since our search for common ancestors is effectively boundless, so is the concept of cousinhood, which means that "the family of man"[25] and "human brotherhood" are more than just metaphors since basically *we are all cousins.*[26]

In fact, "all living creatures are cousins,"[27] since millions of generations ago humans', pigs', and spiders' ancestors were one and the same individuals! We are actually related to every other living organism because we basically all descend from a loosely knit cluster of cells commonly known as the Last Universal Common Ancestor

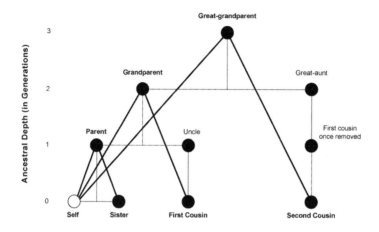

Figure 3.4. Ancestral Depth and Genealogical Distance.

(LUCA) that lived more than three billion years ago.[28] One can thus depict all living organisms on a single family tree (the so-called Tree of Life).

The idea that all organisms have a single origin and are thus genealogically interconnected was first introduced by Charles Darwin in 1859 in *The Origin of Species*.[29] All forms of life have a common ancestor (that is, are monophyletic), claimed Darwin, and are therefore "cousins to the . . . millionth degree."[30]

Common descent is arguably the most important concept in Darwin's theory of evolution.[31] Aptly dubbed "the theory of descent,"[32] the theory adds a critical genealogical dimension to the way we view nature. "The natural system is founded on descent," it famously asserts, and is therefore ultimately "genealogical in its arrangement."[33]

Darwin's theory of evolution is quite different from Lamarck's in that it basically revolves around the notion of diversification rather than transformation.[34] As such, it marked the significant move away from Lamarck's inherently unilinear anagenetic model[35] to the essentially multilinear cladogenetic model of evolution. (The latter's seeds, however, were sown as early as 1750 in botanist Vitaliano Donati's call to replace the unilinear vision of nature implicit in the notion of the "Great Chain of Being" with a pronouncedly two-dimensional one,[36] and even Buffon and Lamarck had already used two-dimensional diagrams to portray the relations among different breeds of dogs as well as between mammals and reptiles or birds.)[37] According to this model, organic populations increasingly diverge until certain parts of them can no longer interbreed and may thus branch off into separate species.[38] Speciation is therefore ultimately a process of genealogical divergence, of organic lineages literally splitting off from one another: "In cladogenesis, new lineages evolve through the splitting of an ancestor."[39]

It was zoologist Ernst Haeckel who in 1866 made the first attempt to reconstruct actual genealogies of organisms, or phylogenies, as he famously called them. And in the process of doing so, explicitly underscoring the arborescent nature of organic evolution,[40] he also introduced the zoological equivalent of the family tree, namely the phylogenetic or evolutionary tree, which has in fact become our standard form of depicting evolutionary processes.[41] Yet in effectively replacing the image of the "ladder of nature" (*scala naturae*) traditionally associated with the "Great Chain of Being" with that of a tree,[42] Haeckel was actually echoing Darwin, who, having explicitly noted that the genealogical affinity of all forms of life can be effectively "represented by a great tree," fully embraced such arborescent imagery:

> The green and budding twigs may represent existing species; and those produced during each former year may represent the long succession of extinct species.... [T]his connexion of the former and present buds by ramifying branches may well represent the classification of all extinct and living species....[43]

In fact, the only actual illustration made by Darwin in *The Origin of Species* is that of a diagrammatic tree.[44]

As a visual metaphor, the tree is the ultimate manifestation of a "cladistic" view of nature that, as etymologically evident (*klados* being the Greek word for "branch"), highlights the patterns of ramification underlying the process of organic evolution, "the peculiar branching character of the evolutionary chronicle."[45] Literally incorporating series of successive bifurcations,[46] trees visually capture the overall branching pattern of phylogeny quite evocatively. As graphic embodiments of Darwin's pronouncedly multilinear vision of organic evolution, tree diagrams thus help us visualize the way organisms are genealogically related to one another.[47] In depicting evolutionary history as a series of successive genealogical splits, the phylogenetic tree (or its diagrammatic offspring, the cladogram) is thus to species what a family tree is to individuals.[48]

Essentially depicting series of historical branching events in the actual order in which they occurred, both phylogenetic trees and cladograms help us visualize genealogical narratives of evolutionary history. In so doing, they visually underscore the fact that genealogical proximity, most typically defined in terms of biological affinity, is directly proportional to, thereby also reflecting, recency of common ancestry.

Biologists have traditionally measured biological affinity in terms of structural resemblance. Since Darwin, however, they view such affinity as the result of descent from a common ancestor, and have therefore been focusing specifically on homologous rather than mere homoplastic resemblance. Whereas homoplasy involves superficially similar observable (phenotypic) features that evolve independently of each other, thereby reflecting merely analogous, parallel patterns of adapting to similar environmental conditions (bird and butterfly wings, frogs' and beavers' webbed feet),[49] homologous features (such as human and dolphins' spinal cords) resemble each other because they have actually been inherited from a common ancestor.[50] Only true homologies, of course, are thus phylogenetically (and therefore genealogically) relevant.[51]

As we move from mere analogy to true homology, which reflects common ancestry, we can in fact measure the genealogical distance between organisms by how much they actually resemble each other. The more homologous features they share, the closer they are genealogically.

Yet even while shifting their focus from mere analogy to true homology, for more than a century after Darwin, biologists continued to measure genealogical distances between organisms in terms of structural resemblance. Today, however, they do so increasingly based on genetic evidence.

As genes are passed on from one generation to the next, certain changes in their chemical structure (that is, mutations) occasionally occur that are then passed on to subsequent generations, thereby altering the genetic makeup of an entire lineage. By producing a permanent genealogical split between those individuals who carry it and pass the mutant gene on to their descendants and those who do not, each such mutation therefore creates "a fork on the family tree."[52]

The mutations organisms inherit from their ancestors thus constitute distinctive genetic markers that, like "badges of descent,"[53] allow us to trace lineages back to when they actually occurred and therefore to the most recent common ancestor of all the individuals who carry the marker.[54] Such tracing is often done through the parts of the organism's genome that are passed down intact from mother to child (mitochondrial DNA, which both sons and daughters inherit yet only the latter transmit to their own progeny) or from father to son (Y-chromosomal DNA). (One's mitochondrial DNA is therefore a copy of one's mother's, her mother's, and so on. By the same token, when one carries a certain mutation in one's Y chromosome, all of one's male descendants, and only they, also carry it.) By examining the genetic makeup of individuals' Y-chromosomal or mitochondrial DNA, we can thus follow a "genetic trail"[55] that allows us to reconstruct their maternal or paternal ancestral lineages. And since both parts of the organism's genome are passed down intact from parent to offspring, a great deal of genetic ancestry testing is indeed based on them.

The more closely related we are, the more similar our genetic makeup, the proportion of genes we share thus reflecting the degree of our genealogical affinity.[56] Our closest relatives are therefore our siblings, since our genomes had only one generation in which to accumulate distinct mutations. Next are our first cousins (two generations), second cousins (three generations), third cousins (four generations), and so on.

By the same token, since genetic (like any other form of biological) affinity is directly proportional to the amount of time that has passed since two groups of organisms shared a common ancestor, we can actually measure genealogical distances not only between individuals but also between entire populations in terms of the amount of genetic change they have undergone since diverging from each other. The earlier two populations split from their common ancestor, the greater the likelihood that each of their members carries certain genetic markers that none of the other's members do.[57] Greater genetic distance between populations thus reflects a longer time since they actually diverged from each other, whereas genetic proximity is the result of having split off from a common ancestor relatively recently and not having had enough time yet to undergo significant differentiation. The more genetically similar two populations are, the more recently they must have therefore split off from each other.

Genetic affinity is thus a measure of "evolutionary kinship."[58] The more similar populations are genetically, the closer they are phylogenetically. As we can see in Figure 3.5, being genetically closer to apes than to frogs means that we must have split off from the former more recently than from the latter.[59]

This was precisely the line of argument used in the early 1960s by Emile Zuckerkandl and Linus Pauling to propose that we actually use

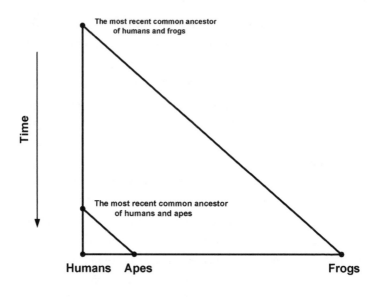

Figure 3.5. Time and Genetic Distance.

molecular evidence to time phylogenetic divergence,[60] that "the chemi-cals of which plants and animals are composed might provide 'clocks' by which to measure genetic distances and to date times of evolu-tionary divergence."[61] And indeed, using such a "molecular clock," we now measure genealogical distances between populations by com-paring their genetic makeup and thereby calculating the amount of time that must have passed since they diverged from each other.[62]

Essentially viewing our DNA as a "molecular parchment on which an account of our species has been written,"[63] geneticists and molecular anthropologists thus try to reconstruct human history by identifying the historical points at which particular genetically rec-ognizable ancestral populations ("haplogroups") sharing particular clusters of genetic markers ("haplotypes") actually split off from each other. By comparing the genetic makeups of region-specific populations such as Central Asians and Native Americans or East Asians and Polynesians, for example, they thus claim to establish when they, in fact, diverged from each other.[64]

Long maintained by biblical tradition, the "monogenist" narrative whereby all humans descend from a common ancestor is now supported by genetic evidence as well.[65] We are by and large a genetically homogeneous species, and most of our genes are essentially identical to those of any other human being. Sicilians and Koreans, for example, have thus much more in common with each other genetically than do some neighboring populations of gorillas or chimpanzees,[66] and the seemingly obvious differences between them involve only skin-deep phenotypic variations that have little genetic significance.[67] "[B]eneath the separate hues of our skins, our various types of hair, and our disparate physiques, our basic biological constitutions are fairly unvarying."[68]

The reason for such remarkably small genetic variation is that even seemingly major "racial" differences in skin color, eye shape, and hair texture are the result of relatively recent environmental adaptations. Genetic diversity, after all, is a function of time, and our genetic commonality attests to our recent common origins. It was relatively recent migrations "that produced the distinct 'racial' morphologies we see in modern humans—not hundreds of thousands of years of separate evolution."[69]

As a growing body of genetic evidence seems to suggest, all modern humans descend from common ancestors who actually lived less than 200,000 years ago,[70] and our differentiation into seemingly distinct region-specific "races" is therefore quite recent. (The genealogical split between Asians and Europeans, for example, occurred less than two thousand generations ago.)[71] That, of course, implicitly makes modern-day Nigerians, Romanians, Samoans, and Panamanians not-so-distant cousins:

The progeny of the people who found Australia 50,000 years ago, and the descendants of the tribes who poured down the Americas 12,000 years ago, as well as the heirs to all those other settlers of Europe, Africa, and Asia . . . are all the children of those Africans who emerged from their homeland only a few ticks ago on our evolutionary clock. They may have . . . developed superficial variations, but underneath our species has scarcely differentiated at all.[72]

Indeed, genetically speaking, we are all almost literally "brothers and sisters."[73]

COMMUNITY AND IDENTITY

Not only does our genealogical vision of co-descent help connect in our minds various "relatives" (from siblings, through second cousins, to any other human beings) as individuals, it also seems to provide the mental cement necessary for constructing actual communities. In other words, it also constitutes a formidable basis for group formation.

The most elemental such "genealogical community" is the one within which our very notions of parenthood, filiation, and sibling-hood actually emerge, namely the family. And as implied in the term *extended family*, we also extend our vision of this community far beyond its basic "nuclear" form. Indeed, the family is the prototypical social group on which larger genealogical communities often model themselves using parenthood, filiation, and siblinghood as foundational templates of social connectedness.

When such communities are only a few generations deep (such as the ones that occasionally gather for "family" reunions),[74] members can usually specify exactly how they are related, but in ones that

go back deeper, visions of common origins often become quite vague. Yet even in such clans, as they are commonly known,[75] all members claim descent from a certain common ("founding," "ultimate," "apical") ancestor that in a way personifies the clan's origins,[76] and clan-based communities (the Somali, the Uzbeks, "the children of Israel") are, in fact, sometimes even named after (thereby effectively deriving their collective identity from) them.[77]

Essentially based on rather vague and often merely putative genealogical ties among their members, most genealogical communities are but extensions of the clan or the group of clans we call a "tribe." The most common such communities are "ethnic" groups, fundamentally past-oriented[78] communities whose members claim common descent despite the fact that it is very often only presumed.[79] Pronouncedly tribal, ethnic sentiments are basically "of the same nature as those encountered between kin, albeit typically . . . more diluted."[80]

Ethnicity also takes the form of peoplehood or nationhood,[81] their envisioned descent from a common ancestor being the foremost image binding the ethnic nation's members together as well as separating them from everyone else.[82] Whereas in predominantly civic nations like France or the United States group membership in the form of citizenship is based on where one was born, in ethnonations such as Japan or Israel it is essentially determined by descent.[83]

In fact, claims sociologist Anthony Smith, "[T]here can be no real 'nation' without its tacit myth of origins and descent, which defines [its] fictive kinship basis . . . and explains [its] network of affective ties and sentiments."[84] That explains the efforts made by many nations to highlight their genealogical foundations and portray their members as co-descending from some common ancestor even when the actual historical evidence for that is rather slim. It also accounts for ethno-nations' self-image as extended families,[85] as so evocatively encapsulated in metaphors like "patriotism," "motherland," "Founding Fathers," and "sons of the nation."

Although they are conventionally viewed as quite distinct from each other, the difference between families and ethno-nations is only a matter of scale. Nationalism, after all, is "a kind of ancestor worship . . . in which national heroes occupy the place of clan elders in defining a nation as a noble lineage."[86] That certainly underscores the tremendous advantage of using a more generic concept like "genealogical community,"[87] which becomes even more pronounced once we realize that even species are mentally clustered based on co-descent, and that the same fundamentally cladistic vision actually underlies both family and evolutionary trees.

The first one to view species as "communities of descent" was Darwin.[88] Unlike earlier taxonomists, who basically grouped organisms according to phenotypic resemblance, he claimed that "all true classification is genealogical" and that "community of descent is the hidden bond which naturalists have been unconsciously seeking, and not . . . the mere putting together and separating objects more or less alike."[89] In other words, he argued, biological taxonomies ought to reflect genealogical realities, and the way taxonomic groups, or taxa, are arranged "must be strictly genealogical in order to be natural":[90]

> Classifications may, of course, be based on any character whatever, as on size, color, or the element inhabited; but naturalists have long felt a profound conviction that there is a natural system. This system, it is now generally admitted, must be, as far as possible, genealogical in arrangement,—that is the co-descendants of the same form must be kept together in one group, apart from the co-descendants of any other form; but if the parent-forms are related, so will be their descendants, and the two groups together will form a larger group. The amount of difference between the several groups—that is the amount of modification which each has undergone—is expressed by such terms as genera, families, orders, and classes.[91]

And indeed, since Darwin, biological taxonomy essentially mirrors the way we envision the phylogenetic history of organic evolution. Taxa are thus viewed primarily as genealogical entities, and systematists basically classify organisms in a way that reflects their presumed genealogical relations to one another.[92]

Such a pronouncedly genealogical approach to biological classification is epitomized by the cladistic or phylogenetic school of systematics,[93] according to whose proponents different organisms should essentially be grouped together only if they share a more recent common ancestor than either of them shares with another organism.[94] Cladists, in other words, basically group organisms "in branching hierarchies defined only by relative times of genealogical connection. Closest, or 'sister-group,' pairs share a unique historical connection: a common ancestor yielding them as its only descendants."[95]

Organisms, in other words, are thus grouped by cladists based on their genealogical proximity as measured in terms of recency of common ancestry. According to Willi Hennig, the founder of cladistics,

The hierarchic system used in phylogenetic systematics is composed of monophyletic groups . . . subordinated to one another according to the temporal distance between their origins and the present; the sequence of subordination corresponds to the "recency of common ancestry" of the species making up each of the monophyletic groups.[96]

Thus, to quote evolutionary biologist Richard Dawkins,

[T]he ultimate criterion for grouping organisms together is closeness of cousinship or, in other words, relative recency of common ancestry. . . . Closely related animals are animals that

share a recent common ancestor. More distantly related animals share an earlier common ancestor. Very distantly related
animals . . . share a very early common ancestor.[97]

More specifically, adds paleoanthropologist Richard Klein,

species that are presumed to share a very recent common ancestor are . . . placed in the same genus; species that are more
distantly related are placed in different genera. . . . [G]enera that
share a relatively recent common ancestor are placed in a
common family; more distantly related genera are placed in different families; and so forth, up to the level of the kingdom.[98]

And that is indeed how biologists now group organisms in what
are essentially genealogical communities such as, for example, kingdoms (animals), phyla (mollusks), subphyla (vertebrates), classes
(insects), infraclasses (marsupials), orders (rodents), families (cats),
genera (African elephants), and species (blue jays). Pronouncedly
monophyletic, each such community consists of all the descendants
of a particular ancestor, and only them.[99]

That also explains the distinctly hierarchical nature of biological
classification, the fact that, as graphically captured in phylogenetic
trees and cladograms,[100] every taxonomic group is nested within, and
thus completely subsumed by, larger, more inclusive ones. With the
discovery of the branching nature of organic evolution, "[t]he entire
Linnean hierarchy suddenly became quite logical, because it was now
apparent that each higher taxon consisted of the descendants of a still
more remote ancestor."[101] In other words, since Darwin, hierarchical
classification has come to

represent the genealogical inclusiveness of taxa found in nature. . . .
Genera consist of multiple species stemming from a common

ancestor. . . . Genera are genealogical parts of families, and so on up the Linnaean hierarchy. . . . [N]ature consists of a series of inclusive genealogical entities.[102]

As exemplified by surnames (which in some languages, such as Korean and Hungarian, actually constitute the first rather than second or third component of a person's name),[103] membership in genealogical communities entails distinct identities. And like those communities themselves,[104] the identities associated with membership in them are also hierarchically nested.[105] A person's various "genealogical identities"[106] are therefore organized in an inclusive hierarchy, each of them being completely subsumed by those above it. As we can see in Figure 3.6,[107] one's identity as a member of the Larsson family, for example, is thus respectively nested within one's identities as a Swede, a human being, a mammal, and an animal.

The unmistakably hierarchical organization of those identities, of course, reflects the fact that the genealogical split between Bengt Larsson's and Gunnar Johansson's ancestors occurred only after the one between Swedes' and Syrians' ancestors, which occurred only after the one between humans' and horses' ancestors, which occurred only after the one between mammals' and insects' ancestors. Yet it also implies that, like the identities they entail, genealogical communities vary in their degree of inclusiveness. After all, the actual size of a genealogical community is directly proportional to the number of generations it encompasses,[108] and the further back its members need to go in search of the common ancestor from whom they all claim descent, the larger that community can be, as distant ancestors tend to have more descendants than recent ones. A deeper sense of co-descent thus usually entails more inclusive genealogical communities.[109]

The further back we go in search of our ancestors, in other words, the greater the number of "relatives" we are likely to identify and the

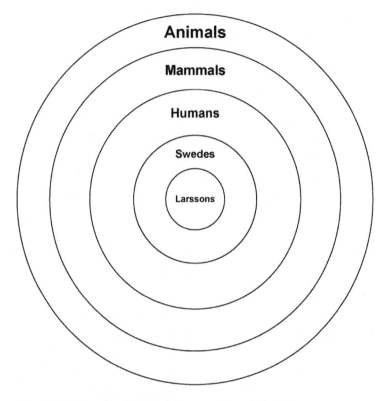

Figure 3.6. Hierarchically Nested Communities and Identities.

more inclusive our genealogical identity is therefore likely to be. Whether one identifies oneself as a Native American or as a Navajo thus depends on how far back one stretches one's genealogical memory. And that, in a nutshell, is the difference between being a Larsson, a Swede, a human being, or an animal.

[4]

NATURE AND CULTURE

It is telling that in our uniquely American taxonomy, Obama is almost always described as a black man with a white mother and never as a white man with a black father.

—Ellis Cose, "It Was Always Headed Here"

BLOOD

As quite evocatively exemplified by a captivating fantasy reported by geneticist Bryan Sykes, we usually view ancestral ties as natural bonds:

> I am on a stage. Before me . . . all the people who have ever lived are lined up . . . stretching far into the distance. . . . I have in my hand the end of the thread which connects me to my ancestral mother way at the back. I pull on the thread and one woman's face in every generation, feeling the tug, looks up at me. . . . These are my ancestors . . . I feel a strong connection. These are all my mothers. . . . The thread becomes an umbilical cord.[1]

Such a view of ancestral ties also affects the way we envision the ties connecting us to our relatives. As Sykes' fantasy continues,

[T]he ancestral mother of my clan . . . pulls on the cord. . . . I feel
the pull in my own stomach. . . . I look to right and left and sense
that others feel it too. These are the other people in [my] clan. . . .
We look at each other and sense our deep umbilical connection.
I am looking at my brothers and sisters. . . . I feel we have something very deep in common. I feel closer to these people than to
the others.[2]

As this fantasy seems to suggest, there is yet a third major element
in arborescent imagery other than a common trunk and branches,
namely roots,[3] which imply permanence. Unlike ties based on physical attraction or political expediency, for example, which are often
quite transient, genealogical ties are considered immutable. A genealogical tie, argued anthropologist David Schneider,

can never be severed. . . . [I]ts nature cannot be terminated. . . .
[I]t is never possible to have an ex-father or an ex-mother, an
ex-sister or an ex-brother, an ex-son or an ex-daughter. . . . The
relationship between parent and child, or between siblings, may
be such that the two never see each other . . . never communicate
in any way [yet nevertheless] remain parent and child or sibling
to each other. Nothing can really terminate [the] relationship
which exists between them.[4]

As Horace Kallen so aptly put it, "Men may change their clothes,
their politics, their wives, their religions, their philosophies [but]
they cannot change their grandfathers."[5]

It is the way we biologize genealogical relatedness that helps us
reify it. When viewed as biological, and therefore natural, genealogical ties seem more real.[6] The affinity they suggest seems inevitable.[7]

The "geneticization of relatedness," the fact that we regard DNA
as "the real substance of kinship,"[8] epitomizes the way we biologize

and thus essentialize genealogical ties. As exemplified by our image of hereditary disease, they are viewed as the actual paths through which biogenetic material is intergenerationally transmitted.[9] To quote sociologist Barbara Katz Rothman,

> [Our] ideas about "really" related people are based on genetic connections. It's a way of reckoning that makes us see adoptive parents as not the real parents, aunts and uncles by marriage as not real aunts and uncles, in-laws as not real relatives.[10]

Yet as implicit in our notion of "blood ties" (and of being "related by blood") and our vision of lineages as "bloodlines," we had already biologized and thereby essentialized ancestry and kinship long before we discovered genetics. Indeed, we have long viewed blood as what actually allows familial, ethno-national, or ethnoracial "essence" to be transmitted from ancestors to their descendants.[11]

Yet blood, we believe, connects not only ancestors and their descendants but also relatives, as evident from our notion of consanguinity (which literally means being "of the same blood"). Whereas affinal ties (as implicit in the term *in-laws*) are viewed as merely contractual, consanguineous ties are considered natural.

Not only do we essentialize "blood ties," we also reify the genealogical communities they help delineate in our minds. A perfect case in point is our image of the family as a "community of blood"[12] (which explains the ritual use of blood mixing as a token of symbolic kinship between "blood brothers" as well as in quasi-familial groups such as the Mafia). As the prototypical instantiation of "blood ties," family ties are considered organic rather than a matter of choice.[13] As such, they are also regarded as permanent and, as culturally embodied in the common cliché "Blood is thicker than water," are indeed expected to outlast political alliances, business partnerships, and even friendships.

The way we essentialize family ties is most strikingly apparent when contrasted with the way we evidently regard adoptive ties as only "as-if-genealogical."[14] Ultimately tying identity to biology, we seem to presume that anyone lacking traceable genetic roots is somehow incomplete,[15] which explains the strong desire many adoptees indeed feel to reunite some day with their "real," "natural" parents.[16]

Furthermore, projecting familial imagery onto other communities (as exemplified by the use of the words *brother* and *sister* among African Americans) helps naturalize them as well,[17] as evident in the way we envision ethnic communities as "extended families bound together through shared biogenetic substance."[18] Effectively viewing ethnicity as a form of kinship, we thus reify ethnic groups and ethnonations as corporeal entities to which we organically belong, as so evocatively suggested by the title of Michael Ignatieff's book *Blood and Belonging.*[19]

Ever since Johann Gottfried von Herder first associated the pronouncedly organicist image of a "community of blood" with the idea of peoplehood, we basically envision members of ethnonations as bound together by consanguinity (and even call the principle of determining citizenship by descent *jus sanguinis*). And ethnicizing nations definitely helps naturalize them.[20] With the Aryanization of Nazi Germany, for example, "[t]he word 'nation' no longer mean[t] a number of citizens living within certain boundaries, but a biological entity."[21]

Particularly critical to the way we view nations as corporeal entities is their "primordialist" image as having existed since time immemorial. The nationalist vision of the tie binding together Egyptians, for example, has thus been based on the notion that "from the dawn of history until the present day, the 'blood' of Egyptians had remained essentially the same," that "[t]he same blood flows in [their] veins which flowed in the veins of [their] ancestors five thousand years ago."[22] Such a seemingly organic tie also implies a strong psychological bond between earlier and current members of the nation. Since "the blood which flowed in [our ancestors'] veins flows in yours," explained Egypt's future Minister of Education Muhammad Husayn Haykal to his fellow countrymen in the 1920s,

> [y]ou are sentenced of necessity, willingly or unwillingly, to surrender to the heritage which has been bequeathed to you. If you should some day . . . examine your character, analyze your nature, and come to know your true temperament, you should discover that the essential nature of your ancestors has been passed on to you.[23]

Such an essentialized vision of peoplehood also draws on notions of indigenousness[24] based on viewing a country's "native" inhabitants as the actual descendants of those who inhabited it thousands (or even millions)[25] of years ago. No wonder ethno-nations (Finland, Israel, Bulgaria, Armenia) often grant "blood-carrying members"[26] a formal right to "return" to the "mother" countries once inhabited by their ancestors.

Such a pronouncedly essentialized vision of genealogical communities also underlies the way we view the particular form of ethnicity we call "race"[27] (in America, for example, the difference between the two basically boils down to whether one's ancestors came from Italy or Liberia, Lithuania or Vietnam) and associate with an intergenerationally transmitted "racial" essence[28] (such as a distinctive racial character) that we can even mathematize, since "the precise degree to which two persons share common heredity can be calculated . . . in specific quantitative terms."[29] After all, since we are 50 percent likely to inherit certain genes from each of our parents, 25 percent from each of our grandparents, and 12 1/2 percent from each of our great-grandparents, it is quite tempting to try to calculate how much of us is actually related by blood to each of those ancestors. That has indeed promoted actual calculations of "racial essence," as explicitly formalized, for example, in the 1910 Louisiana ruling that a person was to be considered "Caucasian or negro in the same proportion in which the two strains of blood [we]re mixed in his veins."[30] Just as noteworthy, in this regard, have been the attempts to pseudo-scientifically calculate how many generations it would take for an "interracial" family "to move from black to white,"[31] not to mention the pronouncedly mathematized notion of the "blood quantum" in terms of which Native Americans' degree of "Indianness" is formally measured to this day.

The most widespread form of such essentialized genealogical calculus has, in fact, been the practice, first introduced in 1705 in Virginia, of portraying a person's "racial essence" in terms of the proportion of his or her blood attributable to a specific ethnoracial ancestry, as explicitly manifested in formalized articulations of racial identity (such as in the above-mentioned case of the so-called Indian blood quantum) in terms of actual fractions (5/32, 3/32, and even 5.75/32 or 3.375/32) of blood.[32] Indeed, in the French Caribbean colonies as well as in the American South, special labels were actually assigned to individuals of seven-eighths (*sacatra* or *mango*), three-quarter (*sambo* or *griffe*), five-eighths (*marabou*), one-quarter (*quadroon*), one-eighth (*mustee* or *octoroon*), one-sixteenth (*meamelouc, quintroon,* or *hexadecaroon*), or one-sixty-fourth (*sang-mêlé*) African ancestry.[33] And in Santo Domingo and South Africa, some Europeans even extended their genealogical calculations nine generations back, actually characterizing people as having literally "1/512" African blood.[34] Only within the context of such highly essentialized ethnoracial calculus would a person facetiously portray oneself as being "52.5 pounds Indian—about 35 pounds Creek and the remainder Cherokee—88 pounds Teutonic,

43.5 pounds some sort of English, and the rest 'undetermined' [or simply] 'human.'"[35]

NATURE OR CULTURE?

And yet, despite the way we naturalize and thereby essentialize the ties connecting us to our ancestors and relatives, nature is only one component of our overall genealogical landscape. The social logic of reckoning relatedness is quite distinct from the biological reality it supposedly reflects, and culture plays an equally important role in how we envision both kinship and descent.

For one thing, genealogical proximity does not always imply actual genetic proximity but only an increased likelihood of sharing the same genes. In other words, it is potential rather than essence that ancestors genetically transmit to their descendants. By the same token, although we often share with our relatives certain genes that we both inherited from our common ancestors, the actual amount of genetic material we share is not always directly proportional to our genealogical proximity to them. Rather than being based on the shared possession of particular genes, "relatedness is [thus] just a mathematical abstraction."[36]

Furthermore, the actual amount of genetic material we inherit from each of our ancestors is quite small, progressively decreasing with each generation.[37] Sykes's existentially captivating fantasy notwithstanding, the genes we inherited from our ancient mitochondrial mothers actually constitute only an infinitesimal fraction of our entire DNA.[38] By the same token, as the genealogical distance between relatives increases, the likelihood of them actually sharing the same genes decreases geometrically. Whereas the likelihood of sharing a particular gene with my siblings is 50 percent, it is only 12.5 percent with my first cousins,

3.125 percent with my second cousins, and .78125 percent with my third cousins.

Our highly reified sense of ethno-national (as well as ethnoracial or any other form of ethnic) "kinship" is therefore essentially contrived, as most of our fellow co-nationals onto whom we project it are genetically quite distant from us. Furthermore, ethno-nations are often also based on mere fictions rather than factual evidence of common descent[39] and thus on fictive rather than real consanguinity, and ethno-nationhood is therefore as much a function of our imagination as of our genes. The common ancestors whose memory holds such communities together (such as the biblical Jacob or the Greek mythological Hellen) are themselves often mythical, and even when they are not, their ties to their alleged descendants often are. The Nazis' fanciful portrayal of the ancient Scythians as their ancestors was a perfect example of such genealogical fantasies, as were their purely imagined blood ties to the Chinese, Japanese, and Tibetan aristocracies.[40]

As exemplified by various competing ways of reckoning relatedness,[41] the genealogical distance based on which we formalize inheritance rights and define incest is ultimately also a social construct. By the same token, even the amount of claimed ancestry formally necessary to determine individuals' genealogical identity varies historically,[42] not to mention cross-culturally. Furthermore, even the fact that we consider blood our most genealogically relevant bodily material is actually based on social convention. Indeed, in many Muslim communities, it is "milk kinship" that is being essentialized, and sexual unions between "milk siblings" suckled as infants by the same wet nurse that are being prohibited.[43]

Moreover, in the genealogical imagination "the facts of nature" are sometimes even "overtaken by the facts of culture."[44] Despite the fact that the genetic distance between ancestors and their descendants actually increases with each generation, for example, we nevertheless attach greater rather than lesser significance to deeper pedigrees and consider remote ancestors far greater sources of legitimacy than recent ones.

The extent to which socially based genealogical reckoning can actually outweigh the biological reality it supposedly reflects is spectacularly evident in the cases of patrilineality and the so-called one-drop rule. As both of those cases clearly demonstrate, not all ancestral ties seem to carry the same social weight. In marked contrast to the fact that "[b]iology is democratic [and] all parents are equal,"[45] culture often promotes a pronouncedly asymmetrical manner of "mental weighing" whereby certain ancestors evidently count disproportionately more than others in determining our genealogical identity.[46]

Many societies, for example, reckon descent in a strictly patrilineal manner, with "only pedigrees made up exclusively of [men] recognized as conferring" it.[47] Effectively assuming that one's essence, and therefore identity, is derived from one's father's sperm, they basically envision lineages as "line[s] of reproductive seed."[48] They thus regard women as merely the soil in which men's seeds grow,[49] so that "[n]either descent nor the [lineage] continues through them,"[50] as quite evident from the way surnames are transmitted there from one generation to the next, as

> children take their "family" name from the line of the father. Half-siblings with the same father share a family name; those with the same mother do not. . . . [C]hildren of brothers share a name. . . . [C]hildren of sisters or of brother and sister do not share a name. They belong to the family line of other men.[51]

Patrilineal narratives, in other words, are "masculinist imaginar[ies] in which women . . . service the intergenerational transfer of men's names and genes" to their seed.[52] In patrilineal societies, children are thus "reckoned as being born to men, out of women. Women [simply] bear the children of men"[53] rather than actually generating them. As mere breeding grounds,[54] they formally have no descendants[55] and are considered genealogically irrelevant. From looking at most biblical genealogies, for example,[56] one would never guess that they actually played even a minor role in that entire process of begetting, thereby inspiring such sardonic remarks as "50% of my forefathers were female."

And yet, as already implied in the old Roman adage *mater certa, pater incertus* (also known today as "Mother's baby, father's maybe"), while there is only rarely any doubt about the identity of a child's mother,[57] that of its father, however, is always somewhat uncertain (which explains the social pressure we may feel to "notice" newborns' resemblance to their legal fathers[58] and thereby solidify the latter's claimed paternity). Indeed, as DNA tests show, "[A] significant percentage of children are not genetically related to the men who think they are their fathers."[59] Despite the fact that it determines the composition of half of our ancestors and therefore also about as many of our relatives, paternity is only putative.[60] Given that, the very idea of reckoning descent patrilineally defies any biologically based logic, and the fact that so many societies nevertheless do so thus underscores the extent to which culturally based genealogical reckoning often outweighs the biological reality it supposedly reflects.

Consider also, along these lines, the American genealogical convention according to which any drop of "black blood, no matter how remote, ma[kes] one black."[61] To understand the social logic underlying this "one-drop rule" one must appreciate the fundamental asymmetry between the ways in which whiteness and blackness are reckoned in America—an asymmetry based on a peculiar "exchange rate" culturally established between "corrupting Senegalese plasma" and "purifying European blood cells."[62] Given this pronouncedly asymmetrical exchange rate, even a single drop of "black blood" is considered a "touch of the tar brush" in one's pedigree, and "no amount of 'white' blood is . . . strong enough to outweigh that stain."[63] Furthermore, whereas blacks can never dilute their offspring's blackness through sexual contact with whites, whites certainly compromise their offspring's whiteness through such contact with blacks.[64] Although "[m]iscegenation has never been a bridge upon which one might cross from the Negro race to the Caucasian," it has definitely been "a thoroughfare from the Caucasian to the Negro."[65]

Thus, despite the fact that they are equally significant genetically, African ancestors clearly affect one's racial identity in America far more than European ones, as nonwhite blood evidently carries much more symbolic weight than white blood.[66] When the terms *quadroon*, *octoroon*, and *quintroon*, for example, were used there as formal racial identity labels, it went without saying that it was people's *black* blood that was being counted.

The standard for claiming a white identity in America is clearly much stricter than the one for being black, as implicitly evident from the fact that, whereas blackness presupposes the presence of black ancestors (so that in the 1923 U.S. Census, for example, a person of mixed European and African ancestry would be formally "classified as a Negro . . . regardless of the amount of white blood" he or she had),[67] whiteness presupposes their absence rather than the presence of white ones.[68] Thus, while a single African great-great-grandparent would often suffice to formally make one black, even fifteen European great-great-grandparents might not be enough to make one white—a biological absurdity inspiring Cherokee activist Jimmie Durham's sarcastic remark "I think I must be a mixed-blood. I claim to be male, although only one of my parents was male."[69] (The symmetrically reverse manner of reckoning descent whereby having even a single European ancestor would suffice to make one white would be inconceivable, of course, in America. When Haitian president François Duvalier once quipped that most Haitians are white, adding "We use the one-drop rule, too,"[70] the latter remark was clearly understood to be facetious.) As Mark Twain described the fair-complexioned quintroon Roxy in *Pudd'nhead Wilson*, "To all intents and purposes Roxy was as white as anybody, but the one-sixteenth of her which was black outvoted the other fifteen parts and made her a negro."[71] Or as Booker Washington put it, "[I]f a person is known to have one per cent of African blood in his veins, he ceases to be a white man. The ninety-nine per cent of Caucasian blood does not weigh by the side of the one per cent of African blood."[72] (There is "considerable irony," of course, "in the fact that the one-drop rule makes black blood immeasurably stronger than white . . . blood, even though . . . this strength consists in an unlimited power to contaminate.")[73]

Such a striking genealogical asymmetry underscores the extent to which the social logic of reckoning descent can outweigh the natural reality it supposedly reflects. It thus explains the "American racial convention that considers a white woman capable of giving birth to a black child but denies that a black woman can give birth to a white child."[74] It also helps us understand why "Obama is almost always described as a black man with a white mother and never as a white man with a black father."[75] It is the sharp contrast between the biological equivalence of these two characterizations and the almost utter cultural inconceivability of the latter, of course, that makes the one-drop rule such an intriguing phenomenon.

Given all the above, we clearly need to disentangle biological realities from the way they are socially narrated, and realize that genealogies are narratives of social descent rather than accurate chronicles or maps of genetic relatedness.[76] In other words, they are formal accounts of social, rather than strictly biological, ties.

Relatedness is therefore not a biological given but a social construct, and genealogies are products of sociocognitive conventions rather than mere reflections of nature. Such conventions, which clearly affect the way we trace our ancestors, are based on certain social norms (and are therefore parts of particular social traditions) of remembering and forgetting.[77] Given these conventions, norms, and traditions, reckoning genealogical relatedness clearly requires more than mere genetic evidence. Indeed, it calls for a sociology of memory.[78]

THE RULES OF GENEALOGICAL LINEATION

Like a river with many tributaries, we have more than just a single genealogical "source" and therefore also many possible paths through which we can trace our origins. After all, we each have two parents, four grandparents, eight great-grandparents, sixteen great-great-grandparents, thirty-two great-great-great-grandparents, and sixty-four great-great-great-great-grandparents, and can thus trace our descent through multiple ancestral lines, the number of which grows exponentially the deeper we go back in time. (The actual number of our ancestors does not always double every generation, however, since there are some from whom we actually descend in more than just one way due to inbreeding. After all, if my parents happen to be third cousins, for example, two of my maternal great-great-great-grandparents then also double as my paternal great-great-great-grandparents, as a result of which I end up having only thirty rather than thirty-two great-great-great-grandparents.)[79] As we can see in Figure 4.1, there are numerous possible ways for Peter to trace his descent—through his father's paternal grandfather Earl, through his father's paternal grandmother Shirley, through his father's maternal grandfather Andrew, through his father's maternal grandmother Sally, through his mother's paternal grandfather Victor, through his mother's paternal grandmother Dorothy, through his mother's maternal grandfather Morris, through his mother's maternal grandmother Jenny, through his paternal grandfather Paul's

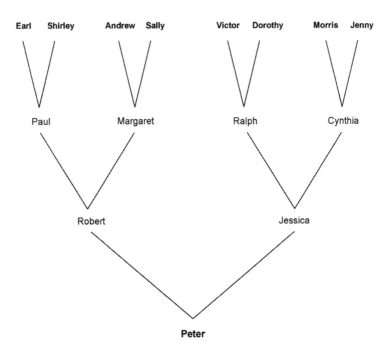

Figure 4.1. Paths of Descent.

paternal grandfather, and so on indefinitely. Indeed, "no family lineage is a single thread. It's more like a broad fan of . . . a million threads coming together."[80]

The visually striking contrast between the conelike and fanlike models of portraying genealogical ties respectively featured in Figures 3.1 and 4.1[81] underscores the fundamental contrast between traditional and modern genealogical awareness. Whereas Figure 3.1, which portrays Peter as one of Margaret's four grandchildren, is explicitly "ancestor-centric,"[82] Figure 4.1, which portrays Margaret as one of Peter's four grandparents, is pronouncedly "descendant-centric." The switch from the former manner of portraying genealogical ties to the latter also represents the historical transition from a predominantly group-centered to a predominantly person-centered conception of genealogy.[83] Whereas Figure 3.1 represents an attempt to depict a family, thereby providing an ideal model for envisioning genealogical *communities*, Figure 4.1 represents an explicitly self-centered vision and is therefore particularly useful as a general model for theorizing genealogical *identities*.

As quite evident from Figure 4.1, when choosing any particular line of descent, we do so out of many different options.[84] Not all of them, however, are always available to us, as our choices are usually made within certain social constraints. After all, of the numerous ancestral paths through which we could possibly trace our origins, only few are socially sanctioned through certain "rules of genealogical lineation" that, by determining the manner in which we envision intergenerational succession, implicitly tell us which of our ancestors we ought to remember and which ones we can actually forget. Rather than mere reflections of nature, ancestral ties are thus products of particular norms of remembrance that basically determine whom we consider our ancestors.

Some societies trace descent bilaterally ("omnilineally"),[85] tying individuals' genealogical identity to both of their parents,[86] which is why in many Spanish-speaking countries, for example, people often have two surnames instead of only one. (Thus, whereas an American credit-card company may use mothers' maiden names as password-like authenticators for verifying its customers' identities, the presumption that those names would not be easily available to identity thieves is not one anyone would ever make in Mexico or Spain.) Most societies, however, do so unilineally, either patrilineally or matrilineally, respectively considering either mothers' or fathers' identities genealogically irrelevant. Thus, for example, in Judaism, "the offspring of a gentile mother and a Jewish father is a gentile, while the offspring of a Jewish mother and a gentile father is a Jew."[87] By the same token, among the Kamea of Papua New Guinea, only maternal siblings are considered blood-related, while the Nayar in India do not even prohibit marriages between children of the same father from different wives as incest.[88]

Unilineal descent systems underscore the social nature of genealogical relatedness, since it is usually society that determines whether we trace descent patrilineally or matrilineally.[89] And only society makes us choose between tracing our origins exclusively through our father's *or* mother's line rather than through both of them.

Unilineal pedigrees, of course, greatly simplify individuals' genealogical makeup. By essentially reducing our entire ancestry to a single line, such "shorthand descriptions of descent"[90] basically transform inherently complex historical realities into much simpler genealogical narratives. As one might expect, that presupposes a considerable amount of "genealogical amnesia,"[91] as most of our ancestors end up being forgotten. When we highlight only one line of descent, we inevitably do so at the expense of all the others, celebrating certain ancestors while forgetting others.[92] Tracing our origins unilineally thus involves a great deal of denial, as most of our ancestors are deemed genealogically irrelevant and formally ignored.[93]

"[E]ither a matrilineal or patrilineal conception of our family histories," in short, "drastically underrepresents the biological range of our ancestry,"[94] and when we consider the ancestors included in any given line of descent (such as Earl, Paul, and Robert in Figure 4.2), it is important to therefore also consider the ones implicitly excluded (Shirley, Andrew, Sally, Victor, Dorothy, Morris, Jenny, Margaret, Ralph, Cynthia, and Jessica). After all, whether I trace my descent matrilineally or patrilineally, one of my two parents, three of my four grandparents, seven of my eight great-grandparents, fifteen of my sixteen great-great-grandparents, thirty-one of my thirty-two great-great-great-grandparents, and sixty-three of my sixty-four great-great-great-great-grandparents are formally relegated to genealogical irrelevance. Furthermore, they become "mnemonic dead-ends,"

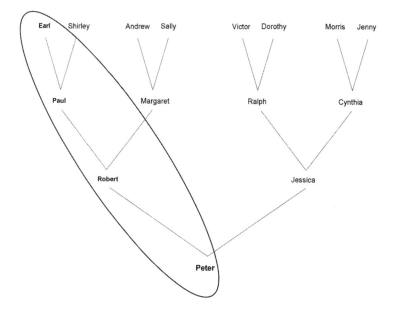

Figure 4.2. Genealogical Denial.

since I end up forgetting their ancestors as well (just as I do not regard their descendants as my relatives.)

That is how Roxy came to be seen as simply black, her tie to her one African great-great-grandparent evidently considered so disproportionately dominant as to outweigh her ties to her fifteen European ones. As her notably lopsided genealogical identity clearly demonstrates, African Americans' complex ethnoracial makeup is greatly distorted by the one-drop rule. Viewing Obama as black, for example, presupposes ignoring the fact that his own mother was actually white. As another product of similarly "mixed" ancestry would lament his existential predicament, "At home I see my mom and dad and I'm part of both of them. But when I walk outside that door, it's like my mom doesn't exist. I'm just Black."[95]

Ironically, a somewhat similar "genealogical tunnel vision" is also inherent in both Y-chromosomal and mitochondrial DNA ancestry tests, which, as we saw earlier, allow us to respectively trace only our paternal or maternal foreparents and thereby reconstruct only strictly male or strictly female ancestral lineages. As such, they can only provide information about one ancestor per generation[96] (such as my father's father's father's father or my mother's mother's mother's mother), implicitly relegating all the others to oblivion. The findings of these genetic tests thus "say absolutely nothing about one's paternal grandmother, maternal grandfather, or, in fact, the vast majority of one's ancestors,"[97] the number of which increases exponentially as one goes back in time. If I go back six generations, sixty-three of my sixty-four great-great-great-great-grandparents would therefore be relegated by either of those tests to oblivion. And if I go back fourteen generations, the test will connect me to only one of the 16,384 ancestors in that generation from whom I actually descend.[98]

As one might expect, that presents a particularly serious problem when tracing one's origins also happens to involve a search for one's ethnoracial "essence." After romantically essentializing his connection to his Jewish ancestors, Steven Pinker, for example, thus soberly notes:

> But my blue eyes remind me not to get carried away with delusions about a Semitic essence. Mitochondrial DNA, and the Y chromosome, do not literally tell you about "your ancestry" but only half of your ancestry a generation ago, a quarter two generations ago and so on, shrinking exponentially the further back you go.[99]

Thus, for example, essentially echoing the general logic (though not the particular racial bias) of the one-drop rule,

> if you had 1 European ancestor in [the fifth preceding] generation, and the rest of your . . . ancestors were African, then you

would be only 1/32 European. . . . But if that European man happened to be your father's father's father's father's father, then Y-chromosome typing would place your ancestry entirely in Europe.[100]

In fact, points out legal scholar Henry Greely,

It is possible for a person to have an eight-times-great-grand-mother who was Japanese, an eight-times-great-grandfather who was Zulu, and 1022 other ancestors in the 10th generation who were Irish. Mitochondrial DNA analysis would suggest that the subject *was* Japanese, or at least East Asian. Y chromosome analysis would suggest that the subject *was* Zulu, or at least sub-Saharan African. Neither would even hint at the Irish origin of 99.8% of the subject's ancestors.[101]

THE RULES OF GENEALOGICAL DELINEATION

Yet society affects not only the number of mental paths through which we trace our descent but also their length (that is, how far back we go in search of our ancestors), which ultimately also determines whom we consider our relatives. Despite the fact that there is nothing, for example, actually stopping us from tracing our origins, as do evolutionary biologists, millions of generations back, certain conventions of remembrance nevertheless keep us from doing so, which is why we rarely consider camels or sardines our distant cousins even though technically they are. While it is the norms, conventions, and traditions of genealogical lineation that determine whom we regard as our ancestors, it is the norms, conventions, and traditions of genealogical *de*lineation that basically determine how inclusively we define our genealogical identity and therefore whom we consider our relatives.

Despite the way we essentialize them, genealogical communities are ultimately products of classification, an unmistakably conventional process of carving supposedly discrete mental constructs out of continuous realities.[102] The family, for example, is an inherently boundless community.[103] Since there is no natural boundary separating recent ancestors from remote ones, there is also no such boundary separating close relatives from distant ones or even relatives from nonrelatives. Any such boundary is therefore a product of social convention alone. Thus, although it is most probably nature that determines that our obligations to others be proportional to our genealogical proximity to them,[104] it is nevertheless unmistakably social norms that specify whose blood or honor we ought to avenge[105] and determine the genealogical reach of family reunification policies. It is likewise social conventions that specify who can claim a share of the blood money paid to relatives of homicide victims[106] and determine whom we invite to family reunions. Thus, whereas the range of other animals' kin recognition is determined by nature,[107] it is social norms, conventions, and traditions of classification that determine how widely humans' range of kin recognition actually extends, and societies indeed often vary in where they draw the line between relatives and nonrelatives.

Just as no natural boundaries exist sharply delineating families and thereby separating relatives from nonrelatives, there are also no natural boundaries sharply delineating ethno-national or ethnoracial communities[108] and thereby distinctly separating Czechs from Slovaks or blacks from whites. Even when membership in such communities is seemingly unambiguously determined by actual "blood quanta," as in the case of Native Americans, it is nevertheless social convention that determines what those should be. We therefore need to be careful not to mistake cultural categories for natural ones, and realize that a sharply delineated "ethnic group" or "nation" is only a reified construct.[109]

Although we often envision ethno-national and ethnoracial communities as discrete entities, none of them actually have natural boundaries distinctly separating their members from nonmembers. Indeed, it is precisely the absence of any such boundaries that may prompt us, as we shall see later, to artificially separate such communities from one another.[110] So-called racial boundaries, for example, are actually but "statistically derived boundaries within gradients of genetic variation,"[111] since what they clearly reveal is not the complete presence or absence of particular population-specific genetic markers[112] but only varying frequencies of such markers in different populations. In other words, even when a specific marker is more frequently present in a particular ethnoracial group, it is by no means unique to it,[113] and scientists have yet to identify, for example, a single "Asian gene" that all and only "Asians" have. To be a member of any ethnoracial community is therefore

> to be a member of a population which exhibits a specified frequency of certain kinds of genes. . . . When a man says "I am white," all that he can mean scientifically is that he is a member of a population which has . . . a high frequency of genes for light skin color, thin lips, heavy body hair.[114]

What we inherit from our ancestors and share with our relatives, in short, is not a certain ethnoracial essence but a certain likelihood of having inherited specific genes that are more frequently present in a particular population. Indeed, it is quite possible that a person who had a Native American great-great-great-grandfather and is thus considered "1/32 Indian," for example, did not actually inherit from him a single typically Native American genetic marker.[115] It is therefore more factually accurate to portray someone as having one grandparent of

African descent than as being "one quarter black."[116] By the same token, having a "46% European," "42% Sub-Saharan African," and "12% Indigenous American" ancestry is only a statistical estimate rather than an accurate description of one's actual genetic makeup.

This is indeed the problem with autosomal DNA ("admixture") tests, where people are actually portrayed in terms of such proportions of racial essence.[117] In the same way that concepts like "biracial" or "multiracial" implicitly perpetuate our view of races as prediscursively discrete entities,[118] the image of "interracial" mixing implies a prior notion of "primary, nonmixed races—in some imagined past."[119] The very idea of admixture, in fact, presupposes distinct populations that had once been reproductively isolated from one another[120]—a somewhat problematic notion given that there is no evidence that such populations ever existed at any point in human history.[121]

Ethnoracial purity is something that never actually existed, and discrete ethnoracial groups are therefore mere abstractions. The reason why there are no natural boundaries separating one such distinct group from others is the long history of interbreeding among (and therefore mixing of) human populations:

> No group of modern humans has ever been reproductively isolated for long. Even island populations such as those of Australia, Hawaii, and Madagascar have absorbed new people, and therefore new mutations. The mixing of populations has helped to ensure that no group of humans has ever become very distinct genetically from any other.[122]

As the actual products of such interbreeding, we are therefore all ethnoracially "mixed."

Since their members can successfully interbreed only with fellow members, however, species, by contrast, do seem to constitute reproductively isolated and therefore also naturally bounded genealogical communities. Yet even species are actually not as sharply delineated as we may think. After all, it is an unbroken chain of ancestors that nevertheless connects "human" beings to their "pre-human" ancestors.[123] We are actually dealing here with an attempt to artificially impose a taxonomy of discontinuous cultural categories on what is essentially a continuous natural reality.[124]

Indeed, were it not for the fact that various intermediate forms between currently extant species happen to already be extinct, we might not have even been able to notice any significant discontinuities between those species.[125] As Dawkins points out,

> A complete fossil record would make it very difficult to classify animals into discrete nameable groups. If we had a complete fossil record, we should have to give up discrete names and resort to some mathematical or graphical notation of sliding scales. The human mind far prefers discrete names, so in one sense it is just as well that the fossil record is poor.[126]

Indeed, "[w]ithout gaps in the fossil record," he concludes,

> our whole system for naming species would break down. . . . [But] this is a human imposition rather than something deeply built into the natural world. Let us use names as if they really reflected a discontinuous reality [yet] remember that . . . it is no more than a convenient fiction.[127]

In real life, in short, there are no sharply delineated, naturally bounded genealogical communities. Families, nations, races, and even species are ultimately products of social traditions of classifying organisms. As such, they exist only in our imagination.[128]

[5]

THE POLITICS OF DESCENT

Mules are always boasting that their ancestors were horses.

—*Ancestors*, 2

Not only are genealogies more than mere reflections of nature, they are also more than mere records of history.[1] Rather than simply documenting who our ancestors were, they are the narratives we construct to actually make them our ancestors. By the same token, rather than simply helping us find out who our relatives are, they are the narratives we construct to actually make them our relatives.

Despite being constrained by various norms, conventions, and traditions of remembering and classifying, we nevertheless have a considerable degree of agency in how we identify ourselves genealogically. "[D]oing genealogy,"

> involves choices about which line or lines to follow and which ancestries matter. In every step of the process, choices continually arise about which line to research . . . the mother's line or the father's, the maternal or paternal grandmother or maternal or paternal grandfather—and so on backwards in time.[2]

Pedigrees and family trees are therefore partly products of the choices we make about which ancestors to remember.[3]

Aside from actually tracing the ancestral lines leading from our parents back to our grandparents and great-grandparents, we sometimes also use essentially fictive ancestors as "genealogical anchors" around which we construct our personal and collective genealogical fantasies. Attempts to trace the origins of the Ethiopian monarchy back to King Solomon and Scotland's kings back to the legendary Egyptian princess Scota are perfect examples of such opportunistic "genealogical appropriation."[4] So, for that matter, are Venezuelan president Hugo Chavez's claim that he descends from the Aztec emperor Montezuma and Pakistani prince Ghazanfar Ali Khan's claim that his Hunza tribesmen are descendants of Alexander the Great's troops.[5] Consider also, in this regard, the Trojan origins claimed by the Romans, Britons, Icelanders, and the early kings of France, not to mention the attempts to trace Jesus back to David and Mohammed all the way back to Abraham.[6]

Yet even when they do not include any fictive elements, the very process of constructing genealogies inevitably distorts the actual historical realities they supposedly reflect. By selectively highlighting certain ancestors (and therefore also ties to certain relatives) while downplaying or even actively suppressing awareness of others, we tactically manipulate genealogies to accommodate both personal and collective agendas. As we shall see, the various tactics we use to manipulate genealogical narratives are part of larger strategies that highlight fundamental tensions between remembering and forgetting, continuity and discontinuity, unilinearity and multilinearity, and social inclusion and exclusion.

STRETCHING

Like foundations of buildings, pedigrees seem more solid the "deeper" they go. "[A]ntiquity is lineage's chief claim to legitimacy; and the older the genealogy, the more prestigious and powerful that claim becomes."[7] Despite the fact that the exact nature of a person's ties to his ancestors becomes increasingly vague[8] and the amount of genetic material he shares with them actually decreases, the more remote from him they are, the more we value those ties. As in the world of canine and equine purebreds, the longer the lineage, the more venerable it is.[9]

In order to enhance our stature and legitimacy, we therefore try to stretch our pedigrees as far back as we can.[10] That explains the tremendous impact of Alex Haley's *Roots*, which, especially given Africans' traditional image as entering history only upon being brought to America as slaves, actually begins with Haley's great-great-great-great-great-grandparents still living as free persons in Africa.[11] It also explains Thomas Jefferson's proposal to place on the Great Seal of the United States replicas of Hengist and Horsa, the semi-legendary chieftains who led the Anglo-Saxon invasion of England in the fifth century and from whom Anglo-Americans would therefore be able to "claim the honor of being descended."[12]

Rulers, too, stretch their pedigrees to enhance their political legitimacy. Emperor Akihito's legitimacy, for example, thus rests on the traditional belief that he is indeed the 125th link in a long ancestral chain that goes back almost twenty-seven centuries to Jimmu, Japan's legendary first emperor, while Jordan's King Abdullah II's and Morocco's King Mohammed VI's are based on the claim that they are direct descendants of the Prophet.[13] Particularly noteworthy, in this regard, is the traditional role of Noah, the mythical survivor of the biblical Flood, as royalty's most universally popular point of genealogical departure.[14] The Russian czar Ivan the Terrible, for example, could not have chosen for himself a more compelling source of legitimacy:

> In order to enhance the glory of his office [he was provided] with an imperial genealogy going back, through Rurik, the Emperor Augustus and a number of fabled characters, to Aeneas and

Noah. No other European monarch . . . could boast of such titles.[15]

Indeed, we often stretch our pedigrees in order to "out-past"[16] others who have shorter ones and thus claim greater legitimacy than them. As exemplified by hereditary societies like the General Society of Mayflower Descendants or the Daughters of the American Revolution, it is far more prestigious to be a tenth-generation than a first-generation American.[17] That is why nativists look down on recent immigrants (as do old-money families on the nouveaux riches) and why some Virginian families, effectively embracing the politics of indigenousness,[18] claim to be descendants of Pocahontas.[19]

Nations, too, try to out-past each other in an effort to claim prior settlement of contested regions.[20] To bolster their claim to Kosovo, for example, Albanians thus claim descent from the ancient Illyrians who had lived there long before its sixth-century conquest by proto-Serbian Slavs.[21] Highlighting their ancestral ties to the ancient Israelites likewise enhances Jews' claim to Palestine,[22] very much like the way in which claiming their Phoenician roots helps Lebanon's Christians draw tacit attention to their country's pre-Muslim past.[23] It also inspires Palestinians, however, to claim descent from its even-earlier inhabitants, the ancient Canaanites.[24]

CUTTING AND PASTING

Constructing pedigrees often involves having to deal with various inconsistencies. In an effort to reconcile Jesus' otherwise patrilineal pedigree with the belief in his virginal conception, Matthew, for example, thus ends his genealogy with "Joseph, the husband of Mary, of whom was born Jesus," while Luke notes that Jesus "was the son, so it was thought, of Joseph."[25] Somewhat similarly, in Islam, since the

Prophet himself had no sons who reached adulthood, his descendants' otherwise strictly patrilineal pedigrees actually reach him only through his daughter, Fatima.[26]

Indeed, constructing pedigrees often involves suppressing such inconsistencies. In an effort to maintain "genealogical purity,"[27] elements that might threaten the sense of continuity such narratives are designed to project are thus sometimes deleted from them. The deliberate omission of foreign rulers from the ancient Assyrian king lists[28] perfectly exemplifies such suppression. So does Matthew's decision to omit from the genealogy of Jesus kings Ahaziah, Joash, and Amaziah, whose inclusion would have more explicitly linked Jesus not only to David but also to Ahab and Jezebel.[29] The very idea of historical continuity, of course, calls for "a past free of such embarrassments."[30]

Such "cutting" is usually complemented by the mental "pasting" together of the resultant noncontiguous stretches of history.[31] Envisioning lineages presupposes visions of temporal contiguity, and even the tiniest gaps in genealogical narratives must therefore be avoided. Projecting a vision of such contiguity between successive members of a lineage is thus critical, and when history itself does not provide actual contiguity, we sometimes fabricate it. As in word processing and film editing, both of which involve pasting together noncontiguous stretches of text or film, by mentally pasting together noncontiguous stretches of history we thus construct seemingly continuous genealogical narratives.

Projecting visions of such illusory continuity presupposes a total denial of the actual chronological gaps inevitably created by suppressing genealogically problematic stretches of history. Only by omitting from the genealogy of Jesus and thereby effectively obliterating from Christian memory kings Ahaziah, (Ahaziah's son) Joash, and (Joash's son) Amaziah, after all, could Matthew actually present (Amaziah's son) King Uzziah as the son, rather than great-great-grandson, of Ahaziah's father, King Jehoram.[32]

Pasting may also take the form of "padding" ancestral chains with some dummy links in order to fill unaccounted-for chronological gaps in genealogical narratives.[33] The persons listed in Genesis and Matthew presumably to help the narrator paste together the otherwise disconnected narrative segments relating to Noah and Abraham or to the last Davidic kings and Jesus[34] are model examples of such "dummy ancestors."[35] So are the high priests whose listed names help the biblical narrator project the vision of a continuous priestly line stretching from David's high priest Zadok to his alleged descendant occupying that office at the time the narrative was constructed several centuries later.[36]

CLIPPING

Yet while pasting is clearly motivated by the wish to project a sense of historical continuity, there are also times when we actually wish to project a sense of rupture with the past.[37] That, however, involves yet a different kind of genealogical tactic. In marked contrast to stretching, where we try to make pedigrees longer, it involves efforts to actually make them shorter by trying to establish more recent, rather than earlier, origins.

Although short pedigrees may also result from a lack of available genealogical information, as is often the case with third-generation immigrants or descendants of slaves, "clipping" pedigrees involves a deliberate attempt to actively curtail our or others' genealogical memory.[38] In an effort to establish "pure" pedigrees, uncontaminated by ancestral ties to individuals or groups from whom one wishes to dissociate oneself, clipping them helps relegate such undesirable ancestors to oblivion. Confining the narrative of human history to the last six thousand years, for example, thus helps creationists ignore our simian origins. Going only two generations back when formally defining Jewishness[39] likewise helped the Nazis avoid realizing how many "Aryan" Germans actually also had Jewish ancestors.

While clipping pedigrees may indeed be motivated by efforts to forget ancestors also shared by undesirable co-descendants (apes, Jews),[40] it is often also part of attempts to establish a new identity, as when new immigrants, for example, try to sever their ancestral ties to a stigmatized ethnic past. Their genealogical myopia[41] is perhaps most striking when the "forgotten" ancestors include even their own parents.

Given surnames' role in helping families project a sense of intergenerational continuity, the very idea of changing one's surname and thereby symbolically severing one's ties to one's parents is particularly noteworthy in this regard. The way many new immigrants to America have Anglicized their "ethnic" surnames is a perfect example. So has been the Zionist practice of Hebraizing traditional Jewish surnames and thereby symbolically severing the ties of new immigrants to Israel to their exilic familial past.[42]

The historical break between Jews' traditional life in exile and modern life in Israel has indeed been one of the underlying themes of Zionism.[43] As Zionist leader Berl Katznelson so explicitly articulated the movement's ideological commitment to rootlessness:

> We cultivate oblivion and are proud of our short memory . . .
> and the depth of our insurrection we measure by our talent to
> forget. . . . The more rootless we see ourselves, the more we
> believe that we are freer. . . . It is roots that delay our upward
> growth.[44]

And indeed, as so dramatically manifested in early portrayals of native-born *sabras* in Israeli literature as parentless,[45] separating "the new Jew" from his ideologically repudiated exilic past might actually require clipping off even his most immediate ancestors from his pedigree.

BRAIDING

Stretching, cutting and pasting, and clipping all presuppose unilinear narratives, but there is yet another genealogical tactic that does acknowledge the inherently multilinear nature of our genealogical condition. Effectively rejecting a strictly unilinear manner of narrating descent, "braiding" produces explicitly multilinear genealogical narratives that highlight our multiple origins. As if interweaving several strands of hair to form a braid, it invokes multiple ancestral strands, thereby ultimately reminding us that we each belong to more than one family and often more than one ethnoracial community. As a way of narrating origins, it thus conveys at the same time a sense of both unity and diversity.[46]

Claiming our multiple roots and thereby acknowledging our genealogical complexity also imply claiming our multiple identities and thereby recognizing our existential complexity, as exemplified when we decide to give children surnames that would provide a bilateral account of their origins. Such practices may include compounding the parents' surnames (as when Ruderman and Wilgoren are compounded into Rudoren, Villar and Raigosa into Villaraigosa, and Dell and Osborne into Delborne),[47] although they usually involve combining them through hyphenation.[48] In both cases, however, the very notion of privileging one line of descent over the others is rejected, and the memory of more than just one ancestral past is formally preserved.

Braiding also promotes viewing ethnoracial identities as adjectivelike rather than nounlike entities[49] and therefore in terms of genealogical fractions[50] rather than unified essences, as exemplified by the way Tiger Woods acknowledges his Dutch (*Ca*ucasian) and Native American (*In*dian) great-grandparents as well as African American (*bl*ack) and both Thai and Chinese (*Asian*) grandparents when he portrays himself as a "Cablinasian."[51] Effectively embracing the spirit of multiculturalism, braiders openly celebrate their "genealogical hybridity."[52] When he introduced himself as "the son of a black man from Kenya and a white woman from Kansas" as well as a "mutt,"[53] the very antithesis of the traditionally revered purebred, Obama was clearly showcasing rather than downplaying, let alone hiding, his ethnoracially mixed origins. It was this spirit, of course, that also led the U.S. Census to introduce its current, unmistakably multilinear "Check One or More" format[54] in 2000.

England's old claim to a braided Trojan-Roman-Celtic-German pedigree[55] reminds us that groups, too, sometimes highlight their multiple origins. Consider, for example, in this regard the 1943 Romanian 5000-lei bill featuring Decebal, Romania's last Dacian ruler, and Trajan, the Roman emperor who defeated him and conquered Dacia in AD 106 (see Figure 5.1).[56] Portraying both of them alongside each other thus presented Romania as heir to both ancient Dacia and imperial Rome. A strikingly similar message is conveyed by a monument at the entrance to the National Museum

Figure 5.1. Genealogical Braiding.

of Anthropology in Mexico City featuring faces representing both the Spanish and Native American roots (and therefore implicitly also the commitment to the ideology of *mestizaje* or mixture)[57] of the society that first formally recognized people as braided products of interethnoracial unions (such as, for example, *mestizos, mulatos, castizos,* and *moriscos*).[58]

LUMPING

While braiding obviously entails a commitment to genealogical inclusiveness, only those directly ancestral to oneself, in fact, are included. Braided pedigrees do not highlight, for example, ties to great-great-uncles and -aunts such as those respectively envisioned by Turkish nationalists and the Nazis as connecting Turks and Germans to the ancient Sumerians and Romans.[59] Nor do they highlight ties to co-descendants, which is what yet another genealogical tactic, "lumping,"[60] essentially does.

As evident from the important role founding ancestors play in clans' and ethno-nations' collective memories,[61] it is their visions of common ancestors that help co-descendants feel that they are actually related.[62] Furthermore, envisioned kinship between their respective founding ancestors helps groups foster a parallel sense of relatedness between their respective members,[63] as exemplified by the ancient association of the Dorian, Aeolian, and Ionian Greeks with the sons (Dorus and Aeolus) and grandson (Ion) of Hellen, the mythical eponymous ancestor of the Hellenic peoples,[64] or by the way Libyan Bedouins have viewed their intertribal relations as reflecting the ties among the children and grandchildren of their founding ancestress Sa'ada.[65] Jacob and his sons may have very well been products of a similar attempt by the authors of the Bible to attribute a common origin to the kingdoms of Judah and Israel.[66]

Since deeper visions of co-descent tend to generate in our minds more inclusive genealogical communities, lumpers stretch their genealogical narratives far back into the past in an effort to build more inclusive genealogical tents. After all, "The further one journeys back, the more one has in common with others."[67] That might explain, for example, why seventh-century archbishop Isidore of Seville would claim that both Spain's native inhabitants and Visigoth rulers actually descended from Noah's grandsons.[68] It also explains the tremendous cultural significance of the mythical patriarch who, having fathered both Ishmael and Isaac, helps foster a sense of symbolic kinship between Arabs and Jews. As soon-to-be New York senatorial hopeful Hillary Clinton announced on a 1999 visit to a Jewish cemetery in Morocco in an attempt to evoke an image of a genealogical tent big enough to include her Arab hosts as well as prospective Jewish voters back home, "We are all children of Abraham."[69]

Such an inclusionary spirit also underlies monogenist narratives emphasizing the genealogical relatedness of all humans, as exemplified by the biblical narrative that traces all the nations of the world to Noah[70] as well as by the currently prevailing "Out of Africa" theory (also known as the "Noah's Ark" model)[71] of human evolution. It is likewise evident in the way we now envision our relatedness to other animals, a vision one may trace back to the great eighteenth-century taxonomist Carolus Linnaeus's historic decision to formally place humans and apes in the same zoological order, Primates, and admit that "as a natural historian I have yet to find any characteristics which enable man to be distinguished on scientific principles from the ape."[72] The genealogical implications of his decision were, in fact, noted by Linnaeus himself, who even referred to apes as the "cousins of man," as well as by Buffon, who actually went as far as to claim that "man and ape have a common origin."[73] They became even clearer, of course, when Darwin effectively provided the theoretical framework necessary for recognizing them as such, and were finally made explicit in 1863 when Huxley, having painstakingly compared human and simian anatomy, concluded that "the structural differences which separate Man from the Gorilla and the Chimpanzee are not so great as those which separate the Gorilla from the lower apes," adding that humans must "have originated . . . by the gradual modification of a man-like ape; or . . . as a ramification of the same primitive stock as those apes."[74]

The idea that we may actually be genealogically integrated into the rest of the animal world received yet another significant boost in 1904, when serologist George Nuttall noted how closely human blood resembles chimpanzees' and gorillas'.[75] "[T]he affinity of man and the anthropoid apes, long established by anatomy," announced Haeckel, "has now been proved physiologically to be in real 'blood-relationship.'"[76] Then, in 1963, biochemist Morris Goodman stunned the world of science when he discovered that *chimpanzees and bonobos are, in fact, closer genetically to humans than they are to gorillas.*[77]

Indeed, the human, bonobo, and chimpanzee genomes are so remarkably similar that the scientists who first sequenced the latter actually referred to chimpanzees as "our siblings."[78] Such genetic affinity indicates that "we cannot have been evolving separately for very long," that "chimpanzees and humans share 99.9999997% of their evolutionary histories," that we "have had only a short history as a species distinct from other apes."[79] Indeed, in 1967, Vincent Sarich and Allan Wilson presented molecular evidence that our proto-human ancestors split from proto-chimpanzees and proto-bonobos only five to six million years ago (see Figure 5.2).[80] Only five to six million years thus separate us from those apes, only five to six million years since our DNA and theirs resided in the very same cells.[81] (The fact that living chimpanzees and bonobos—as well as gorillas and orangutans, for that matter—are actually our contemporaries precludes, of course, the popular view of human evolution as a uni-linear series of successive stages of development leading from apes to modern humans.[82] As one can tell from Figure 5.2, having evolved alongside us, those apes are clearly our distant cousins rather than "less evolved" ancestors.)

As we can see in Figure 5.3, before the 1960s, taxonomists used to subdivide the zoological superfamily Hominoidea into three families: the Hylobatidae (which included the gibbon), the Pongidae (which included the orangutan, the gorilla, the chimpanzee, and the

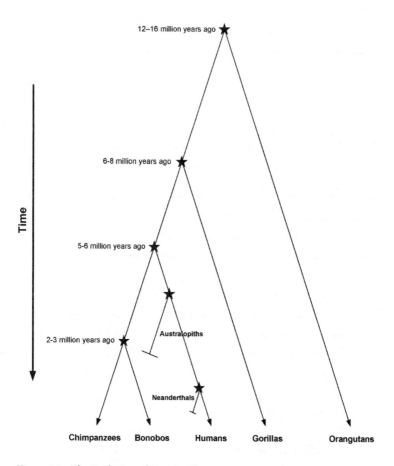

Figure 5.2. The Evolution of Hominoids.

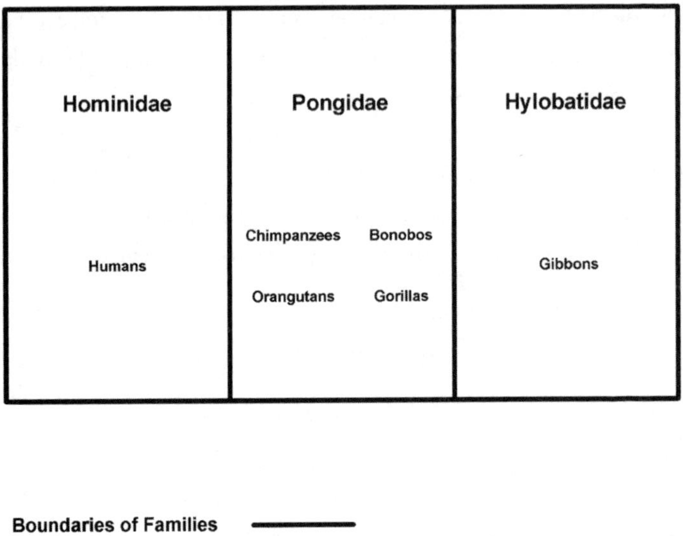

Figure 5.3. The Pre-1960s Taxonomic Relations between Humans and Apes.

bonobo), and the Hominidae (which included humans). The line separating "human" from "ape" was thus drawn at the taxonomic family level. Goodman's findings, however, presented a major challenge to this taxonomy, as they defy the notion

> that there is somehow some special distinctness and separateness between humans and other animals. Molecular data and the revisions to phylogeny, taxonomy, and divergence times that they imply undermine the validity of that distinctness and separateness.[83]

As Goodman himself pointed out,

> This traditional anthropocentric view . . . ignores (1) the overwhelming evidence that the African great apes share their more

recent common ancestry with humans rather than with orangutans and (2) the mounting evidence that . . . chimpanzees and
bonobos . . . shar[e] a more recent common ancestry with
humans than with gorillas.[84]

Goodman's findings, in other words, showed that proto-chimpanzees
and proto-bonobos split from proto-humans only after having
already split earlier from proto-gorillas (see Figure 5.2), which means
that chimpanzees and gorillas have no common ancestor that they do
not also share with humans.[85] And since we now group species together only if they share a more recent common ancestor than either
of them shares with other species, that certainly makes our conventional category "apes" a genealogical absurdity. After all, while we
would never consider ourselves genealogically closer to our cousins
than to our siblings, we actually "make exactly such a statement when
we argue that chimps are closer to gorillas than to humans."[86] Indeed,
if chimpanzees knew genetics, they would find it inconceivable that
they are actually being lumped together with gorillas rather than
with humans!

Goodman's finding that chimpanzees and bonobos are genealogically closer to us than they are to gorillas thus seemed to imply
that "[i]t is past time when humans could bask in the inflated ideas
of our separation from the rest of the living world."[87] Indeed, the fact
that only "the narrowest of genetic crevices" actually separates us
from our simian cousins[88] led him to question the very distinction
between the categories "hominid" and "pongid" and propose that
the former be expanded to also include the gorilla, chimpanzee,
bonobo, and orangutan, and the latter be eliminated altogether (see
Figure 5.4).[89] Essentially dividing the new Hominidae family into
two subfamilies, the Ponginae (which includes the orangutan) and
the Homininae (which includes the gorilla, the bonobo, and the
chimpanzee along with humans), and subdividing the latter into

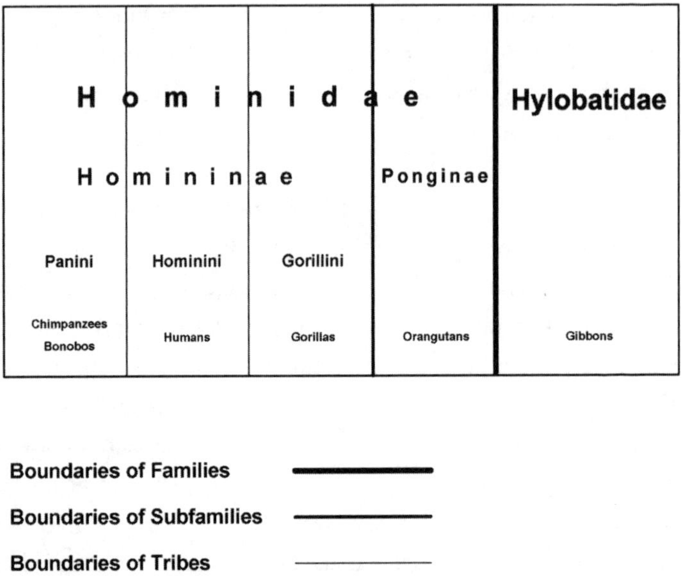

Hominidae				Hylobatidae
Homininae			Ponginae	
Panini	Hominini	Gorillini		
Chimpanzees Bonobos	Humans	Gorillas	Orangutans	Gibbons

Boundaries of Families ━━━━━━

Boundaries of Subfamilies ─────

Boundaries of Tribes ────

Figure 5.4. The Post-1960s Taxonomic Relations between Humans and Apes.

three taxonomic tribes—the Gorillini (which includes the gorilla), the Panini (which includes the chimpanzee and the bonobo), and the Hominini (which includes humans)[90]—he thus effectively redrew the line separating humans from other animals at the taxonomic tribe level.

Scientists have since by and large accepted this unmistakably bold taxonomic recommendation, essentially moving the formal distinction between "human" and "animal" from the zoological family to the tribe level. And since chimpanzees and bonobos are genetically (and therefore also genealogically) closer to us than are "sibling" species of bears, mice, or frogs to one another,[91] some (notably biogeographer Jared Diamond as well as Goodman himself) have even gone so far as to include both of them in the genus *Homo*, thereby effectively daring taxonomists to follow Linnaeus and draw the line between "human" and "ape" already at the species level.[92] After all,

> [g]enetic differences between human, chimpanzee, and gorilla are within the range of distances between species within the same genus in the animal world. It is, therefore, no longer defensible . . . that humans should be in a separate genus while equally or even more distant mammal species of, for example, antelope, seal, or gibbon are in the same genus.[93]

Such a radical taxonomic revision would require, however, giving up our exceptionalist self-image as "human" beings, thereby essentially acknowledging our inevitably simian identity. Indeed, as Linnaeus himself explained already back in 1747 his far-from-casual decision to place humans and apes in the same genus,

> [i]t matters little to me what names we use; but I demand of you . . . that you show me a generic character, one that is according to generally accepted principles of classification, by which to distinguish between man and ape. . . . I myself most assuredly know of none. . . . But, if I had called man an ape, or vice-versa, I should have fallen under the ban of all the ecclesiastics. It may be that as a naturalist I ought to have done so.[94]

Linnaeus's mea culpa underscores the important role of language in the mental act of lumping.[95] As exemplified by the way we use surnames, a common label clearly helps signal genealogical affinity. It was, in fact, their critique of our self-image as somehow separate from the rest of the animal world that made Desmond Morris and Diamond pick for their anti-exceptionalist portrayals of humans such provocative titles as *The Naked Ape* and *The Third Chimpanzee*, and Matt Cartmill and Fred Smith title the chapters of their textbook on human evolution "The Bipedal Ape," "The Migrating Ape," "The Big-Brained Ape," "Talking Apes," and "The Symbolic Ape."[96]

Lumpers also use other effectively inclusionary linguistic tactics such as lexical compounding and hyphenation.[97] Thus, in the 1860s, strongly suspecting our genealogical ties to apes, Haeckel, for example, essentially compounded the Greek words for "ape" (*pithekos*) and "man" (*anthropos*) and named the hypothetical missing link he postulated between them *Pithecanthropus* (later renamed by archaeologist Gabriel de Mortillet *Anthropopithecus*).[98] Later, when Raymond Dart discovered the first australopithecine fossil with its distinctive blend of human and simian features, he likewise assigned it to a new family of primates that he formally named *Homo-simiadae*.[99]

Indeed, part of the reason we actually envision such a wide gap supposedly separating us from chimpanzees and bonobos is that *Ardipithecus ramidus, Australopithecus afarensis, Homo erectus*, as well as every other intermediate species between us are already extinct. To quote anthropologist Robin Dunbar,

> [T]he apparent size of the gulf separating us from our nearest relatives is largely a consequence of the absence of any intermediate species alive today. . . . It is not that there have never been any intermediate species. Such species have existed in plenty. . . . Rather, our problem is that they are all extinct. . . . If any of these species were alive today, the gulf between ourselves and the chimpanzees would almost certainly seem a lot less dramatic than it does at present.[100]

In other words, there have never been any actual gaps in the ancestral chain going back to the common ancestors of humans and apes. Therefore, if we do envision such a gap, it must be in our own minds.[101]

MARGINALIZING

Lumping, of course, is expressly inclusionary, but there are other genealogical tactics specifically designed to exclude various "others." One such tactic is marginalizing.

Marginalizers acknowledge sharing their ancestral tree with those whom they try to exclude, but they view themselves as part of its actual trunk yet those others only as its side branches.[102] While admitting that they both descend from the same ancestors, they nevertheless distinguish between "main" and "side" lines of descent and try to figuratively sideline those whom they wish to exclude.

Marginalizing thus presupposes a fundamental distinction between "true" successors (and therefore rightful heirs) and supposedly lesser descendants (see Figure 5.5). In yet another instance where the logic of reckoning genealogical relatedness clearly distorts the biological and historical reality it supposedly reflects, not all descendants are evidently created equal. Effectively regarding the mythical Abraham-Isaac-Jacob line as the trunk, yet the Abraham-Ishmael one as a mere offshoot, of their ancestral tree, for example,[103] ultranationalist Jews can thus conveniently forget that the so-called Promised Land was actually "promised" to all of Abraham's descendants and not just Jacob's.

We likewise sideline our aunts and uncles as well as other predecessors deemed not directly ancestral to us. A perfect example are the Neanderthals, in contrast to whom we often view our own humanity. While we may not be able to define what "human" is,

it is increasingly evident that we can agree on what it is *not*— Neandertal! With native peoples no longer available for that role, it is the Neandertals who have become "other." How better to define ourselves than in comparison with these folk?[104]

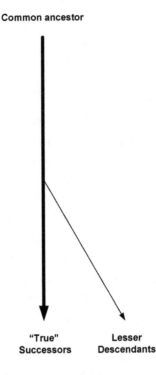

Common ancestor

"True"   **Lesser**
Successors   **Descendants**

Figure 5.5. Marginalizing.

Such contrast is implicit, for example, in popular depictions of their exaggeratedly stooped posture[105] (that are somewhat evocative of the pronouncedly apelike features which we associate with the australopiths, yet much less so with even the earliest members of *Homo*)[106] as well as in the way we often withhold attributing to them humanlike qualities such as having language, technology, morality, or art. And indeed, despite the increasingly compelling genetic evidence that they may actually be ancestral to some modern Europeans,[107] only few scholars today consider the Neanderthals a subspecific variant of our own species, which they even formally label *Homo sapiens neanderthalensis*,[108] while everyone else essentially

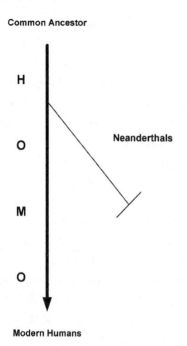

Figure 5.6. The Marginalization of the Neanderthals.

regards them as a distinct species (*Homo neanderthalensis*), a mere side branch of *Homo* that was not ancestral to any modern humans (see Figure 5.6).[109] Rather than consider them our conspecific great-great-uncles and -aunts (not to mention great-great-grandparents), we thus sideline them as strictly congeneric and therefore much more distant relatives.

SPLITTING

In order to marginalize others, we often push the ancestors we share with them as far back as we can, since greater distance from a common ancestor implies weaker genealogical ties among his or her co-descendants. Whereas lumpers reach back as far as they can into the past in an attempt to identify common ancestors that would help them build more inclusive genealogical tents, marginalizers do so in the hope that they would not encounter any recent ones. In an effort to distance themselves from undesirable co-descendants, they therefore try to establish protective temporal buffers that would help dilute the contaminative effect of their common origins. Pushing the historical point at which their ancestral lines split as far back as possible is designed to help make those contaminative origins less relevant.

That explains, for example, the great anxiety evidently generated by the finding that the lineages ultimately leading to humans and modern apes actually diverged only relatively recently. After all, "One of the ways in which man separates himself from the rest of nature is to put his origins as far back in time as he can," thereby "safely distancing him from the other animals,"[110] but the genetic evidence we now have clearly erodes this essentially illusory sense of safety. As Sarich, the person perhaps most singularly responsible for unveiling this evidence, points out, "Many people do not like the idea that one of our ancestors was similar to a living ape. The more recent our divergence from the common ancestor, the more likely that this is true."[111]

Yet an even more effective exclusionary tactic than just pushing back the historical point at which two populations must have split from each other is their portrayal as never having shared any ancestor. Whereas marginalizers acknowledge shared origins even with those whom they try to exclude (see Figure 5.5 and 5.6), "splitters"[112] explicitly deny any common ancestry. Rather than presenting them as trunks and branches of essentially the same trees, they portray their respective lineages as altogether separate trees, and their respective populations (the French elites and the French masses, the Polish elites and the Polish masses, humans and apes)[113] as therefore totally distinct from each other.

Splitting is the ultimate expression of purist visions of pedigrees that "can be traced back to an untainted origin"[114] and are not contaminated by ties to any undesirable co-descendants. Some classic manifestations of this exclusionary tactic were the *limpieza de sangre* ("purity of blood") laws introduced by the Spanish Inquisition in the fifteenth century. Under those laws, in order to differentiate themselves from mere descendants of converts (also known as "New Christians"), "Old Christians" had to officially establish their genealogical purity by proving that they had no Jewish or Muslim ancestors.[115] To ensure that their pedigrees were not contaminated by even a single drop of non-Christian blood, there was no limit on how far back they had to go in order to demonstrate the absence of any such "genealogical stains." Being an Old Christian evidently required a pedigree that was pure "since time immemorial."[116]

It is in reference to Spain's "New Christians" that the word *race* was probably first used in its modern sense,[117] and it is indeed within the context of race that the tactic of splitting has been carried to its ultimate extreme. The alleged Neanderthal origins attributed to the Irish (by the English), the Germans (by the French), as well as Europeans in general (by Afrocentrists)[118] offer a great example of such "genealogical apartheid," as do practically all other manifestations of the "polygenist" vision of humanity as made up of separate "races."[119] To underscore their supposedly distinct essences, polygenists attribute separate origins to those "races." In order to maximally widen the genealogical gulf supposedly separating them from one another,[120] they portray them as having evolved totally independently of one another through essentially parallel ancestral lines (see Figure 5.7).[121]

The greater the antiquity attributed to "racial" divisions (as exemplified by the "multiregionalist" claim that modern East Asians, Southeast Asians, and Australian Aborigines evolved not only from bands of *Homo sapiens* who came out of Africa 50,000–100,000 years

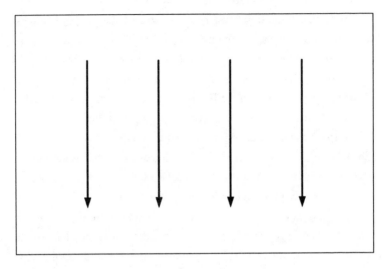

Figure 5.7. The Polygenist Vision of Human Descent.

ago but also from regional variants of *Homo erectus* who had preceded them by almost two million years),[122] the more compelling the image of the various "races" as actually distinct from one another.[123] As Alabama Governor Chauncey Sparks, effectively echoing Arthur de Gobineau's claim that the racial divisions were fixed "immediately after the creation,"[124] articulated segregationists' vision of the genealogical relations between blacks and whites in the 1940s: "[T]he two races are distinct. They . . . began in different origins . . . and should remain separate, as they have always been since the Creation."[125]

The notion of polygenesis dates back to the Renaissance, when some Europeans who found it difficult to reconcile the extent of human diversity to which they were exposed in their encounters with sub-Saharan Africa, America, and Melanesia[126] with the biblical theory that all humans descend from Adam and Eve proceeded to trace sub-Saharan Africans, Native Americans, and Melanesians back to some mythical protohuman "pre-Adamites."[127] It later acquired a somewhat more scientific veneer, however, when polygenists began to portray the various "races" as distinct species designated by taxonomic labels such as *Homo europeus*, *Homo australis*, and *Homo mongolus*,[128] thus effectively essentializing racial divisions by implying their supposedly zoological basis. "If Negroes and Caucasians were snails," contended paleontologist Friedrich Quenstedt, "zoologists would universally agree that they represented two very distinct species, which could never have originated from one pair by gradual divergence."[129] Modern anthropology, claimed Hermann Klaatsch, could therefore no longer

> support the idea of [human brotherhood] that had been suggested by religious and sentimental considerations. Modern science cannot confirm the exaggerated humanitarianism which sees brothers and sisters in all the lower races.[130]

In fact, concluded zoologist Karl Vogt in what may very well have been the ultimate expression of the spirit of genealogical splitting, Africans, Asians, and Europeans must have respectively evolved from the gorilla, the orangutan, and the chimpanzee![131]

PRUNING

While marginalizers sideline the genealogical branches they wish to exclude and splitters place them on a separate tree, there is yet a third form of genealogical exclusion that involves "pruning" them. And like both cutting and clipping, it requires some forgetting.

Yet whereas both cutting and clipping genealogical narratives make them shorter, pruning is designed to make them narrower. By effectively erasing certain ancestral branches from our genealogical memory, it basically reduces multilinear and therefore structurally complex historical realities to simpler, unilinear genealogical narratives. Essentially denying multiple origins,[132] it is indeed the antithesis of braiding.

"Mules are always boasting that their ancestors were horses," observes a wise proverb,[133] yet they rarely mention their own fathers, who were mere donkeys. Effectively applying the principle of "hyperdescent," we thus usually highlight our more esteemed ancestors while pruning off our lesser ones. The efforts made by some Australians to suppress their embarrassing ties to their country's early European settlers, who were convicts,[134] are a classic example of that. So, of course, has been the practice of whitening ("bleaching") one's pedigree by pruning off African ancestral branches in order to pass as a white person in the United States or Brazil.[135]

However, while the principle of hyperdescent may seem almost self-evident, there is also the reverse situation when we reckon descent according to a person's *least* esteemed ancestors while essentially disregarding his or her more esteemed ones. The most spectacular manifestation of this principle of "hypodescent"[136] is the aforementioned one-drop rule, where it is one's white rather than black ancestors who are actually being disregarded.

Although later also embraced by affirmative-action officers as well as black nationalists who "hate every drop of that white rapist's blood" in them,[137] the one-drop rule was originally designed to help white slave owners deny their sexual encounters with their female slaves and thereby also keep the products of those unions as slaves.[138] Yet even long after the end of slavery, it still remains the ultimate expression of Americans' obsession with racial purity, as it reflects their deep anxiety about racially ambiguous persons,[139] whose very existence threatens the notion that one is either black or white. Such ambiguity, indeed, was actually legislated out of existence in 1930 by formally reclassifying former "mulattoes" as "Negroes" and thereby eliminating any middle category between "black" and "white."[140] By effectively considering anyone with any black ancestors black, the one-drop rule thus "makes black unhyphenable" since there is basically "no such category as anything-black people. There are only black people."[141] As such, it certainly helps Americans maintain their view of whiteness and blackness as mutually exclusive.[142] But in order to bolster this binary schema and protect whites' alleged racial purity, it also requires carefully pruning any white branch off any "black" person's family tree.

As we saw in the cases of the *limpieza de sangre* and polygenism, how far back we actually delve into the past to protect our purity is a good barometer of our racist sentiments. Consider, for example, in this regard Virginia, where, starting in 1930, "any Negro blood at all"[143] would suffice to make one black. That was also true in Georgia ("any ascertainable trace of Negro blood"), Arkansas ("any negro blood whatever"), and Alabama, where anyone with any "negro ancestors, without . . . limit of time or number of generations" was considered black.[144]

The notion that "any known African ancestry renders one black"[145] explains why even today, long after the end of slavery and Jim Crow as well as the introduction of somewhat more nuanced genealogical categories such as "biracial," most Americans still consider Obama black despite his hardly negligible white roots. As James McBride, who is also considered a "black author" despite having been raised by a white mother, laments such existential predicament: "Why can't I be a white author? I'm half white."[146]

[6]

THE GENEALOGY OF THE FUTURE

*The cross between a white man and an Indian is an Indian; the cross
between a white man and a Negro is a Negro; the cross between a white
man and a Hindu is a Hindu; and the cross between any of the three
European races and a Jew is a Jew.*

—Madison Grant, *The Passing of the Great Race*, 15

GENEALOGICAL ENGINEERING

Although usually seen as an attempt to reconstruct the past, genealogy also plays an important role in efforts to shape the future. Effectively projecting our visions of relatedness not only back but also
forward, we thus use our genealogical imagination retrospectively as
well as prospectively.

As exemplified by teknonymy, the practice of naming someone
after his or her children, grandchildren, and even great-grandchildren,[1]
thinking genealogically involves not only ancestors and relatives but
also descendants. Indeed, given the reality of Jewish-Christian intermarriage, for example, Jews may soon be defined not by who their
grandparents were but rather by who their grandchildren will be.

Our prospective genealogical visions certainly affect the way we
reproduce ourselves, and as evidenced by the eugenics movement,

which has carried the connection between the two to its extreme, such "genealogical engineering" is actually modeled after the basic philosophy and techniques used by animal breeders. (Indeed, eugenicists dream of a future "when a woman would no more accept a man 'without knowing his biologico-genealogical history' than a stockbreeder would take 'a sire for his colts or calves . . . without pedigree.'")[2] As such, it involves the use of various genealogical tactics that are but the prospective forms of lumping, braiding, splitting, and pruning.

INTEGRATION

The first and most basic prospective genealogical tactic is integration, the fusion of two or more hitherto unrelated elements into a single genealogical community. In the same way that sharing common ancestors helps make their co-descendants feel related, the very prospect of sharing common descendants, and therefore becoming "co-ancestors," transforms hitherto unrelated individuals into prospective relatives. After all, only by co-generating children do otherwise unrelated sexual partners become kin.[3]

Envisioning a common genealogical future, of course, is one of the most important factors underlying the decision to get married. Yet marriage unites more than just individuals,[4] since the prospect of sharing common descendants can also help meld hitherto separate genealogical communities into one. Indeed, marriage has traditionally been viewed as a bond between two families based on the grand-progeny they anticipate sharing as future in-laws (see Figure 6.1).

As one might expect, genealogical integration is greatly enhanced by outbreeding (and particularly its institutionalized form, exogamy), or the practice of mating only outside one's own genealogical community, which is designed to prevent excessive inbreeding

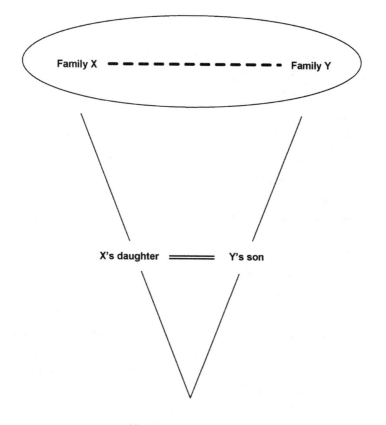

Figure 6.1. Co-Ancestry.

by formally disqualifying potential mates considered genealogically too close to us. Its ultimate manifestation, of course, has been the establishment of the incest taboo as a way to ensure that we would never mate with any member of our immediate family. Effectively fostering reproductive ties across rather than within families,[5] it thus clearly expands our web of genealogical affiliations.

Outbreeding further manifests itself in intermarriage, the practice of mating across not only families but also ethnoracial communities. As a prospective form of lumping, it involves envisioning those hitherto separate communities eventually relinquishing their distinct identities (like the ingredients of a chemical compound or a blended soup) to form a "post-ethnic"[6] society whose members would no longer be Korean Americans or Mexican Americans but simply Americans. As a prospective form of braiding, however, it involves projecting onto the future a pronouncedly multicultural vision of a "salad bowl" or "cultural mosaic," an ethnoracial mixture (rather than a compound) that preserves the distinct identities of its multiple ancestral components.

Prior to the rise of multiculturalism in the 1970s, the United States was considered the prime example of the first form of genealogical integration, also known as assimilation. As early as 1782, John Hector St. John de Crèvecoeur invoked the metallurgical metaphor with which it has since come to be associated when he portrayed American society as one where "individuals of all nations are melted into a new race of men,"[7] a vision later also shared by Ralph Waldo Emerson, who believed that

> in this continent . . . the energy of Irish, Germans, Swedes, Poles, and Cossacks, and all the European tribes,—of the Africans, and of the Polynesians,—will construct a new race . . . which will be as vigorous as the new Europe which came out of the smelting-pot of the Dark Ages.[8]

Such characterization of Americanness as a product of the amalgamation of different ethnic origins was famously popularized in Israel Zangwill's 1909 play *The Melting-Pot.*[9]

The assimilationist melting-pot and multicultural salad-bowl metaphors certainly capture the pronouncedly contrasting prospective visions fueling modern nation-states' genealogical culture wars. Invoking the metaphor of a Caribbean dish where several distinct food ingredients are effectively blended into one stew, Trinidad thus celebrates itself as a melting-pot-like "callaloo nation,"[10] yet as evident from the very title of anthropologist Viranjini Munasinghe's book *Callaloo or Tossed Salad?* such a prospective genealogical vision is by no means uncontroversial. Indo-Trinidadian politicians, for example,

> draw on Indo-Trinidadian sentiments against what they perceive to be a forced . . . integration . . . by counterpoising the image of a tossed salad to that of a callaloo, a popular local dish in the Caribbean in which a number of distinct ingredients are boiled down to a homogeneous mush. The callaloo is a clear analogy to the melting-pot model of assimilation; the imagery of the tossed salad, in which each piece of lettuce and cucumber retains its "true" identity despite being mixed with "other" ingredients, draws on the plural society model.[11]

Given this contrasting symbolism, Indo-Trinidadians are indeed "quick to opt for a tossed salad analogy" of that island nation's genealogical identity "over that of a callaloo."[12]

SEGREGATION

As a major symbol of the boundary-defying spirit of universalism,[13] intermarriage is highly romanticized by advocates of genealogical integration. "A marital union . . . across boundaries that are considered significant, and often in defiance of . . . old descent antagonisms," argues Werner Sollors, "is what constitutes melting-pot love."[14] No wonder it is so intensely opposed by those who object to the very idea of integration.

It is the fact that its members mate with one another more than with members of other groups, of course, that makes any group (a tribe, a nation, a species) a genealogical community. Therefore, with intermarriage, ethnicity tends to fade,[15] and ethnic groups face the danger of being assimilated into their social surroundings and thereby ceasing to exist as distinct communities.[16]

That explains why many ethnic minorities are so threatened by intermarriage. As their members intermarry, they risk losing their social visibility,[17] the imaginary boundaries delineating them as supposedly discrete, and therefore distinct,[18] entities. No wonder Jews, Armenians, Parsis, Druzes, and other pronouncedly "unmeltable"[19] ethnic communities often discourage or even prohibit intermarriage.

Yet it is not only ethnic minorities who fear intermarriage. So, in fact, do ethnic majorities who nevertheless consider themselves endangered by genealogical integration. As evident from the very title of his 1916 bestselling book *The Passing of the Great Race*, nativist Madison Grant's great horror was the imminent death of "the Nordic race" as a result of America's melting-pot ideology.[20] Indeed, it is both black separatists[21] and white supremacists who abhor "interracial" unions.

Yet whereas ethnic minorities fear that intermarriage will effectively obliterate them as distinct communities, supremacists worry that it will dilute, and thereby degrade, their supposedly superior blood.[22] As anthropologist Georges Vacher de Lapouge articulated such a lopsided view of intergroup mating, "bad blood drives out good."[23] Such imagined asymmetry was manifested, for example, in the Nazis' belief that "an Aryan woman, if only once soiled by a Jew, was destined to breed only Jewish . . . children,"[24] as portrayed in Artur Dinter's bestselling proto-Nazi anti-Semitic novel *Sin Against the Blood* about

a "racially pure," blonde, blue-eyed German woman who was seduced by a Jew. Although she . . . subsequently married an

"Aryan," she and her husband nonetheless produced "typically Jewish-looking" children. Her "hereditary properties" had been permanently corrupted by a casual encounter with a Jew.[25]

(A Jew who defiles an Aryan woman with his blood, wrote Hitler in *Mein Kampf*, therefore effectively "steal[s] her from her people.")[26] It was likewise explicitly evident in then Vice President Calvin Coolidge's claim that "Nordics deteriorate when mixed with other races,"[27] and is perhaps most famously captured in Grant's assertion that

> the cross between a white man and an Indian is an Indian; the cross between a white man and a Negro is a Negro; the cross between a white man and a Hindu is a Hindu; and the cross between any of the three European races and a Jew is a Jew.[28]

There is a rather pronounced gender asymmetry, however, in the way we view intergroup mating given the fact that it is much more difficult to disavow maternity than paternity.[29] In trying to secure their future, ethnoracial groups therefore try to prevent particularly their female members from breeding with nonmembers.[30] That explains why sexual unions between black men and white women seem to have always threatened white supremacists far more than any such unions between white men and black women,[31] and why a Serbian soldier who raped a Bosnian woman would not be considered impure, whereas she would.

As Hitler's use of the word *defiles* seems to imply, the notion of genealogical purity plays a major role in the way we think about intermarriage, as do the notions of genealogical impurity and contamination.[32] Indeed, it is ethnoracial communities' genealogical purity that intermarriage clearly threatens.

It is their strong objection to ethnoracial mixing, or "mixophobia,"[33] of course, that characterizes genealogical purists.[34] "The dream of the ethnic purist is . . . the eternal perpetuation of the boundaries between races or stocks or groups,"[35] thereby keeping ethnoracial communities separate. Such segregation can be accomplished spatially through ethnic "cleansing" as well as zoning ordinances and immigration restrictions. (In the words of one of the founders of America's early-twentieth-century Immigration Restriction League, "[I]nferior stocks can be prevented from . . . diluting . . . good stocks. Just as we isolate bacterial invasions . . . so we can compel an inferior race to remain in its native habitat").[36] Yet it is most often accomplished by controlling mate choice. In the same way that intermarriage helps erase ethnic boundaries and thereby enhance genealogical integration, banning it helps solidify those boundaries, thus enhancing genealogical segregation. In other words, just as the prospect of sharing common descendants transforms unrelated individuals into kin, preventing such a common future helps produce ethnoracially pure communities (in the same way that inability to produce common progeny often implies membership in different species).[37]

Whereas genealogical integration presupposes outbreeding, genealogical segregation requires inbreeding. In marked contrast to exogamy, endogamy thus disqualifies potential mates considered genealogically too distant from (rather than too close to) us, thereby ensuring that we mate only with members of our own clan or ethnoracial community and not venture sexually beyond its confines. Thus, whereas in exogamous societies marrying one's cousin is often considered incestuous, in highly endogamous groups it is actually a rather common practice. More than 80 percent of all Samaritan marriages, in fact, are between first or second cousins.[38]

Formal bans on intermarriage have been documented as early as twenty-four centuries ago when Ezra and Nehemiah, effectively invoking the Deuteronomic admonition "Thy daughter thou shalt not give unto his son, nor his daughter shalt thou take unto thy son," prohibited fellow Jews from marrying non-Jews.[39] (As the Talmud explicitly spells out the actual genealogical implications of this ban, "Thy son by a heathen is not called thy son.")[40] Consider also, in this regard, France's 1778 and Italy's 1938 laws prohibiting "interracial" marriages, the 1949 Prohibition of Mixed Marriages Act and 1950 Immorality Act banning sexual unions between blacks and whites in South Africa, and Nazi Germany's 1935 Law for the Protection of German Blood and Honor, explicitly designed to promote "the biological separation of the Jewish and German races."[41] In a similar vein, consider, finally, America's "anti-miscegenation" laws dating back to the seventeenth-century ban on "interracial" unions in Maryland and Virginia,[42] many of which were still in effect as late as the mid-1960s.

EXTINCTION

Its ultimate goal being the reproductive isolation of ethnoracial communities from one another, genealogical segregation, in effect, simulates the natural process of speciation.[43] "Once cultural differences have achieved this initial separation, with the consequence that there is no gene flow to hold them together, the groups would subsequently evolve apart genetically"[44] like geographically separated conspecific populations that can no longer interbreed, ultimately diverging into separate species.[45] Segregated ethnoracial communities are thus "species in the making," and ethnoracial boundaries are essentially "an early version of the barriers against interbreeding that establish distinct species."[46] Indeed, had America's anti-miscegenation laws not been abolished, they would have ultimately produced biologically discrete, and thus genetically distinct, populations.

Yet making black and white Americans biologically distinct would have required hundreds of thousands of generations of absolute reproductive isolation.[47] After all, despite having been geographically separated for thousands of years, Maoris and Basques, for example, can nevertheless still interbreed. So can Zulus and Finns.

There is, however, a much faster, not to mention more effective, way to prevent genealogical integration, namely genocide. Whereas segregation is the prospective form of genealogical splitting, the prospective form of genealogical pruning is extinction.

One can effectively extinguish a genealogical community, for example, by removing its children from it, as Euro-Australians indeed tried to do to the Aborigines.[48] (That may also explain objections to transnational and "transracial" adoption, as exemplified by the National Association of Black Social Workers' denunciation of adoptions of African American children by white families as essentially genocidal.)[49] Somewhat similar genealogical reasoning, in fact, also explains organized rape. Carrying the notion of patrilineal descent to its violent logical conclusion, the systematic raping of Bosnian women by Serbian soldiers in the 1990s, for example, was cynically designed to ensure that they would no longer bear Bosnian children.[50]

One could, of course, also try to prevent such children from even being born, and genealogical communities can, in fact, also be extinguished by eugenic means. After all, like animal breeders, eugenicists can effectively hinder community members' ability to reproduce, as infamously exemplified by their use of prospective pruning tactics like vasectomy and sterilization.[51]

Yet as evidenced by the Nazis' efforts to "suppress all sources which might 'dilute' or 'taint'" their "Nordic blood,"[52] an even more effective way to prevent the birth of any future members of a genealogical community is by actually exterminating its current members. And in attempting to push their purist genealogical vision to its logical extreme and essentially wipe out Europe's entire Jewish and Gypsy populations, they thus gave us a chilling demonstration of the potential implications of the very idea of genealogical engineering.

[7]

THE FUTURE OF GENEALOGY

*[W]hether social parentage is or is not identical with genetic parentage
does not matter, for both follow the same logical model.*
—J. A. Barnes, "Genealogies," 102

Given their social nature, the contours of our genealogical landscape
are also affected by various (demographic, cultural, technological)
forms of social change. Several such recent changes in particular
affect the way we now envision genealogical relatedness.

Increasing immigration, for example, entails increased contact
among hitherto more isolated ethnoracial communities. Such contact, in turn, is also increasing our rates of intermarriage, thereby
"destroying the old, regional patterns of genetic diversity [and]
replacing them with cosmopolitan melting pots of markers"[1] as well
as more "braided" genealogical identities.

Further acknowledging their multiethnic makeup, modern nation-
states are also increasingly held together by civic rather than tribal notions of nationhood, thereby essentially embracing "post-ethnicity."[2]
In such a "post-tribal"[3] world, of course, one would expect visions of
a common future to supersede those of a common past as a basis for
social solidarity, or in the words of John Quincy Adams, social

communities whose members actually look "forward to their posterity rather than backward to their ancestors."[4]

Modern birth-control practices (such as the use of oral contraceptive pills) and policies (such as China's one-child rule) are also changing our micro-genealogical landscape, as families are getting smaller. If this trend continues, the very notion of siblinghood, for example, may ultimately become obsolete.[5] At the same time, however, our traditional notion of having only one set of parents and siblings is constantly being challenged by increasing rates of remarriage[6] that have given rise to the "stepfamily" or "blended" ("reconstituted," "recomposed," "recombinant") family,[7] a new form of genealogical community based on new kinds of genealogical ties such as step-parenthood and half-siblinghood. Membership in such communities implies having multiple sets of ancestors and therefore also multiple sets of relatives as well as multiple genealogical identities. It also raises new definitional dilemmas. After all, how exactly is one genealogically related to one's mother's new husband's ex-wife's stepchildren?[8]

New reproductive technologies such as surrogacy further complexify our genealogical landscape by introducing a major new distinction between the genetic mother who donates the egg and the gestational mother who carries it to term,[9] thereby also posing new dilemmas such as whether Jewish identity, for example, which is conferred matrilineally, is "embedded in bodily substance [or] created in gestational environment."[10] Indeed, as we may soon be able to produce a child with genetic contributions from more than just two biological parents,[11] he or she would actually have several "fractional parents," as biological parenthood may become "just a matter of degree."[12]

Assisted reproductive technology has also given rise to some rather intriguing genealogical paradoxes. If a man donates his sperm to his daughter-in-law, for example, should he then be considered her child's father, grandfather, or both?[13] Indeed, surrogacy has already made it possible for a woman to carry her daughter's fertilized egg to term and thus to actually give birth to her own grandchild, whose genetic mother was therefore also its sister![14]

Other new technological possibilities may soon also create new genealogical realities that would have been considered pure science fiction only a few years ago. As we can freeze embryos, for example, siblings may someday be born centuries apart from one another, thus further complicating the way we delineate generations. Someday, indeed, we may also be able to have human eggs gestate in simian wombs, and simian eggs in human wombs,[15] or to even fertilize eggs parthenogenetically, thereby producing biologically fatherless children.

Since it ultimately involves duplication instead of filiation, thereby deeming the very notions of ancestry and descent irrelevant, cloning, of course, poses the ultimate challenge to the genealogical imagination. With clones, who would be effectively parentless, we would actually no longer even be dealing with genealogical relatedness anymore.[16]

Indeed, it may thus seem as if genealogical relatedness might lose some of its traditional significance, and that ironically, as we are getting better in being able to trace as well as measure it, how much it will even matter to us is unclear. Yet as the growing number of websites and software programs designed to help us construct our family trees and discover previously unknown relatives (including even sperm-bank "siblings")[17] as well as of companies offering "genealogical tours" or genetic ancestry tests seems to indicate, our fascination with genealogy is far from waning. Furthermore, the way we now use it clearly transcends its original role as a framework for reckoning only strictly biological proximity.

Indeed, we have long viewed certain kinds of nonbiological ties through a quasi-familial lens.[18] As strictly symbolic forms of ancestry explicitly modeled after parenthood, both adoption and fostering (and to a lesser extent also godparenthood) exemplify our ability to formally transform nonkin into "as-if kin."[19] And in effectively pulling individuals away from their supposedly natural familial, ethnoracial, and ethno-national environments, they also challenge our conventional, highly essentialized notions of family, ethnicity, race, and nationhood.

As I first realized when my then-four-year-old son asked me if apricots are "baby peaches," genealogy has in fact become a general framework, or template, for conceptualizing various forms of relatedness that include, but are by no means confined to, biological ancestry, descent, and consanguinity. Thus, whether or not a particular form of social relatedness is actually based on biogenetic relatedness does not really matter, as "both follow the same logical model."[20]

As exemplified by quasi-intergenerational envisioned lines of "great-grand big sisters," "grand big sisters," "big sisters," and "little sisters" in American college sororities,[21] not all the ties we consider "ancestral" are always blood-based. The blood tie so suggestively represented by the wine Christians drink during Communion to mark their spiritual "descent" from Jesus is clearly only symbolic, as was the one, so explicitly invoked in a poem that opens with the line "Her blood runs in my veins," linking Israeli poet Rachel Bluwstein to her biblical namesake Rachel the Matriarch.[22]

Modern organizational succession, in fact, presupposes the notion of a nonhereditary "office"[23] (the musical directorship of the New York Philharmonic, a seat on the United States Supreme Court) effectively occupied by a quasi-intergenerational "line" (see Figure 7.1) of nonbiologically related incumbents.[24] (As evidenced by the nickname "41" given to President George H. W. Bush, assigning their members successive numbers certainly helps reify such imaginary lines.) Yet the cognitive role of parenthood and filiation as templates for conceptualizing even purely symbolic forms of

ancestry and descent is most strikingly manifest in the way we come to envision chains of spiritual and other modes of cultural transmission such as exemplified by centuries-long lines of Dalai Lamas, Sikh Gurus, and popes. And as particularly evident in the case of the envisioned quasi-intergenerational lines of mentors and disciples constituting chains of intellectual transmission, such strictly symbolic lineages are nevertheless modeled after bloodlines. Thus, in traditional Islamic scholarship, for example, scholars are viewed as spiritually linked

> to the Prophet Muhammad . . . through an uninterrupted chain of teachers. . . . Through direct aural instruction, the teacher gives birth to the student into the world of religious scholarship, and the student becomes like the teacher's child.[25]

In a similar manner, we seem to envision quasi-filial ties between doctoral students and their dissertation advisors,[26] and use unmistakably genealogical diagrams to portray the flow of intellectual influence from Charles Peirce to John Dewey, Benedetto Croce to Antonio Gramsci, and Jeremy Bentham to John Stuart Mill.[27] As I envision the quasi-intergenerational chain of mentors (Robert Park, Everett Hughes, and Erving Goffman) effectively "connecting" me to Georg Simmel, one of the "founding fathers" of modern sociology (see Figure 7.2), I therefore consider myself his "great-great-grandstudent."

We often invoke our symbolic ancestors (as I saw Jordi Bonet do in 2004 by presenting himself as the ninth link in a chain of chief architects of Barcelona's Sagrada Familia cathedral going back 121 years to Antonio Gaudí) to activate our cultural capital. As Heidi's piano teacher reminds her in an attempt to boost her professional self-confidence in the film *The Competition*, "Ludwig van Beethoven taught Carl Czerny, who taught Leschetizky, who taught Schnabel, who taught Renaldi, who taught me, and now the

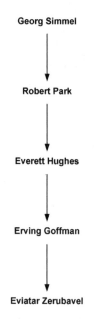

Georg Simmel

Robert Park

Everett Hughes

Erving Goffman

Eviatar Zerubavel

Figure 7.2. A Chain of Intellectual Transmission.

sixth pianist in a direct line from Beethoven is standing here staring at me."[28] Indeed, in an effort to enhance Brian Williams's journalistic authority during his early years on the *Nightly News*, NBC would open the newscast with a montage of photos and voices of former program anchors (David Brinkley, John Chancellor, Tom Brokaw) effectively offering their figurative coattails to their symbolic descendant.

Along with symbolic ancestors we also envision symbolic relatives, effectively projecting the notion of consanguinity onto non-biological ties as well.[29] We thus use arboreal imagery to depict quasi-fraternal ties among fellow students of the same mathematician or martial arts instructor, or portray modern artists Yves Tanguy, Willem de Kooning, and Marc Chagall as symbolic cousins.[30]

As exemplified by Ted Koppel's narration of the history of television newsmagazines ("And so *60 Minutes* begat *20/20,* and then *20/20* begat *Dateline,* and *Dateline* begat *Primetime Live*"),[31] our notions of symbolic ancestry and descent also transcend personal ties, so that we actually envision "fourth-generation" computers, consider the modern piano a descendant of the harpsichord,[32] and view the bossa nova as a cross between samba and jazz. So, in fact, does our notion of symbolic consanguinity, and we thus view Romanesque architecture not only as ancestral to Renaissance architecture but also as consanguineous with Byzantine architecture (see Figure 7.3).[33] Such a notion of consanguinity, of course, also makes the actual historical relations among different hand copies of the same manuscript or between rock-and-roll and rhythm-and-blues much more evident.[34]

Similar genealogical imagery helps us conceptualize relations between languages. Ever since the great Renaissance scholar Joseph Scaliger first envisioned French and Spanish co-descending from Latin,[35] we have been using metaphors such as language "family," "parent" language, "sister" languages, and "cousin" languages to portray the way in which different languages are related. We likewise refer to words presumed to have derived from the same "ancestral" word (the Spanish [*corazón*] and Portuguese [*coração*] words for "heart," the Finnish [*kissa*] and Estonian [*kass*] words for "cat") as "cognates" (that is, related by descent). And ever since 1853, when August Schleicher first used a tree diagram to portray the evolution of the Indo-European languages,[36] we have been explicitly theorizing linguistic relatedness cladistically. We thus consider French a sister language, yet Swedish only a distant cousin, of Italian because French is presumed to have diverged from their common ancestor more recently than Swedish (see Figure 7.4).[37]

Furthermore, the very same tactics we use to construct biologically based genealogical narratives also help us construct symbolic

BANISTER FLETCHER. INV.

This Tree of Architecture shows the main growth or evolution of the various styles, but must be taken as suggestive only, for minor influences cannot be indicated on a diagram of this kind.

Figure 7.3. Symbolic Ancestry and Consanguinity.

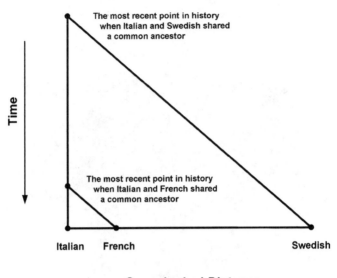

Figure 7.4. Linguistic Relatedness.

ones. Clipping their symbolic pedigrees by changing their names (such as from "the Italian Communist Party" to Italy's "Democratic Party of the Left" or from "Dutch Guiana" to "Suriname"), for example, helps transformed organizations and newly independent countries distance themselves from their immediate symbolic ancestors. Pasting, by contrast, helps make fundamentally discontinuous symbolic lineages seem continuous. Essentially glossing over those periods in its history (such as from 304 to 308, during the persecution of Diocletian) when the papal chair was actually vacant, the Catholic Church thus portrays Pope Benedict XVI as the 265th link in a seemingly unbroken apostolic chain going back to Saint Peter.

The actual historical gaps glossed over in such cases often involve much longer periods, as when Charlemagne, effectively presenting the 324-year period since the abdication of Emperor Romulus Augustus in 476 as a mere pause in the history of a single political entity, proclaimed himself in 800 a "Roman" emperor. Such audacious disregard for conventional notions of genealogical continuity was superseded, however, in 1971 when Iran's Shah Mohammed Reza Pahlavi staged the 2,500th anniversary of the Persian monarchy, thereby trying to invoke an image of a continuous dynastic chain implicitly linking him to Cyrus the Great despite the fact that the Pahlavi "dynasty" actually went back only to his own father. Depictions of imaginary "transhistorical encounters"[38] between Saddam Hussein and ancient Mesopotamian rulers (see, for example, Figure 7.5)[39] likewise exemplify efforts to effectively delete even actual 2,600-year gaps separating the links constituting such symbolic ancestral chains from one another.

Names play a major role in genealogical pasting, and as exemplified by the practice of naming kings and popes after earlier links in their symbolic ancestral chain, pairing them with successive ordinal numbers helps create the illusion of continuity even between noncontiguous links in the chain. The name "Menelik II," for example, helped Ethiopians ignore the 2,800-year gap actually separating their nineteenth-century emperor from the mythical founder of their kingdom, while the name "Boris III" helped Bulgarians mentally link their twentieth-century czar to his ninth- and tenth-century namesakes.

The upcoming "30th Olympic Games" remind us that this applies to nonpersonified lineages as well. France's Second Republic, for example, was thus envisioned as the symbolic heir to its First Republic despite the 44-year actual historical gap (1804–48) separating them from each other, while the vision of a Third Reich was part of the Nazis' effort to effectively delete the Weimar period (1918–33) from Germany's collective memory and symbolically link their regime to its imperial Second Reich. Current plans to build the Third Temple[40]

Figure 7.5. A Transhistorical Encounter.

likewise reveal Jewish fundamentalists' desire to resume a fundamentally continuous national-spiritual project only temporarily interrupted by the destruction of the Second Temple in AD 70.

Consider, next, the way we use genealogical lumping to form symbolic genealogical communities. By presenting themselves in 2006 as "the 265th successor of St. Peter" and "the 269th successor of St. Andrew" (that is, as those apostles' spiritual descendants), thereby implicitly pointing to the Roman Catholic and Eastern Orthodox Churches' common roots (see Figure 7.6)[41], for example,

Pope Benedict XVI, the 265th successor of the St. Peter, joining hands in solidarity with Ecumenical Patriarch Bartholomew, the 269th successor of St. Andrew, the first called Apostle and the older brother of St. Peter, at the Patriarchal Cathedral of St. George, Istanbul, Turkey, November 30, 2006 during the historic Papal Visitation to the Ecumenical Patriarchate.

Figure 7.6. Symbolic Kinship.

Pope Benedict XVI and Ecumenical Patriarch Bartholomew I thus reminded their respective memberships that like distant cousins, despite the 952-year rift between them, they are actually branches of a single "family" tree. By the same token, as exemplified by the way children of Nigerian and Cambodian immigrants to America are socialized to consider themselves symbolic descendants of their adoptive nation's "Founding Fathers,"[42] even civic (that is, pronouncedly nonethnic) nations nevertheless try to cultivate a sense of symbolic kinship among their members.

But the relations between Catholics and Eastern Orthodox Christians also provide a window into the equally fascinating politics of genealogical marginalization. After all, as so explicitly portrayed in Figure 7.7,[43] the Roman Catholic Church is conventionally considered the actual trunk of Christianity's symbolic family tree, while all the other Christian denominations are essentially sidelined as mere offshoots, very much the way psychoanalysts often portray Jungians, or the way the Soviet Communist Party used to portray Trotskyites,

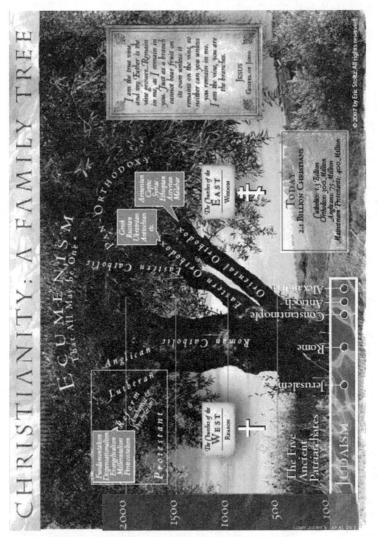

Figure 7.7. Christianity's "Family Tree." Courtesy Eric Stoltz, www.ericstoltz.com.

as having betrayed the true spirit, and thereby effectively disqualified themselves from being considered the true successors, of their common symbolic ancestor (Freud, Lenin). As one might expect, the status of rightful symbolic heirs in such situations is usually essentialized, as so explicitly exemplified by the way former members of the Provisional Irish Republican Army who have refused to participate in the Northern Ireland peace process actually call themselves "The Real Irish Republican Army."[44]

Eastern Orthodox Christians, however, consider their own church the trunk of the tree of Christianity, and the Roman Catholic Church but a side branch (see Figure 7.8). In the words of

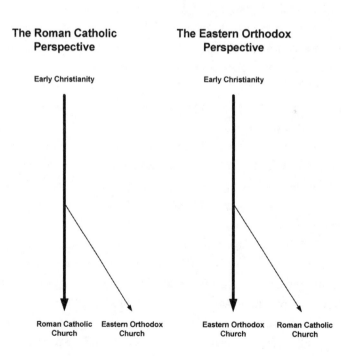

Figure 7.8. Trunk or Side Branch?

one Eastern Orthodox Christian, "Eastern Orthodox Christians do not consider themselves part of a 'denomination' . . . but rather the Church itself."[45] Such claims, in fact, are not uncommon. Mormons too, for example, consider their church the authentic heir to early Christianity, as do Jehovah's Witnesses, while according to the Samaritans, it is they and not the Jews who are "the true Israel."

Whether a particular community constitutes the actual trunk or a mere schismatic branch of a family tree, of course, is a symbolic rather than a factual matter. And the fact that long after China's president Chiang Kai-shek had fled to Taiwan his Nationalist Party kept insisting that the small island nation with its population of twenty million represented "the true China" whereas the People's Republic with its population of over a billion was but a breakaway offshoot reminds us that no factual evidence can ever conclusively resolve such a symbolic dispute, which is rooted, after all, in our genealogical imagination.

Ancestry, descent, and consanguinity, in short, are obviously not the only kinds of ties of which we seem to be genealogically aware, as we evidently envision biological as well as nonbiological forms of being "related." Besides blood ties, we have also developed various visions of quasi-ancestral as well as quasi-consanguineal ties, and how we construct our genealogical identity thus clearly depends on more than just our genetic makeup.

In fact, the ways in which we are related to our ancestors and relatives have come to constitute the fundamental templates we also use to conceptualize other forms of relatedness, as genealogy has clearly become the predominant framework within which we now think about relatedness in general. The way we envision the relations between French and Italian or the harpsichord and the piano is thus rooted in a distinctly genealogical view of the world. So, for that matter, is the manner in which Jungian psychoanalysts and Eastern Orthodox Christians are being socially marginalized.

Genealogy, in short, is first and foremost a way of thinking. Indeed, thinking genealogically is one of the distinctive characteristics of human cognition. As the very objects of our genealogical imagination, ancestors and relatives therefore deserve a prominent place among the foundational pillars of the human condition.

NOTES

Chapter 1

1. http://www.nbc.com/who-do-you-think-you-are (accessed on June 3, 2010).
2. http://ancestry.com (accessed on June 6, 2010); http://www.familytreedna.com (accessed on November 5, 2010); www.familysearch.org (accessed on June 3, 2010).
3. See, for example, http://en.wikipedia.org/wiki/Comparison_of_genealogy_software (accessed on June 16, 2010).
4. Margot Hornblower et al., "Roots Mania," *Time*, April 19, 1999, 54–67; Alondra Nelson, "Bio Science: Genetic Genealogy Testing and the Pursuit of African Ancestry," *Social Studies of Science* 38 (2008): 759–83; Alondra Nelson, "The Factness of Diaspora: The Social Sources of Genetic Genealogy," in Barbara A. Koenig et al. (eds.), *Revisiting Race in a Genomic Age* (New Brunswick, NJ: Rutgers University Press, 2008), 253–68.
5. Robert M. Taylor and Ralph J. Crandall, "Historians and Genealogists: An Emerging Community of Interest," in *Generations and Change: Genealogical Perspectives in Social History* (Macon, GA: Mercer University Press, 1986), 3–27.
6. Spencer Wells, *The Journey of Man: A Genetic Odyssey* (Princeton, NJ: Princeton University Press, 2002); Spencer Wells, *Deep Ancestry: Inside the Genographic Project* (Washington, DC: National Geographic, 2006).
7. Richard Clogg, *A Concise History of Greece* (Cambridge, UK: Cambridge University Press, 2002 [1992]), 2.
8. See, for example, Richard S. Caldwell, *Hesiod's Theogony* (Newburyport, MA: Focus Classical Library, 1987), and the first eight chapters of I Chronicles.

9. See also John R. Gillis, *A World of Their Own Making: Myth, Ritual, and the Quest for Family Values* (New York: Basic Books, 1996), 6, 75; Karla B. Hackstaff, "Who Are We? Genealogists Negotiating Ethno-Racial Identities," *Qualitative Sociology* 32 (2009): 177–78.

10. Tamara K. Hareven, "The Search for Generational Memory: Tribal Rites in Industrial Society," *Daedalus* 107 (Fall 1978): 138. See also Hornblower et al., "Roots Mania."

11. See, for example, Kaja Finkler, "The Kin in the Gene: The Medicalization of Family and Kinship in American Society," *Current Anthropology* 42 (2001): 235–49.

12. See, for example, Bryan Sykes, *Saxons, Vikings, and Celts: The Genetic Roots of Britain and Ireland* (New York: W.W. Norton, 2006).

13. See, for example, http://www.dnaheritage.com (accessed on July 6, 2009); http://rootsforreal.com (accessed on July 6, 2009); http://www.africanancestry.com (accessed on July 6, 2009); http://dnaancestryproject.com (accessed on May 26, 2010); http://www.familytreedna.com (accessed on June 3, 2010); https://www.23andme.com/ancestry (accessed on June 10, 2010). See also Mark D. Shriver and Rick A. Kittles, "Genetic Ancestry and the Search for Personalized Genetic Histories," *Nature Review: Genetics* 5 (2004): 611–18; Henry T. Greely, "Genetic Genealogy: Genetics Meets the Marketplace," in Barbara A. Koenig et al. (eds.), *Revisiting Race in a Genomic Age* (New Brunswick, NJ: Rutgers University Press, 2008), 215–34; Deborah A. Bolnick, "Individual Ancestry Inference and the Reification of Race as a Biological Phenomenon," in Barbara A. Koenig et al. (eds.), *Revisiting Race in a Genomic Age* (New Brunswick, NJ: Rutgers University Press, 2008), 70–85; Nelson, "Bio Science."

14. See, for example, Tony N. Frudakis, *Molecular Photofitting: Predicting Ancestry and Phenotype Using DNA* (Amsterdam: Elsevier, 2008), 305ff.

15. See, for example, http://oxfordancestors.com (accessed on July 6, 2009); http://genographic.nationalgeographic.com/genographic/index.html (accessed on May 26, 2010); http://genebase.com (accessed on June 3, 2010); www.ethnoancestry.com (accessed on June 3, 2010). See also Bryan Sykes, *The Seven Daughters of Eve: The Science That Reveals Our Genetic Ancestry* (London: W.W. Norton, 2001); Wells, *The Journey of Man*; Wells, *Deep Ancestry*; Jennifer A. Hamilton, "The Case of the Genetic Ancestor: DNA Ancestry Testing, Legal Subjectivity and Race in America," paper presented at the DNA, Race, and History Conference, Rutgers University, New Brunswick, NJ, April 2008.

16. Henry L. Gates Jr., "Family Matters: When Science Clashes with Ancestral Lore," *The New Yorker*, December 1, 2008, 37.

17. http://original.britannica.com/eb/topic-256452/Hasan (accessed on July 9, 2008).

18. See, for example, Paul Spruhan, "A Legal History of Blood Quantum in Federal Indian Law to 1935," *South Dakota Law Review* 51 (2006): 1–50. See also Terry P. Wilson, "Blood Quantum: Native American Mixed Bloods," in Maria P. P.

Root (ed.), *Racially Mixed People in America* (Newbury Park: CA: SAGE, 1992), 108–25; Pauline T. Strong and Barrik van Winkle, "'Indian Blood': Reflections on the Reckoning and Refiguring of Native North American Identity," *Cultural Anthropology* 11 (1996): 547–76; Eva Marie Garroutte, "The Racial Formation of American Indians: Negotiating Legitimate Identities within Tribal and Federal Law," *American Indian Quarterly* 25 (2001): 224–39; Circe Sturm, *Blood Politics: Race, Culture, and Identity in the Cherokee Nation of Oklahoma* (Berkeley: University of California Press, 2002).

19. Sturm, *Blood Politics*, 87. See also David E. Wilkins, *American Indian Politics and the American Political System* (Lanham, MD: Rowman & Littlefield, 2007), 29.

20. See also Kwame Owusu-Bempah, *Children and Separation: Socio-Genealogical Connectedness Perspective* (London: Routledge, 2007), 33, 45, 98; Hackstaff, "Who Are We?" 183.

21. Back cover of *African American Lives 2* (PBS Home Video, 2008). Emphasis added.

22. In the fourth episode ("The Past Is Another Country") of *African American Lives 2*. See also Gates's interviews with Meryl Streep in *Faces of America* (PBS Home Video, 2010).

23. Catherine Nash, "'They're Family!': Cultural Geographies of Relatedness in Popular Genealogy," in Sara Ahmed et al. (eds.), *Uprootings/Regroundings: Questions of Home and Migration* (Oxford: Berg, 2003), 179.

24. Ibid., 188–89.

25. See, for example, the last episodes of both *African American Lives* (PBS Home Video, 2006) and *African American Lives 2*.

26. See, for example, Nash, "'They're Family!'," 188–93; Paul Basu, *Highland Homecomings: Genealogy and Heritage Tourism in the Scottish Diaspora* (Abingdon, UK: Routledge, 2007). See also Signe Howell, *The Kinning of Foreigners: Transnational Adoption in a Global Perspective* (New York: Berghahn Books, 2006), 112–20; David C. Mountain and Jeanne K. Guelke, "Genetics, Genealogy, and Geography," in Dallen J. Timothy and Jeanne K. Guelke (eds.), *Geography and Genealogy: Locating Personal Pasts* (Aldershot, UK: Ashgate, 2008), 153–73; Dallen J. Timothy, "Genealogical Mobility: Tourism and the Search for a Personal Past," in Timothy and Guelke, *Geography and Genealogy*, 115–35.

27. See, for example, Henry Louis Gates, *In Search of Our Roots: How 19 Extraordinary African Americans Reclaimed Their Past* (New York: Crown Publishers, 2009), 5–9. See also Hortense J. Spillers, "Mama's Baby, Papa's Maybe: An American Grammar Book," *Diacritics* 17 (Summer 1987): 65–81; Nancy Bentley, "The Fourth Dimension: Kinlessness and African American Narrative," *Critical Inquiry* 35 (Winter 2009): 270–92. On the similar predicament of many children of genocide survivors, see also Arlene Stein, "Trauma and Origins: Post-Holocaust Genealogists and the Work of Memory," *Qualitative Sociology* 32 (2009): 293–309.

28. Gates, *In Search of Our Roots*, 374–75.
29. See also Cynthia Winston and Rick A. Kittles, "Psychological and Ethical Issues Related to Identity and Inferring Ancestry of African Americans," in Trudy R. Turner (ed.), *Biological Anthropology and Ethics: From Repatriation to Genetic Identity* (Albany: State University of New York Press, 2005), 211; Nelson, "Bio Science."
30. A. J. Turner and A. Coyle, "What Does It Mean to Be a Donor Offspring? The Identity Experiences of Adults Conceived by Donor Insemination and the Implications for Counseling and Therapy," *Human Reproduction* 15 (2000): 2047. See also Betsy Streisand, "Who's Your Daddy?" http://health.usnews.com/usnews/health/articles/060213/13donor (accessed on July 7, 2009).
31. Russ Castronovo, *Fathering the Nation: American Genealogies of Slavery and Freedom* (Berkeley: University of California Press, 1995), 201; Nadine Lefaucheur, "Fatherless Children and Accouchement Sous X, From Marriage to Demarriage: A Paradigmatic Approach," *Journal of Family History* 28 (2003): 175; James D. Faubion and Jennifer A. Hamilton, "Sumptuary Kinship," *Anthropological Quarterly* 80 (2007): 551. See also Carey Goldberg, "DNA Offers Link to Black History," *New York Times*, August 28, 2000, A10.
32. Owusu-Bempah, *Children and Separation*.
33. Ibid., 22.
34. On the navel as a metaphor of genealogical embeddedness, see Martin Gardner, "Did Adam and Eve Have Navels?" in *Did Adam and Eve Have Navels? Debunking Pseudoscience* (New York: W.W. Norton, 2001 [1998]), 7–14. See also Ernest Gellner, "Reply: Do Nations Have Navels?" *Nations and Nationalism* 2 (1996): 367; Anthony D. Smith, *The Antiquity of Nations* (Cambridge, UK: Polity, 2004), 63–67.
35. Alex Shoumatoff, *The Mountain of Names: A History of the Human Family* (New York: Simon and Schuster, 1985), 50.
36. See Hugh Baker, *Chinese Family and Kinship* (New York: Columbia University Press, 1979), 95.
37. H. J. Sants, "Genealogical Bewilderment in Children with Substitute Parents," *British Journal of Medical Psychology* 37 (1964): 133–41. See also John Triseliotis, *In Search of Origins: The Experiences of Adopted People* (London: Routledge and Kegan Paul, 1973), 18–19.
38. Triseliotis, *In Search of Origins*, 88–89.
39. Ibid., 87. See also Judith S. Modell, *Kinship with Strangers: Adoption and Interpretations of Kinship in American Culture* (Berkeley: University of California Press, 1994), 137, 143, 149.
40. Betty J. Lifton, *Journey of the Adopted Self: A Quest for Wholeness* (New York: Basic Books, 1994). See also Turner and Coyle, "What Does It Mean to Be a Donor Offspring?" 2047.
41. See, for example, Turner and Coyle, "What Does It Mean to Be a Donor Offspring?" 2046.

42. See also Richard Tutton, "'They Want to Know Where They Came From': Population Genetics, Identity, and Family Genealogy," *New Genetics and Society* 23 (2004): 110–12.

43. Zora N. Hurston, *Dust Tracks on a Road: An Autobiography* (Urbana: University of Illinois Press, 1984 [1942]), 235. See also Gates, *In Search of Our Roots*, 99–100, 148, 376.

44. In the fourth episode ("The Past Is Another Country") of *African American Lives 2.*

45. Ibid.

46. See also Sants, "Genealogical Bewilderment," 135–37.

47. See also Shriver and Kittles, "Genetic Ancestry," 616.

48. http://www.bbcwhodoyouthinkyouaremagazine.com/episode/us/sarah-jessica-parker (accessed on June 27, 2010).

49. See, for example, *African American Lives, African American Lives 2, Faces of America*, as well as the television series *Who Do You Think You Are?*

50. Gates, *In Search of Our Roots*, 222.

51. Shriver and Kittles, "Genetic Ancestry," 616. See also Winston and Kittles, "Psychological and Ethical Issues," 221.

52. Rachelle Germana, personal communication.

53. http://lyricsplayground.com/alpha/songs/s/shameandscandalinthefamily.shtml (accessed on June 11, 2010).

54. Charles Darwin, *On the Origin of Species* (New York: Sterling, 2008 [1859]), 440, 443. See also Charles Darwin, *The Descent of Man and Selection in Relation to Sex* (Amherst, NY: Prometheus, 1998 [1871]), 153–55; Peter J. Bowler, *Life's Splendid Drama: Evolutionary Biology and the Reconstruction of Life's Ancestry, 1860–1940* (Chicago: University of Chicago Press, 1996), 49.

55. Marc Ereshefsky, *The Poverty of the Linnaean Hierarchy: A Philosophical Study of Biological Taxonomy* (Cambridge, UK: Cambridge University Press, 2001), 209; Niles Eldredge and Joel Cracraft, *Phylogenetic Patterns and the Evolutionary Process: Method and Theory in Comparative Biology* (New York: Columbia University Press, 1980), 12.

56. Eviatar Zerubavel, *Social Mindscapes: An Invitation to Cognitive Sociology* (Cambridge, MA: Harvard University Press, 1997).

57. Ibid., 84, 87.

58. Charles H. Cooley, *Human Nature and the Social Order* (New York: Schocken, 1964 [1922]), 121. See also 120.

59. This term was first introduced by Andrew Shryock in *Nationalism and the Genealogical Imagination: Oral History and Textual Authority in Tribal Jordan* (Berkeley: University of California Press, 1997). See also Katharine Tyler, "The Genealogical Imagination: The Inheritance of Interracial Identities," *The Sociological Review* 53 (2005): 476–94; Judith Shulevitz, "Roots and Branches," *The Book: An Online Review at the New Republic*, April 2, 2010.

60. See also Robin Fox, *Kinship and Marriage: An Anthropological Perspective* (Cambridge, UK: Cambridge University Press, 1983 [1967]), 30.

61. See also Benedict Anderson, *Imagined Communities: Reflections on the Origin and Spread of Nationalism* (London: Verso, 1983).

62. See also Eviatar Zerubavel, "Generally Speaking: The Logic and Mechanics of Social Pattern Analysis," *Sociological Forum* 22 (2007): 134–39.

63. Ibid., 135–36.

64. See Fox, *Kinship and Marriage*, 125; Quentin D. Atkinson and Russell D. Gray, "Are Accurate Dates an Intractable Problem for Historical Linguistics?" in Carl P. Lipo et al. (eds.), *Mapping Our Ancestors: Phylogenetic Approaches in Anthropology and Prehistory* (New Brunswick, NJ: AldineTransaction, 2006), 282; Morris Goodman et al., "Toward a Phylogenetic Classification of Primates Based on DNA Evidence Complemented by Fossil Evidence," *Molecular Phylogenetics and Evolution* 9 (1998): 591. See also Edward E. Evans-Pritchard, *The Nuer: A Description of the Modes of Livelihood and Political Institutions of a Nilotic People* (London: Oxford University Press, 1940), 201; Luigi L. Cavalli-Sforza and Francesco Cavalli-Sforza, *The Great Human Diasporas: The History of Diversity and Evolution* (Reading, MA: Addison-Wesley, 1995 [1993]), 38.

65. See also Eviatar Zerubavel, "The Rigid, the Fuzzy, and the Flexible: Notes on the Mental Sculpting of Academic Identity," *Social Research* 62 (1995): 1093–1106.

Chapter 2

1. See also W. Lloyd Warner, *The Living and the Dead: A Study of the Symbolic Life of Americans* (New Haven, CT: Yale University Press, 1959); Peter L. Berger and Thomas Luckmann, *The Social Construction of Reality: A Treatise in the Sociology of Knowledge* (Garden City, NY: Doubleday Anchor, 1967 [1966]), 33–34; Alfred Schutz and Thomas Luckmann, *The Structures of the Life-World* (Evanston, IL: Northwestern University Press, 1973), 87–92; Karen A. Cerulo, "Nonhumans in Social Interaction," *Annual Review of Sociology* 35 (2009): 542.

2. See Raymond L. Schmitt, "Symbolic Immortality in Ordinary Contexts: Impediments to the Nuclear Era," *Omega* 13 (1982–83): 95–116.

3. See also Kathryn Coe, *The Ancestress Hypothesis: Visual Art as Adaptation* (New Brunswick, NJ: Rutgers University Press, 2003), 33–46.

4. On genealogical "depth," see also Meyer Fortes, "The Structure of Unilineal Descent Groups," in *Time and Social Structure and Other Essays* (London: Athlone Press, 1970 [1953]), 85; David P. Henige, *The Chronology of Oral Tradition: Quest for a Chimera* (Oxford: Clarendon Press, 1974), 101.

5. See also Eviatar Zerubavel, *Social Mindscapes: An Invitation to Cognitive Sociology* (Cambridge, MA: Harvard University Press, 1997), 89–93.

6. See also Julia Watson, "Ordering the Family: Genealogy as Autobiographical Pedigree," in Sidonie Smith and Julia Watson (eds.), *Getting a Life: Everyday Uses of Autobiography* (Minneapolis: University of Minnesota Press, 1996), 298.

7. See also Richard D. Alford, *Naming and Identity: A Cross-Cultural Study of Personal Naming Practices* (New Haven, CT: HRAF Press, 1988), 55.

8. See also Rex Taylor, "John Doe, Jr.: A Study of His Distribution in Space, Time, and the Social Structure," *Social Forces* 53 (1974): 11–21.

9. Hugh Baker, *Chinese Family and Kinship* (New York: Columbia University Press, 1979), 26–27.

10. Henry Kendall, *The Kinship of Men: An Argument from Pedigrees, or Genealogy Viewed as a Science* (Boston: Cupples and Hurd, 1888), 43.

11. Baker, *Chinese Family and Kinship*, 27. See also pp. 71–74.

12. See, for example, Richard Dawkins, *River out of Eden: A Darwinian View of Life* (New York: Basic Books, 1995); Guy Murchie, *The Seven Mysteries of Life: An Exploration in Science and Philosophy* (New York: Mariner Books, 1999 [1978]), 357; Gabrielle M. Spiegel, "Genealogy: Form and Function in Medieval Historical Narrative," *History and Theory* 22 (1983): 49; Margaret Mead, *Sex and Temperament in Three Primitive Societies* (New York: William Morrow, 1935), 176–77; Judith S. Modell, *Kinship with Strangers: Adoption and Interpretations of Kinship in American Culture* (Berkeley: University of California Press, 1994), 167.

13. Baker, *Chinese Family and Kinship*, 26.

14. See, for example, Daniel Rosenberg and Anthony Grafton, *Cartographies of Time: A History of the Timeline* (New York: Princeton Architectural Press, 2010), 13–15, 36.

15. See also R. Howard Bloch, *Etymologies and Genealogies: A Literary Anthropology of the French Middle Ages* (Chicago: University of Chicago Press, 1983), 84, 93.

16. See, for example, Ernest H. Wilkins, "The Genealogy of the Genealogy Trees of the *Genealogia Deorum*," *Modern Philology* 23 (1925): 62; Arthur Watson, *The Early Iconography of the Tree of Jesse* (London: Oxford University Press, 1934), 37; Tim Ingold, *Lines: A Brief History* (London: Routledge, 2007), 104.

17. See, for example, Schutz and Luckmann, *The Structures of the Life-World*, 91; Randall Collins, *The Sociology of Philosophies: A Global Theory of Intellectual Change* (Cambridge, MA: Harvard University Press, 1998), 5–6, 65.

18. Stanley Milgram, "The Small World Problem," in *The Individual in a Social World: Essays and Experiments* (New York: McGraw-Hill, 1992 [1967]), 259–75; Ithiel de Sola Pool and Manfred Kochen, "Contacts and Influence," in Manfred Kochen (ed.), *The Small World* (Norwood, NJ: Ablex, 1989 [1978]), 3–51.

19. See, for example, *African American Lives* (PBS Home Video, 2006); *African American Lives 2* (PBS Home Video, 2008); Henry L. Gates Jr., *In Search of Our Roots: How 19 Extraordinary African Americans Reclaimed Their Past* (New York: Crown Publishers, 2009); *Faces of America* (PBS Home Video, 2010).

20. See, for example, Patricia Polacco, *Pink and Say* (New York: Philomel Books, 1994).
21. See also Tamara K. Hareven, "The Search for Generational Memory: Tribal Rites in Industrial Society," *Daedalus* 107 (Fall 1978): 139; Spiegel, "Genealogy," 49.
22. Bryan Sykes, *The Seven Daughters of Eve: The Science That Reveals Our Genetic Ancestry* (London: W.W. Norton, 2001), 288. See also Ruth Simpson, "I Was There: Establishing Ownership of Historical Moments" (paper presented at the Annual Meeting of the American Sociological Association, Los Angeles, 1994).
23. Edward Shils, *Tradition* (Chicago: University of Chicago Press, 1981), 37; Donald Johanson and Blake Edgar, *From Lucy to Language* (New York: Simon and Schuster, 1996), 112. See also Pitirim A. Sorokin, *Social and Cultural Dynamics*, Vol. 4: *Basic Problems, Principles, and Methods* (New York: Bedminster Press, 1941), 505–26; Richard Lewontin, *Human Diversity* (New York: Scientific American Books, 1982), 162.
24. Milgram, "The Small World Problem"; John Guare, *Six Degrees of Separation* (New York: Random House, 1990).
25. Avraham S. Friedberg, *Zikhronot le-Veit David* (Ramat Gan, Israel: Masada, 1958 [1893–1904]).
26. See also Kenneth W. Wachter, "Ancestors at the Norman Conquest," in Bennett Dyke and Warren T. Morrill (eds.), *Genealogical Demography* (New York: Academic Press, 1980 [1978]), 92.
27. Don Cheadle, in Gates, *In Search of Our Roots*, 345.
28. See also Alex Shoumatoff, *The Mountain of Names: A History of the Human Family* (New York: Simon and Schuster, 1985), 73.
29. See, for example, Robin Fox, *The Tory Islanders: A People of the Celtic Fringe* (Cambridge, UK: Cambridge University Press, 1978), 99–126.
30. See also Watson, *The Early Iconography of the Tree of Jesse*, 38; Marshall D. Johnson, *The Purpose of the Biblical Genealogies with Special Reference to the Setting of the Genealogies of Jesus* (London: Cambridge University Press, 1969), 79; Henige, *The Chronology of Oral Tradition*.
31. See also Eviatar Zerubavel, *Time Maps: Collective Memory and the Social Shape of the Past* (Chicago: University of Chicago Press, 2003), 16–18.
32. See also Bloch, *Etymologies and Genealogies*, 85; Ingold, *Lines*, 109, 111.
33. For lists of such groups, see, for example, http://www.hereditary.us/list_date.htm (accessed on July 6, 2009); http://en.wikipedia.org/wiki/List_of_hereditary_and_lineage_organizations (accessed on September 14, 2009). See also Virginia R. Domínguez, *White by Definition: Social Classification in Creole Louisiana* (New Brunswick, NJ: Rutgers University Press, 1986), 237–38; Watson, "Ordering the Family," 306.
34. Engseng Ho, *The Graves of Tarim: Genealogy and Mobility Across the Indian Ocean* (Berkeley: University of California Press, 2006), 324–26.

35. Johnson, *The Purpose of the Biblical Genealogies*, 255–56.

36. See, for example, Shoumatoff, *The Mountain of Names*, 64. See also Anthony Wagner, "Bridges to Antiquity," in *Pedigree and Progress: Essays in the Genealogical Interpretation of History* (London: Phillimore, 1975), 50–75.

37. See, for example, Robert R. Wilson, *Genealogy and History in the Biblical World* (New Haven, CT: Yale University Press, 1977), 42; Shoumatoff, *The Mountain of Names*, 73.

38. See, for example, Ronald D. Lambert, "Reclaiming the Ancestral Past: Narrative, Rhetoric, and the 'Convict Stain,'" *Journal of Sociology* 38 (2002): 111–27.

39. Israel B. Levner, *Kol Agadot Yisrael* (Tel-Aviv: Achiasaf, 1982 [1902]), Vol. iv, no. 56, p. 76.

40. Exodus 34:7. See also 20:5; Numbers 14:18; Deuteronomy 5:9, 23:4.

41. See María E. Martínez, *Genealogical Fictions: Limpieza de Sangre, Religion, and Gender in Colonial Mexico* (Stanford, CA: Stanford University Press, 2008), 47–52, 63, 69.

42. I Chronicles 6:18–23.

43. See, for example, Gísli Pálsson, "The Life of Family Trees and the Book of Icelanders," *Medical Anthropology* 21 (2002): 344.

44. Luke 3:23–38.

45. See, for example, Seth Faison, "Qufu Journal: Not Equal to Confucius, but Friends to His Memory," *New York Times*, October 10, 1997. See also Maurice Freedman, *Chinese Lineage and Society: Fukien and Kwangtung* (London: Athlone Press, 1966), 26–27; Shoumatoff, *The Mountain of Names*, 66.

46. See also Dwight W. Read, "What Is Kinship?" in Richard Feinberg and Martin Ottenheimer (eds.), *The Cultural Analysis of Kinship: The Legacy of David M. Schneider* (Urbana: University of Illinois Press, 2001), 91–92.

47. J. A. Barnes, "Genealogies," in A. L. Epstein (ed.), *The Craft of Social Anthropology* (London: Tavistock, 1967), 102.

48. See, for example, Richard Dawkins, *The Ancestor's Tale: A Pilgrimage to the Dawn of Evolution* (Boston: Mariner Books, 2005).

49. On the discovery of "deep time," see also Stephen J. Gould, *Time's Arrow, Time's Cycle: Myth and Metaphor in the Discovery of Geological Time* (Cambridge, MA: Harvard University Press, 1987).

50. Donald K. Grayson, *The Establishment of Human Antiquity* (New York: Academic Press, 1983), 34–36.

51. Ibid., 79. See also p. 84.

52. Ibid., 149. See also pp. 162–64, 168.

53. Jacob W. Gruber, "Brixham Cave and the Antiquity of Man," in Melford E. Spiro (ed.), *Context and Meaning in Cultural Anthropology* (New York: Free Press, 1965), 374.

54. See also Henri Breuil, "The Discovery of the Antiquity of Man: Some of the Evidence," *Journal of the Royal Anthropological Institute of Great Britain and*

Ireland 75 (1945): 24; Thomas R. Trautmann, "The Revolution in Ethnological Time," *Man* 27 (1992): 379–97.

55. Breuil, "The Discovery of the Antiquity of Man," 23; Gruber, "Brixham Cave and the Antiquity of Man," 379–82; Grayson, *The Establishment of Human Antiquity*, 91–92, 101, 109–11, 120–32; Peter J. Bowler, *Theories of Human Evolution: A Century of Debate, 1844–1944* (Baltimore: Johns Hopkins University Press, 1986), 24–25.

56. Gruber, "Brixham Cave and the Antiquity of Man," 378–79; Grayson, *The Establishment of Human Antiquity*, 55–84, 89ff.

57. Trautmann, "The Revolution in Ethnological Time," 383. See also Gruber, "Brixham Cave and the Antiquity of Man," 396; Grayson, *The Establishment of Human Antiquity*, 186–87.

58. Charles Lyell, *Geological Evidences of the Antiquity of Man* (London: John Murray, 1863). See also Grayson, *The Establishment of Human Antiquity*, 78–82.

59. See also Daniel L. Smail, *On Deep History and the Brain* (Berkeley: University of California Press, 2008).

60. Thomas H. Huxley, *Evidence as to Man's Place in Nature* (Ann Arbor: University of Michigan Press, 2003 [1863]), 184.

61. Breuil, "The Discovery of the Antiquity of Man," 31.

62. Trautmann, "The Revolution in Ethnological Time," 380.

63. For the latter, see, for example, Floyd N. Jones, *The Chronology of the Old Testament* (Green Forest, AR: Master Books, 2005). See, however, Thomas H. Jukes, "Random Walking," *Journal of Molecular Evolution* 34 (1992): 469.

64. See, for example, Carl Woese, "The Universal Ancestor," *Proceedings of the National Academy of Sciences of the United States of America* 95 (1998): 6854–59; Mark Ridley, "The Search for LUCA," *Natural History* 109, no. 9 (November 2000): 82–85.

65. See Arthur O. Lovejoy, *The Great Chain of Being: A Study of the History of an Idea* (Cambridge, MA: Harvard University Press, 1936).

66. Ibid., 242–87. See also Ernst Mayr, *The Growth of Biological Thought: Diversity, Evolution, and Inheritance* (Cambridge, MA: Harvard University Press, 1982), 359.

67. Richard W. Burkhardt, *The Spirit of System: Lamarck and Evolutionary Biology* (Cambridge, MA: Harvard University Press, 1977), 81, 203; Raymond Corbey, *The Metaphysics of Apes: Negotiating the Animal-Human Boundary* (Cambridge, UK: Cambridge University Press, 2005), 62.

68. See, for example, Mayr, *The Growth of Biological Thought*, 352; Ernst Mayr, "Darwin's Five Theories of Evolution," in David Kohn (ed.), *The Darwinian Heritage* (Princeton, NJ: Princeton University Press, 1985), 758.

69. Jean-Baptiste Lamarck, *Zoological Philosophy: An Exposition with Regard to the Natural History of Animals* (New York: Hafner, 1963 [1809]), 39. See also John C. Greene, *The Death of Adam: Evolution and Its Impact on Western Thought*

(Ames: Iowa State University Press, 1959), 159; Mayr, *The Growth of Biological Thought*, 346–49; Milford Wolpoff and Rachel Caspari, *Race and Human Evolution* (Boulder, CO: Westview Press, 1997), 71.

70. Lamarck, *Zoological Philosophy*, 170. See also pp. 172–73.
71. Mayr, *The Growth of Biological Thought*, 359. See also George G. Simpson, *Principles of Animal Taxonomy* (New York: Columbia University Press, 1961), 51.

Chapter 3

1. Lewis H. Morgan, *Systems of Consanguinity and Affinity of the Human Family* (Lincoln: University of Nebraska Press, 1997 [1871]), 17.
2. Sharon Begley, "Beyond Stones and Bones," *Newsweek*, March 19, 2007, 55.
3. I Chronicles 2:36–41.
4. See also Robert R. Wilson, *Genealogy and History in the Biblical World* (New Haven, CT: Yale University Press, 1977), 18–20, 40–44, 194.
5. On "tunnel vision," see Eviatar Zerubavel, *Social Mindscapes: An Invitation to Cognitive Sociology* (Cambridge, MA: Harvard University Press, 1997), 40–42. See also Eviatar Zerubavel, *The Fine Line: Making Distinctions in Everyday Life* (Chicago: University of Chicago Press, 1993 [1991]), 116.
6. On the difference between the unilinear and multilinear manners of mapping time, see Eviatar Zerubavel, *Time Maps: Collective Memory and the Social Shape of the Past* (Chicago: University of Chicago Press, 2003), 20–23.
7. See Ian Tattersall, "Once We Were Not Alone," *Scientific American* 282 (January 2000): 56–62. See also Michael Hammond, "The Expulsion of the Neanderthals from Human Ancestry: Marcellin Boule and the Social Context of Scientific Research," *Social Studies of Science* 12 (1982): 5, 14; Richard G. Klein, *The Human Career: Human Biological and Cultural Origins* (Chicago: University of Chicago Press, 1999), 395, 489–90; Bernard Wood and Mark Collard, "The Human Genus," *Science*, 284 (April 2, 1999): 65; Carl Zimmer, *Smithsonian Intimate Guide to Human Origins* (New York: HarperCollins, 2005), 6–7, 138, 140, 142.
8. Rachel Brekhus, personal communication.
9. See also Mary Bouquet, "Family Trees and Their Affinities: The Visual Imperative of the Genealogical Diagram," *Journal of the Royal Anthropological Institute*, n.s., 2 (1996): 59; Uli Linke, *Blood and Nation: The European Aesthetics of Race* (Philadelphia: University of Pennsylvania Press, 1999), 58–62; James W. Valentine, *On the Origin of Phyla* (Chicago: University of Chicago Press, 2004), 13.
10. Emile Durkheim, *The Division of Labor in Society* (New York: Free Press, 1984 [1893]), 84.
11. See also Wilson, *Genealogy and History in the Biblical World*, 34.

12. See also C. Cannings and E. A. Thompson, *Genealogical and Genetic Structure* (Cambridge, UK: Cambridge University Press, 1981), 5.

13. See, for example, Maurice Freedman, *Lineage Organization in Southeastern China* (London: Athlone Press, 1965 [1958]), 81–91; Maurice Freedman, *Chinese Lineage and Society: Fukien and Kwangtung* (London: Athlone Press, 1966), 141–54.

14. Hugh Baker, *Chinese Family and Kinship* (New York: Columbia University Press, 1979), 90–91. See also Ernest L. Schusky, *Variation in Kinship* (New York: Holt, Rinehart, and Winston, 1974), 53; Nancy Jay, *Throughout Your Generations Forever: Sacrifice, Religion, and Paternity* (Chicago: University of Chicago Press, 1992), 46.

15. See, for example, Morgan, *Systems of Consanguinity and Affinity*, 95, 533–34. See also pp. 552, 555.

16. See also David M. Schneider, *American Kinship: A Cultural Account* (Englewood Cliffs, NJ: Prentice-Hall, 1980), 65; Bernard Farber, *Conceptions of Kinship* (New York: Elsevier, 1981), 7, 40–42.

17. See, for example, Ernest H. Wilkins, "The Genealogy of the Genealogy Trees of the *Genealogia Deorum*," *Modern Philology* 23 (1925): 62–63; Arthur Watson, *The Early Iconography of the Tree of Jesse* (London: Oxford University Press, 1934), 39–40; Christiane Klapisch-Zuber, "The Genesis of the Family Tree," in *I Tatti Studies: Essays in the Renaissance,* Vol. 4 (Florence, Italy: Villa I Tatti, 1991), 105–29; Tim Ingold, *Lines: A Brief History* (London: Routledge, 2007), 105–06.

18. See also Schneider, *American Kinship*, 73; Irwin Bernstein, "The Correlation Between Kinship and Behavior in Non-Human Primates," in Peter G. Hepper (ed.), *Kin Recognition* (Cambridge, UK: Cambridge University Press, 1991), 7.

19. See also David M. Schneider and Calvert B. Cottrell, *The American Kin Universe: A Genealogical Study* (Chicago: University of Chicago Press, 1975), 41, 92–94.

20. See, for example, Zuleyma T. Halpin, "Kin Recognition Cues of Vertebrates," in Peter G. Hepper (ed.), *Kin Recognition* (Cambridge, UK: Cambridge University Press, 1991), 231–47; Michael D. Beecher, "Successes and Failures of Parent-Offspring Recognition in Animals," in Hepper, *Kin Recognition*, 95, 97; Pierre Jaisson, "Kinship and Fellowship in Ants and Social Wasps," in Hepper, *Kin Recognition*, 61, 66; Bruce Waldman, "Kin Recognition in Amphibians," in Hepper, *Kin Recognition*, 165.

21. See also Edward E. Evans-Pritchard, *The Nuer: A Description of the Modes of Livelihood and Political Institutions of a Nilotic People* (London: Oxford University Press, 1940), 106, 200–01.

22. See also Schneider, *American Kinship*, 67–68.

23. See also Alex Shoumatoff, *The Mountain of Names: A History of the Human Family* (New York: Simon and Schuster, 1985), 245; Craig T. Palmer and Lyle

B. Steadman, "Human Kinship as a Descendant-Leaving Strategy: A Solution to an Evolutionary Puzzle," *Journal of Social and Evolutionary Systems* 20 (1997): 43.

24. See also Alfred R. Radcliffe-Brown, "The Study of Kinship Systems," in *Structure and Function in Primitive Society* (New York: Free Press, 1965 [1941]), 52.

25. See Edward Steichen, *The Family of Man* (New York: Museum of Modern Art, 1955). See also Shoumatoff, *The Mountain of Names*, 244; David A. Hollinger, *Postethnic America: Beyond Multiculturalism* (New York: Basic Books, 1995), 10.

26. See also Guy Murchie, *The Seven Mysteries of Life: An Exploration in Science and Philosophy* (New York: Mariner Books, 1999 [1978]), 351; Spencer Wells, *The Journey of Man: A Genetic Odyssey* (Princeton, NJ: Princeton University Press, 2002); Spencer Wells, *Deep Ancestry: Inside the Genographic Project* (Washington, DC: National Geographic, 2006).

27. Richard Dawkins, *The Ancestor's Tale: A Pilgrimage to the Dawn of Evolution* (Boston: Mariner Books, 2005), 13. See also Murchie, *The Seven Mysteries of Life*, 357–59; Ernst Mayr, *The Growth of Biological Thought: Diversity, Evolution, and Inheritance* (Cambridge, MA: Harvard University Press, 1982), 582; Ernst Mayr, "Darwin's Five Theories of Evolution," in David Kohn (ed.), *The Darwinian Heritage* (Princeton, NJ: Princeton University Press, 1985), 761; Richard Dawkins, *River out of Eden: A Darwinian View of Life* (New York: Basic Books, 1995), 12; Bernard Wood, *Human Evolution: A Very Short Introduction* (Oxford: Oxford University Press, 2005),1.

28. Carl Woese, "The Universal Ancestor," *Proceedings of the National Academy of Sciences of the United States of America* 95 (1998): 6854–59; Mark Ridley, "The Search for LUCA," *Natural History* 109, no. 9 (November 2000): 82–85.

29. See also Mayr, *The Growth of Biological Thought*, 581.

30. Charles Darwin, *On the Origin of Species* (New York: Sterling, 2008 [1859]), 440. See also Robert J. Richards, *The Meaning of Evolution: The Morphological Construction and Ideological Reconstruction of Darwin's Theory* (Chicago: University of Chicago Press, 1992), 165; Peter J. Bowler, *Life's Splendid Drama: Evolutionary Biology and the Reconstruction of Life's Ancestry, 1860–1940* (Chicago: University of Chicago Press, 1996), 41.

31. Mayr, *The Growth of Biological Thought*, 435. See also Stephen G. Alter, *Darwinism and the Linguistic Image: Language, Race, and Natural Theology in the Nineteenth Century* (Baltimore: Johns Hopkins University Press, 1999), 5–6.

32. Ernst Haeckel, *The History of Creation: On the Development of the Earth and Its Inhabitants by the Action of Natural Causes* (New York: D. Appleton, 1876), Vol. 1, p. xiii, and Vol. 2, pp. 2–3, 44–47, 123, 130–31.

33. Darwin, *The Origin of Species*, 440, 443. See also Charles Darwin, *The Descent of Man and Selection in Relation to Sex* (Amherst, NY: Prometheus, 1998 [1871]), 153–55; Ian Tattersall, *The Fossil Trail: How We Know What We Think*

We Know about Human Evolution (New York: Oxford University Press, 1995), 19; Bowler, *Life's Splendid Drama*, 49.

34. See also Mayr, *The Growth of Biological Thought*, 400–01; Mayr, "Darwin's Five Theories of Evolution," 759.

35. See, for example, Milford Wolpoff and Rachel Caspari, *Race and Human Evolution* (Boulder, CO: Westview Press, 1997), 116, 319; R. Lee Lyman and Michael J. O'Brien, "Seriation and Cladistics: The Difference between Anagenetic and Cladogenetic Evolution," in Carl P. Lipo et al. (eds.), *Mapping Our Ancestors: Phylogenetic Approaches in Anthropology and Prehistory* (New Brunswick, NJ: AldineTransaction, 2006), 66.

36. Rulon S. Wells, "The Life and Growth of Language: Metaphors in Biology and Linguistics," in Henry M. Hoenigswald and Linda F. Wiener (eds.), *Biological Metaphor and Cladistic Classification: An Interdisciplinary Perspective* (Philadelphia: University of Pennsylvania Press, 1987), 72. See also W. Keith Percival, "Biological Analogy in the Study of Language before the Advent of Comparative Grammar," in Hoenigswald and Wiener, *Biological Metaphor and Cladistic Classification*, 26.

37. Jean-Baptiste Lamarck, *Zoological Philosophy: An Exposition with Regard to the Natural History of Animals* (New York: Hafner, 1963 [1809]), 178–79; John C Greene, *The Death of Adam: Evolution and Its Impact on Western Thought* (Ames: Iowa State University Press, 1959), 149–51; Mayr, *The Growth of Biological Thought*, 351; Mayr, "Darwin's Five Theories of Evolution," 759; Percival, "Biological Analogy in the Study of Language," 26; Wells, "The Life and Growth of Language," 74–76; Konrad Koerner, "On Schleicher and Trees," in Henry M. Hoenigswald and Linda F. Wiener (eds.), *Biological Metaphor and Cladistic Classification: An Interdisciplinary Perspective* (Philadelphia: University of Pennsylvania Press, 1987), 111; Richards, *The Meaning of Evolution*, 108–11.

38. See, for example, Niles Eldredge and Joel Cracraft, *Phylogenetic Patterns and the Evolutionary Process: Method and Theory in Comparative Biology* (New York: Columbia University Press, 1980), 114, 121, 125; Luigi L. Cavalli-Sforza and Francesco Cavalli-Sforza, *The Great Human Diasporas: The History of Diversity and Evolution* (Reading, MA: Addison-Wesley, 1995 [1993]), 113; Franco Moretti, *Graphs, Maps, Trees: Abstract Models for a Literary History* (London: Verso, 2005), 69.

39. Marc Ereshefsky, *The Poverty of the Linnaean Hierarchy: A Philosophical Study of Biological Taxonomy* (Cambridge, UK: Cambridge University Press, 2001), 53. See also Julian Huxley, "The Three Types of Evolutionary Process," *Nature* 180 (1957): 454; Stephen J. Gould, "Bushes and Ladders in Human Evolution," in *Ever Since Darwin: Reflections in Natural History* (New York: W.W. Norton, 1979 [1976]), 61–62; Roger Lewin and Robert A. Foley, *Principles of Human Evolution* (Malden, MA: Blackwell, 2004), 103.

40. Ernst Haeckel, *The Evolution of Man: A Popular Exposition of the Principal Points of Human Ontogeny and Phylogeny* (New York: D. Appleton, 1879

[1874]), 102; Ernst Haeckel, *Anthropogenie oder Entwickelungsgeschichte des Menschen* (Leipzig: Wilhelm Engelmann, 1874), 496; Haeckel, *The History of Creation*, Vol. 1, p. 314 and Vol. 2, pp. 222, 353.

41. See Stephen J. Gould, *Ontogeny and Phylogeny* (Cambridge, MA: Harvard University Press, 1977), 76–77; Jane M. Oppenheimer, "Haeckel's Variations on Darwin," in Henry M. Hoenigswald and Linda F. Wiener (eds.), *Biological Metaphor and Cladistic Classification: An Interdisciplinary Perspective* (Philadelphia: University of Pennsylvania Press, 1987), 123–35; Peter J. Bowler, *The Invention of Progress: The Victorians and the Past* (Oxford: Basil Blackwell, 1989), 155; Stephen J. Gould, *Wonderful Life: The Burgess Shale and the Nature of History* (New York: W.W. Norton, 1989), 263; Bouquet, "Family Trees and Their Affinities," 56–57; Donald Johanson and Blake Edgar, *From Lucy to Language* (New York: Simon and Schuster, 1996), 37; Bowler, *Life's Splendid Drama*, 57–58; Alter, *Darwinism and the Linguistic Image*, 110–17.

42. See also Raymond Corbey, *The Metaphysics of Apes: Negotiating the Animal-Human Boundary* (Cambridge, UK: Cambridge University Press, 2005), 65.

43. Darwin, *The Origin of Species*, 140. See also pp. 131–33; Richards, *The Meaning of Evolution*, 110–11.

44. Darwin, *The Origin of Species*, 126–27.

45. Robert J. O'Hara, "Telling the Tree: Narrative Representation and the Study of Evolutionary History," *Biology and Philosophy* 7 (1992): 143.

46. Moretti, *Graphs, Maps, Trees*, 107.

47. See also Mayr, *The Growth of Biological Thought*, 230.

48. Klein, *The Human Career*, 9.

49. R. S. Bigelow, "Classification and Phylogeny" *Systematic Zoology* 7, no. 2 (1958): 54; Valentine, *On the Origin of Phyla*, 11; Matt Cartmill and Fred H. Smith. *The Human Lineage* (Hoboken, NJ: Wiley-Blackwell, 2009), 32. See also Klein, *The Human Career*, 13.

50. Darwin, *The Origin of Species*, 440–50; George G. Simpson, *Principles of Animal Taxonomy* (New York: Columbia University Press, 1961), 78, 81; Willi Hennig, *Phylogenetic Systematics* (Urbana: University of Illinois Press, 1999 [1966]), 93–94; Eldredge and Cracraft, *Phylogenetic Patterns and the Evolutionary Process*, 7–8; Mayr, *The Growth of Biological Thought*, 45, 464–65; Stephen J. Gould, "Evolution and the Triumph of Homology, or Why History Matters," *American Scientist* 74 (February 1986): 66; Ereshefsky, *The Poverty of the Linnaean Hierarchy*, 68; Carl P. Lipo et al., "Cultural Phylogenies and Explanation: Why Historical Methods Matter," in *Mapping Our Ancestors: Phylogenetic Approaches in Anthropology and Prehistory* (New Brunswick, NJ: AldineTransaction, 2006), 3, 7; Carl P. Lipo, "The Resolution of Cultural Phylogenies Using Graphs," in *Mapping Our Ancestors*, 89.

51. Klein, *The Human Career*, 222.

52. Nicholas Wade, *Before the Dawn: Recovering the Lost History of Our Ancestors* (New York: Penguin, 2006), 56. See also Steve Olson, *Mapping Human History: Discovering the Past through Our Genes* (Boston: Houghton Mifflin, 2002), 36–37.

53. *Journey of Man* (PBS Home Video, 2003).

54. See also Lewin and Foley, *Principles of Human Evolution*, 411; Wells, *Deep Ancestry*, 230.

55. *Journey of Man.*

56. See also Pierre L. van den Berghe, *The Ethnic Phenomenon* (Westport, CT: Praeger, 1987 [1981]), 20.

57. See also Bryan Sykes, *The Seven Daughters of Eve: The Science That Reveals Our Genetic Ancestry* (London: W.W. Norton, 2001), 48.

58. John H. Relethford, *Reflections of Our Past: How Human History Is Revealed in Our Genes* (Boulder, CO: Westview Press, 2003), 30. See also p. 33.

59. See also Cavalli-Sforza and Cavalli-Sforza, *The Great Human Diasporas*, 38.

60. See Gregory J. Morgan, "Emile Zuckerkandl, Linus Pauling, and the Molecular Evolutionary Clock, 1959–1965," *Journal of the History of Biology* 31 (1998): 155–78.

61. Jared Diamond, *The Third Chimpanzee: The Evolution and Future of the Human Animal* (New York: HarperCollins, 1992), 18.

62. See also Cavalli-Sforza and Cavalli-Sforza, *The Great Human Diasporas*, 34–37.

63. Olson, *Mapping Human History*, 5.

64. See, for example, Cavalli-Sforza and Cavalli-Sforza, *The Great Human Diasporas*; Luigi L. Cavalli-Sforza et al., *The History and Geography of Human Genes* (Princeton, NJ: Princeton University Press, 1996); Luigi L. Cavalli-Sforza, *Genes, Peoples, and Languages* (New York: North Point Press, 2000); Sykes, *The Seven Daughters of Eve*; Wells, *The Journey of Man*; Mark D. Shriver and Rick A. Kittles. "Genetic Ancestry and the Search for Personalized Genetic Histories," *Nature Review: Genetics* 5 (2004): 611–18; Wells, *Deep Ancestry*. For maps showing the global distribution of the different haplogroups, see, for example, Tony N. Frudakis, *Molecular Photofitting: Predicting Ancestry and Phenotype Using DNA* (Amsterdam: Elsevier, 2008), 152, 155. See also John C. Avise, "Phylogeography: Retrospect and Prospect," *Journal of Biogeography* 36 (2009): 3–15.

65. See, for example, Jun Z. Li et al., "Worldwide Human Relationships Inferred from Genome-Wide Patterns of Variation," *Science* 319 (2008): 1100–04.

66. Ann Gibbons, "The Mystery of Humanity's Missing Mutations," *Science* 267 (January 6, 1995): 35; Relethford, *Reflections of Our Past*, 119.

67. See, for example, Rebecca L. Cann et al., "Mitochondrial DNA and Human Evolution," *Nature* 325 (1987): 31–36; Maryellen Ruvolo et al., "Mitochondrial COII Sequences and Modern Human Origins," *Molecular Biology and Evolution* 10 (1993): 1115–35; Cavalli-Sforza and Cavalli-Sforza, *The Great*

Human Diasporas, 114–15, 123–25; Alan R. Rogers and Lynn B. Jorde, "Genetic Evidence on Modern Human Origins," *Human Biology* 67 (1995): 21; Johanson and Edgar, *From Lucy to Language*, 56; Christopher Stringer and Robin McKie, *African Exodus: The Origins of Modern Humanity* (New York: Henry Holt, 1997 [1996]), 116, 182; Frudakis, *Molecular Photofitting*, 43.

68. Stringer and McKie, *African Exodus*, 117. See also Natalie Angier, "Do Races Differ? Not Really, Genes Show," *New York Times*, August 22, 2000, 1, 6.

69. Wells, *The Journey of Man*, 191. See also Stringer and McKie, *African Exodus*, 117, 162.

70. See, for example, Richard Lewontin, *Human Diversity* (New York: Scientific American Books, 1982), 161–62; Cann et al., "Mitochondrial DNA and Human Evolution"; Alan C. Wilson and Rebecca L. Cann, "The Recent African Genesis of Humans," *Scientific American* 266 (April 1992): 68–73; Gibbons, "The Mystery of Humanity's Missing Mutations," 35; Michael F. Hammer, "A Recent Common Ancestry for Human Y Chromosomes," *Nature* 378 (1995): 376–78.

71. Cavalli-Sforza and Cavalli-Sforza, *The Great Human Diasporas*, 121–23; Cavalli-Sforza, *Genes, Peoples, and Languages*, 62; Wade, *Before the Dawn*, 106–09.

72. Stringer and McKie, *African Exodus*, 177. See also Dawkins, *River out of Eden*, 52.

73. Geneticist Spencer Wells, in *Journey of Man*.

74. See, for example, Robert M. Taylor, "Summoning the Wandering Tribes: Genealogy and Family Reunions in American History," *Journal of Social History* 16 (Winter 1982): 21–37; Gwen K. Neville, *Kinship and Pilgrimage: Rituals of Reunion in American Protestant Culture* (New York: Oxford University Press, 1987), 57–65.

75. See, for example, Edward E. Evans-Pritchard, "The Nuer of the Southern Sudan," in Robert Parkin and Linda Stone (eds.), *Kinship and Family: An Anthropological Reader* (Malden, MA: Blackwell, 2004 [1940]), 71; Robin Fox, *Kinship and Marriage: An Anthropological Perspective* (Cambridge, UK: Cambridge University Press, 1983 [1967]), 90, 124–27; Pierre L. van den Berghe, *Man in Society: A Biosocial View* (New York: Elsevier, 1975), 74.

76. Evans-Pritchard, *The Nuer*, 106, 195; Robin Fox, *The Tory Islanders: A People of the Celtic Fringe* (Cambridge, UK: Cambridge University Press, 1978), 32, 35, 70; Anthony D. Smith, "National Identity and Myths of Ethnic Descent," in *Myths and Memories of the Nation* (Oxford: Oxford University Press, 1999 [1984]), 64; Neville, *Kinship and Pilgrimage*, 60, 88.

77. See also Meyer Fortes, "The Significance of Descent in Tale Social Structure," in *Time and Social Structure and Other Essays* (London: Athlone Press, 1970 [1943–44]), 41.

78. See also Richard D. Alba, *Ethnic Identity: The Transformation of White America* (New Haven, CT: Yale University Press, 1990), 37.

79. Max Weber, *Economy and Society: An Outline of Interpretive Sociology* (Berkeley: University of California Press, 1978 [1925]), 389. See also van den Berghe, *The Ethnic Phenomenon*, 16; Smith, "National Identity and Myths of Ethnic Descent," 60; Kwame Gyekye, *Tradition and Modernity: Philosophical Reflections on the African Experience* (New York: Oxford University Press, 1997), 96; Catherine Lee, "'Race' and 'Ethnicity' in Biomedical Research: How Do Scientists Construct and Explain Differences in Health?" *Social Science and Medicine* 30 (2009): 2.

80. van den Berghe, *The Ethnic Phenomenon*, 239. See also pp. xi, 18; Pierre L. van den Berghe, "Ethnies and Nations: Genealogy Indeed," in Atsuko Ichijo and Gordana Uzelac (eds.), *When Is the Nation? Towards an Understanding of Theories of Nationalism* (Abingdon, UK: Routledge, 2005), 114.

81. See also van den Berghe, *The Ethnic Phenomenon*, 61; van den Berghe, "Ethnies and Nations," 115–16; Andreas Wimmer, "The Making and Unmaking of Ethnic Boundaries: A Multilevel Process Theory," *American Journal of Sociology* 113 (2008): 973–74; Rogers Brubaker, "Ethnicity, Race, and Nationalism," *Annual Review of Sociology* 35 (2009): 21–42.

82. See also Weber, *Economy and Society*, 395.

83. On the fundamental distinction between "civic" and "ethnic" nations, see, for example, Rogers Brubaker, *Citizenship and Nationhood in France and Germany* (Cambridge, MA: Harvard University Press, 1992); Michael Ignatieff, *Blood and Belonging: Journeys into the New Nationalism* (New York: Farrar, Straus, and Giroux, 1994 [1993]), 5–9; David A. Hollinger, "National Culture and Communities of Descent," *Reviews in American History* 26 (1998): 312–28.

84. Anthony D. Smith, *The Antiquity of Nations* (Cambridge, UK: Polity, 2004), 47. See also pp. 43–46; Anthony D. Smith, *The Ethnic Origins of Nations* (Oxford: Basil Blackwell, 1986), 24–25; Brubaker, *Citizenship and Nationhood in France and Germany*, 2, 114–37; Hollinger, *Postethnic America*, 21–22, 165; Anthony D. Smith, "The Genealogy of Nations: An Ethno-Symbolic Approach," in Atsuko Ichijo and Gordana Uzelac (eds.), *When Is the Nation? Towards an Understanding of Theories of Nationalism* (Abingdon, UK: Routledge, 2005), 98.

85. See, for example, Catherine Nash, "Genetic Kinship," *Cultural Studies* 18, no.1 (2004): 3, 6. See also Benedict Anderson, *Imagined Communities: Reflections on the Origin and Spread of Nationalism* (London: Verso, 1983), 131; Israel Gershoni and James P. Jankowski, *Egypt, Islam, and the Arabs: The Search for Egyptian Nationhood, 1900–1930* (New York: Oxford University Press, 1986), 165; Carol Delaney, "Father State, Motherland, and the Birth of Modern Turkey," in Sylvia Yanagisako and Carol Delaney (eds.), *Naturalizing Power: Essays in Feminist Cultural Analysis* (New York: Routledge, 1995), 177–99; Katherine Verdery, *What Was Socialism, and What Comes Next?* (Princeton, NJ: Princeton University Press, 1996), 233; Patricia H. Collins, "It's All in the Family:

Intersections of Gender, Race, and Nation," *Hypatia* 13 (Summer 1998): 69–71; Catherine Nash, *Of Irish Descent: Origin Stories, Genealogy, and the Politics of Belonging* (Syracuse, NY: Syracuse University Press, 2008), 20, 32–34.

86. Katherine Verdery, *The Political Lives of Dead Bodies: Reburial and Postsocialist Change* (New York: Columbia University Press, 1999), 41.

87. See also Eviatar Zerubavel, "Generally Speaking: The Logic and Mechanics of Social Pattern Analysis," *Sociological Forum* 22 (2007): 135–36, 141–42.

88. Darwin, *The Origin of Species*, 440, 447, 450.

89. Ibid., 440.

90. Ibid. See also p. 443.

91. Darwin, *The Descent of Man*, 153–54.

92. See also Simpson, *Principles of Animal Taxonomy*, 50, 53; Ereshefsky, *The Poverty of the Linnaean Hierarchy*, 67, 209–12.

93. See also Mayr, *The Growth of Biological Thought*, 226.

94. See also Ereshefsky, *The Poverty of the Linnaean Hierarchy*, 67, 75.

95. Gould, "Evolution and the Triumph of Homology," 66.

96. Hennig, *Phylogenetic Systematics*, 83. See also p. 154; Bigelow, "Classification and Phylogeny," 49.

97. Richard Dawkins, *The Blind Watchmaker: Why the Evidence of Evolution Reveals a Universe Without Design* (New York: W.W. Norton, 2006 [1986]), 367–68.

98. Klein, *The Human Career*, 11. See also p. 69; Mark Ridley, *Evolution and Classification: The Reformation of Cladism* (London: Longman, 1986), 184, 190, 192.

99. See, for example, Dawkins, *The Blind Watchmaker*, 398; Wolpoff and Caspari, *Race and Human Evolution*, 254.

100. See also Ereshefsky, *The Poverty of the Linnaean Hierarchy*, 71.

101. Mayr, "Darwin's Five Theories of Evolution," 760. See also Cartmill and Smith, *The Human Lineage*, 32–33.

102. Ereshefsky, *The Poverty of the Linnaean Hierarchy*, 47.

103. See also Richard D. Alford, *Naming and Identity: A Cross-Cultural Study of Personal Naming Practices* (New Haven, CT: HRAF Press, 1988), 55.

104. See, for example, Freedman, *Lineage Organization in Southeastern China*, 34–35.

105. See also Charles E. Keyes, "Towards a New Formulation of the Concept of Ethnic Group," *Ethnicity* 3 (1976): 206–07.

106. See also Catherine Nash, "Genealogical Identities," *Environment and Planning D: Society and Space* 20 (2002): 27–52.

107. See also van den Berghe, *The Ethnic Phenomenon*, 21.

108. See also Fortes, "The Significance of Descent in Tale Social Structure," 37; Wilson, *Genealogy and History in the Biblical World*, 20.

109. See also Evans-Pritchard, *The Nuer*, 106, 195–201; Fortes, "The Significance of Descent in Tale Social Structure," 37–38, 43.

Chapter 4

1. Bryan Sykes, *The Seven Daughters of Eve: The Science That Reveals Our Genetic Ancestry* (London: W.W. Norton, 2001), 289. On such "umbilical" ties, see also Catherine Nash, "Genetic Kinship," *Cultural Studies* 18 (2004), 17.

2. Sykes, *The Seven Daughters of Eve*, 289.

3. See also Gilles Deleuze and Felix Guattari, *A Thousand Plateaus: Capitalism and Schizophrenia* (Minneapolis: University of Minnesota Press, 1987), 3–28; Liisa H. Malkki "National Geographic: The Rooting of Peoples and the Territorialization of National Identity Among Scholars and Refugees," *Cultural Anthropology* 7 (1992): 34.

4. David M. Schneider, *American Kinship: A Cultural Account* (Englewood Cliffs, NJ: Prentice-Hall, 1980), 24. See also Barbara K. Rothman, *Recreating Motherhood* (New Brunswick, NJ: Rutgers University Press, 2000 [1989]), 17; Dorothy Nelkin and Susan Lindee, *The DNA Mystique: The Gene as a Cultural Icon* (New York: W. H. Freeman, 1995), 60.

5. Horace M. Kallen, "Democracy versus the Melting-Pot: A Study of American Nationality," *The Nation*, February 25, 1915, http://www.expo98.msu.edu/people/Kallen.htm.

6. See also Eviatar Zerubavel, *The Seven-Day Circle: The History and Meaning of the Week* (Chicago: University of Chicago Press, 1989 [1985]), 139–41; Eviatar Zerubavel, *The Fine Line: Making Distinctions in Everyday Life* (Chicago: University of Chicago Press, 1993 [1991]), 28–29.

7. See also Jennifer Mason, "Tangible Affinities and the Real Life Fascination of Kinship," *Sociology* 42 (2008): 33–34.

8. Nash, "Genetic Kinship," 4; James D. Faubion and Jennifer A. Hamilton, "Sumptuary Kinship," *Anthropological Quarterly* 80 (2007): 550.

9. See also C. Cannings and E. A. Thompson, *Genealogical and Genetic Structure* (Cambridge, UK: Cambridge University Press, 1981), 1.

10. Rothman, *Recreating Motherhood*, 18.

11. See also Melissa L. Meyer, *Thicker Than Water: The Origins of Blood as Symbol and Ritual* (New York: Routledge, 2005), 8, 49–64.

12. Lewis H. Morgan, *Systems of Consanguinity and Affinity of the Human Family* (Lincoln: University of Nebraska Press, 1997 [1871]), 10; Ferdinand Tönnies, *Community and Society* (New York: Harper Torchbooks, 1963 [1887]), 42.

13. Tönnies, *Community and Society*, 42, 192; Werner Sollors, *Beyond Ethnicity: Consent and Descent in American Culture* (New York: Oxford University Press, 1986), 151; Mason, "Tangible Affinities."

14. Judith S. Modell, *Kinship with Strangers: Adoption and Interpretations of Kinship in American Culture* (Berkeley: University of California Press, 1994), 2. See also p. 226.

15. See, for example, Betty J. Lifton, *Journey of the Adopted Self: A Quest for Wholeness* (New York: Basic Books, 1994).

16. See, for example, Nelkin and Lindee, *The DNA Mystique*, 66–72.

17. Carol Delaney, "Father State, Motherland, and the Birth of Modern Turkey," in Sylvia Yanagisako and Carol Delaney (eds.), *Naturalizing Power: Essays in Feminist Cultural Analysis* (New York: Routledge, 1995), 177.

18. Catherine Nash, *Of Irish Descent: Origin Stories, Genealogy, and the Politics of Belonging* (Syracuse, NY: Syracuse University Press, 2008), 20.

19. Michael Ignatieff, *Blood and Belonging: Journeys into the New Nationalism* (New York: Farrar, Straus, and Giroux, 1994 [1993]). See also Benedict Anderson, *Imagined Communities: Reflections on the Origin and Spread of Nationalism* (London: Verso, 1983), 131; Patricia H. Collins, "It's All in the Family: Intersections of Gender, Race, and Nation," *Hypatia* 13 (Summer 1998): 69–71.

20. See also Craig Calhoun, "Nationalism and Ethnicity," *Annual Review of Sociology* 19 (1993): 221.

21. Edwin Black, *War Against the Weak: Eugenics and America's Campaign to Create a Master Race* (New York: Four Walls Eight Windows, 2003), 343.

22. Israel Gershoni and James P. Jankowski, *Egypt, Islam, and the Arabs: The Search for Egyptian Nationhood, 1900–1930* (New York: Oxford University Press, 1986), 165.

23. Ibid., 167.

24. See also Eviatar Zerubavel, *Time Maps: Collective Memory and the Social Shape of the Past* (Chicago: University of Chicago Press, 2003), 105.

25. See, for example, Claudio Tuniz et al., *The Bone Readers: Atoms, Genes, and the Politics of Australia's Deep Past* (Crows Nest, Australia: Allen & Unwin, 2009), 214.

26. David A. Hollinger, *Postethnic America: Beyond Multiculturalism* (New York: Basic Books, 1995), 133.

27. On race as a particular form of ethnicity, see also Stanley Lieberson and Mary C. Waters, *From Many Strands: Ethnic and Racial Groups in Contemporary America* (New York: Russell Sage Foundation, 1988), 14; Joane Nagel, "Constructing Ethnicity: Creating and Recreating Ethnic Identity and Culture," *Social Problems* 41 (1994): 152–76; Roger Waldinger and Mehdi Bozorgmehr, "The Making of a Multicultural Metropolis," in *Ethnic Los Angeles* (New York: Russell Sage Foundation, 1996), 30; Orlando Patterson, *The Ordeal of Integration: Progress and Resentment in America's "Racial" Crisis* (New York: Basic Civitas, 1997), 173; Richard Alba and Victor Nee, "Rethinking Assimilation Theory for a New Era of Immigration," *International Migration Review* 31 (1997): 834; Andreas Wimmer, "The Making and Unmaking of Ethnic Boundaries: A Multilevel Process Theory," *American Journal of Sociology* 113 (2008): 973–74.

28. See also Naomi Zack, "Life After Race," in *American Mixed Race: The Culture of Microdiversity* (Lanham, MD: Rowman & Littlefield, 1995), 302; Pauline T.

Strong and Barrik van Winkle, "'Indian Blood': Reflections on the Reckoning and Refiguring of Native North American Identity," *Cultural Anthropology* 11 (1996): 560–62; Stephen Howe, *Afrocentrism: Mythical Pasts and Imagined Homes* (London: Verso, 1998), 25, 85, 265.

29. Schneider, *American Kinship*, 25.
30. David T. Goldberg, *The Racial State* (Malden, MA: Blackwell, 2002), 185.
31. Werner Sollors, *Neither Black Nor White Yet Both: Thematic Explorations of Interracial Literature* (Cambridge, MA: Harvard University Press, 1997), 119. On Thomas Jefferson's calculations, see also pp. 113–14, 140.
32. See, for example, Frank W. Sweet, *Legal History of the Color Line: The Rise and Triumph of the One-Drop Rule* (Palm Coast, FL: Backintyme, 2005), 127, 171–72; Virginia R. Domínguez, *White by Definition: Social Classification in Creole Louisiana* (New Brunswick, NJ: Rutgers University Press, 1986), 46. See also Michael A. Elliott, "Telling the Difference: Nineteenth-Century Legal Narratives of Racial Taxonomy," *Law and Social Inquiry* 24 (1999): 611–36; Catherine Nash, "Genealogical Identities," *Environment and Planning D: Society and Space* 20 (2002): 38.
33. See, for example, Joel Williamson, *New People: Miscegenation and Mulattoes in the United States* (New York: Free Press, 1980), 24; Sollors, *Neither Black Nor White Yet Both*, 118, 120, 153.
34. See, for example, Sollors, *Neither Black Nor White Yet Both*, 121, 459.
35. Ward Churchill, quoted in Strong and van Winkle, "'Indian Blood,'" 551.
36. Jonathan Marks, *What It Means to Be 98% Chimpanzee: Apes, People, and Their Genes* (Berkeley: University of California Press, 2002), 251. See also F. James Davis, *Who Is Black? One Nation's Definition* (University Park: Pennsylvania State University Press, 1991), 166–67; Naomi Zack, *Race and Mixed Race* (Philadelphia: Temple University Press, 1993), 187; G. Reginald Daniel, *More Than Black? Multiracial Identity and the New Racial Order* (Philadelphia: Temple University Press, 2002), xii.
37. See also Henry Kendall, *The Kinship of Men: An Argument from Pedigrees, or Genealogy Viewed as a Science* (Boston: Cupples and Hurd, 1888), 24–25; Nash, *Of Irish Descent*, 196.
38. See also Francisco J. Ayala, "The Myth of Eve: Molecular Biology and Human Origins," *Science* 270 (December 22, 1995): 1934.
39. See, for example, Patrick J. Geary, *The Myth of Nations: The Medieval Origins of Europe* (Princeton, NJ: Princeton University Press, 2002). See also Jennifer Jackson Preece, *Minority Rights: Between Diversity and Community* (Cambridge, UK: Polity Press, 2005), 138–39.
40. See, for example, Heather Pringle, *The Master Plan: Himmler's Scholars and the Holocaust* (New York: Hyperion, 2006), 145–46, 175, 225. See also David P. Henige, *The Chronology of Oral Tradition: Quest for a Chimera* (Oxford: Clarendon Press, 1974), 59–64; Nash, *Of Irish Descent*, 114.

41. See, for example, Morgan, *Systems of Consanguinity*, 25; Bernard Farber, *Conceptions of Kinship* (New York: Elsevier, 1981), 4–12, 21–32, 189. See also Jack Goody, *The Development of the Family and Marriage in Europe* (Cambridge, UK: Cambridge University Press, 1983), 136–38.
42. See, for example, Sweet, *Legal History of the Color Line*.
43. Janet Carsten, "The Substance of Kinship and the Heat of the Hearth: Feeding, Personhood, and Relatedness among Malays in Pulau Langkawi," in Robert Parkin and Linda Stone (eds.), *Kinship and Family: An Anthropological Reader* (Malden, MA: Blackwell, 2004 [1995]), 313; Peter Parkes, "Fosterage, Kinship, and Legend: When Milk Was Thicker Than Blood?" *Comparative Studies in Society and History* 46 (2004): 590–92; Peter Parkes, "Milk Kinship in Islam: Substance, Structure, History," *Social Anthropology* 13 (2005): 307–29; Morgan Clarke, "The Modernity of Milk Kinship," *Social Anthropology* 15 (2007): 287–304.
44. Jonathan Marks, "Race: Past, Present, and Future," in Barbara A. Koenig et al. (eds.), *Revisiting Race in a Genomic Age* (New Brunswick, NJ: Rutgers University Press, 2008), 26.
45. Anthony Appiah, "The Uncompleted Argument: DuBois and the Illusion of Race," in Henry L. Gates Jr. (ed.), *"Race," Writing, and Difference* (Chicago: University of Chicago Press, 1986), 26.
46. See also Sollors, *Neither Black Nor White Yet Both*, 43, 121. On mental weighing, see Jamie L. Mullaney, "Making It 'Count': Mental Weighing and Identity Attribution," *Symbolic Interaction* 22 (1999): 269–83. On cognitive asymmetry, see Wayne Brekhus, "Social Marking and the Mental Coloring of Identity: Sexual Identity Construction and Maintenance in the United States," *Sociological Forum* 11 (1996): 497–522; Eviatar Zerubavel, "The Social Marking of the Past: Toward a Socio-Semiotics of Memory," in Roger Friedland and John Mohr (eds.), *Matters of Culture: Cultural Sociology in Practice* (Cambridge, UK: Cambridge University Press, 2004), 184–95; Karen A. Cerulo, *Never Saw It Coming: Cultural Challenges to Envisioning the Worst* (Chicago: University of Chicago Press, 2006).
47. Meyer Fortes, "Descent, Filiation, and Affinity," in *Time and Social Structure and Other Essays* (London: Athlone Press, 1970 [1959]), 108.
48. Carol Delaney, *The Seed and the Soil: Gender and Cosmology in Turkish Village Society* (Berkeley: University of California Press, 1991), 152. See also p. 156; Carol Delaney, "Cutting the Ties that Bind: The Sacrifice of Abraham and Patriarchal Kinship," in Sarah Franklin and Susan McKinnon (eds.), *Relative Values: Reconfiguring Kinship Studies* (Durham, NC: Duke University Press, 2001), 453–54; María E. Martínez, *Genealogical Fictions: Limpieza de Sangre, Religion, and Gender in Colonial Mexico* (Stanford, CA: Stanford University Press, 2008), 49–50.
49. Rothman, *Recreating Motherhood*, 16–20; Carol Delaney, *The Seed and the Soil*.

50. Carol Delaney, *The Seed and the Soil*, 150.
51. Rothman, *Recreating Motherhood*, 16–17. See also Colleen Nugent, "Children's Surnames, Moral Dilemmas: Accounting for the Predominance of Fathers' Surnames for Children," *Gender and Society* 24 (2010): 500.
52. Nash, *Of Irish Descent*, 261.
53. Rothman, *Recreating Motherhood*, 15.
54. Marc Shell, *The End of Kinship: "Measure for Measure," Incest, and the Ideal of Universal Siblinghood* (Baltimore: Johns Hopkins University Press, 1995 [1988]), 204.
55. Nancy Jay, *Throughout Your Generations Forever: Sacrifice, Religion, and Paternity* (Chicago: University of Chicago Press, 1992), 47.
56. See, for example, the first eight chapters of *I Chronicles*.
57. Sykes, *The Seven Daughters of Eve*, 292.
58. See, for example, Martin Daly and Margo I. Wilson, "Whom Are Newborn Babies Said to Resemble?" *Ethology and Sociobiology* 3 (1982): 70, 73–74.
59. Henry T. Greely, "Genetic Genealogy: Genetics Meets the Marketplace," in Barbara A. Koenig et al. (eds.), *Revisiting Race in a Genomic Age* (New Brunswick, NJ: Rutgers University Press, 2008), 228–29. See also Ruth Padawer, "Losing Fatherhood," *New York Times Magazine*, November 22, 2009, pp. 38–62.
60. See also Shell, *The End of Kinship*, 4–5; David Lowenthal, *Possessed by the Past: The Heritage Crusade and the Spoils of History* (New York: Free Press, 1996), 50; John Seabrook, "The Tree of Me," in *Flash of Genius and Other True Stories of Invention* (New York: St. Martin's Griffin, 2008 [2001]), 111–37.
61. Williamson, *New People*, p. 65.
62. Léon-François Hoffmann, quoted in Sollors, *Neither Black Nor White Yet Both*, 121.
63. Cecile A. Lawrence, "Racelessness," in Naomi Zack (ed.), *American Mixed Race: The Culture of Microdiversity* (Lanham, MD: Rowman & Littlefield, 1995), 28. See also Paul R. Spickard, *Mixed Blood: Intermarriage and Ethnic Identity in Twentieth-Century America* (Madison: University of Wisconsin Press, 1989), 332.
64. Zack, "Life After Race," 305. See also Stephen Satris, "What Are They?" In Naomi Zack (ed.), *American Mixed Race: The Culture of Microdiversity* (Lanham, MD: Rowman & Littlefield, 1995), 312–13; Winthrop D. Jordan, *White over Black: American Attitudes toward the Negro, 1550–1812* (New York: W. W. Norton, 1977), 170.
65. Gilbert T. Stephenson, *Race Distinctions in American Law* (New York: AMS Press, 1969 [1910]), 19.
66. See also Sollors, *Neither Black Nor White Yet Both*, 121; Wayne Brekhus et al., "On the Contributions of Cognitive Sociology to the Sociological Study of Race," *Sociology Compass* 4 (2010): 61–76.
67. Goldberg, *The Racial State*, 189.

68. Zack, *Race and Mixed Race*, 11.
69. Strong and van Winkle, "'Indian Blood,'" 551.
70. Harold P. Freeman, "Commentary on the Meaning of Race in Science and Society," *Cancer Epidemiology, Biomarkers and Prevention* 12 (March 2003): 236s. See also Mary T. Bassett, "The Pursuit of Equity in Health: Reflections on Race and Public Health Data in Southern Africa," *American Journal of Public Health* 90 (2000): 1690.
71. Mark Twain, *Pudd'nhead Wilson* (Mineola, NY: Dover, 1999 [1894]), 7.
72. Booker T. Washington, *The Future of the American Negro* (Boston: Small, Maynard, and Co., 1900), 158.
73. Patrick Wolfe, "Land, Labor, and Difference: Elementary Structures of Race," *American Historical Review* 106 (2001): 882.
74. Barbara J. Fields, "Ideology and Race in American History," in J. Morgan Kousser and James M. McPherson (eds.), *Region, Race, and Reconstruction: Essays in Honor of C. Vann Woodward* (New York: Oxford University Press, 1982), 149. See also Sweet, *Legal History of the Color Line*, 92.
75. Ellis Cose, "It Was Always Headed Here," *Newsweek*, March 31, 2008, p. 33.
76. Meyer, *Thicker Than Water*, 172; Brackette F. Williams, "A Class Act: Anthropology and the Race to Nation Across Ethnic Terrain," *Annual Review of Anthropology* 18 (1989): 416. See also Northcote W. Thomas, *Kinship Organisations and Group Marriage in Australia* (New York: Humanities Press, 1966 [1906]), 3–4; George P. Murdock, *Social Structure* (New York: Macmillan, 1949), 15–16, 42–44.
77. On norms, conventions, and traditions of remembering and forgetting, see Eviatar Zerubavel, *Social Mindscapes: An Invitation to Cognitive Sociology* (Cambridge, MA: Harvard University Press, 1997), 81–99.
78. Ibid.
79. See also Kendall, *The Kinship of Men*, 101–08; J. D. Freeman, "On the Concept of the Kindred," in Paul Bohannan and John Middleton (eds.), *Kinship and Social Organization* (Garden City, NY: American Museum of Natural History, 1968 [1961]), 258; Kenneth W. Wachter, "Ancestors at the Norman Conquest," in Bennett Dyke and Warren T. Morrill (eds.), *Genealogical Demography* (New York: Academic Press, 1980 [1978]), 85–87; John H. Relethford, *Reflections of Our Past: How Human History Is Revealed in Our Genes* (Boulder, CO: Westview Press, 2003), 6; Steven Pinker, "Strangled by Roots: The Genealogy Craze in America," *New Republic*, August 6, 2007, p. 33.
80. Richard Conniff, "The Family Tree, Pruned," *Smithsonian*, 38 (July 2007): 95.
81. See also Katherine Verdery, *The Political Lives of Dead Bodies: Reburial and Postsocialist Change* (New York: Columbia University Press, 1999), 119.
82. See also Robin Fox, *The Tory Islanders: A People of the Celtic Fringe* (Cambridge, UK: Cambridge University Press, 1978), 31–33; Gwen K. Neville, *Kinship and Pilgrimage: Rituals of Reunion in American Protestant Culture* (New York: Oxford University Press, 1987), 60.

83. See also Verdery, *The Political Lives of Dead Bodies*, 118.
84. Mary C. Waters, *Ethnic Options: Choosing Identities in America* (Berkeley: University of California Press, 1990). See also Millicent R. Ayoub, "The Family Reunion," *Ethnology* 5 (1966): 430; Domínguez, *White by Definition*, 262–63.
85. Paul Bohannan, *Social Anthropology* (New York: Holt, Rinehart and Winston, 1963), 126–29; Pierre L. van den Berghe, *Man in Society: A Biosocial View* (New York: Elsevier, 1975), 73, 76.
86. On bilateral or "cognatic" descent, see, for example, Murdock, *Social Structure*, 57; George P. Murdock, "Cognatic Forms of Social Organization," in Paul Bohannan and John Middleton (eds.), *Kinship and Social Organization* (Garden City, NY: American Museum of Natural History, 1968 [1960]), 236–37; Edmund Leach, "On Certain Unconsidered Aspects of Double Descent Systems," *Man* 62 (1962): 132; Robin Fox, *Kinship and Marriage: An Anthropological Perspective* (Cambridge, UK: Cambridge University Press, 1983 [1967]), 147, 149; Ernest L. Schusky, *Variation in Kinship* (New York: Holt, Rinehart, and Winston, 1974), 26–39.
87. Shaye J. D. Cohen, "The Matrilineal Principle in Historical Perspective," *Judaism* 34 (Winter 1985): 5.
88. Sandra Bamford, "Conceiving Relatedness: Non-Substantial Relations Among the Kamea of Papua New Guinea," *Journal of the Royal Anthropological Institute* (New Series) 10 (2004): 291; Rothman, *Recreating Motherhood*, 18–19. See also Susan M. Kahn, *Reproducing Jews: A Cultural Account of Assisted Conception in Israel* (Durham, NC: Duke University Press, 2000), 105.
89. See, for example, Alfred R. Radcliffe-Brown, "Patrilineal and Matrilineal Succession," in *Structure and Function in Primitive Society* (New York: Free Press, 1965 [1935]), 32–48.
90. Nash, *Of Irish Descent*, 58. See also p. 74.
91. Hildred Geertz and Clifford Geertz, "Teknonymy in Bali: Parenthood, Age-Grading and Genealogical Amnesia," *Journal of the Royal Anthropological Institute of Great Britain and Ireland* 94 (1964), no. 2: 94–108; Alex Shoumatoff, *The Mountain of Names: A History of the Human Family* (New York: Simon and Schuster, 1985), 37; Lowenthal, *Possessed by the Past*, 51. See also Freeman, "On the Concept of the Kindred," 262; Julie M. Gricar, "How Thick Is Blood? The Social Construction and Cultural Configuration of Kinship" (PhD diss., Columbia University, New York, 1991), 323; Johanna E. Foster, "Feminist Theory and the Politics of Ambiguity: A Comparative Analysis of the Multiracial Movement, the Intersex Movement and the Disability Rights Movement as Contemporary Struggles over Social Classification in the United States" (PhD diss., Rutgers University, New Brunswick, NJ, 2000), 73–74.
92. See also Waters, *Ethnic Options*, 21.
93. On the process of such mental "filtering," see also Asia Friedman, "Toward a Sociology of Perception: Sight, Sex, and Gender," *Cultural Sociology* 5 (2011): 187–206.

94. Appiah, "The Uncompleted Argument," 26.
95. Paul R. Spickard, "The Illogic of American Racial Categories," in Maria P. P. Root (ed.), *Racially Mixed People in America* (Newbury Park: CA: SAGE, 1992), 21.
96. Mark D. Shriver and Rick A. Kittles, "Genetic Ancestry and the Search for Personalized Genetic Histories," *Nature Review: Genetics* 5 (2004): 614.
97. Greely, "Genetic Genealogy," 225.
98. Carl Elliott and Paul Brodwin, "Identity and Genetic Ancestry Tracing," *British Medical Journal* 325 (2002): 1469–70.
99. Steven Pinker, "My Genome, My Self," *New York Times Magazine*, January 11, 2009, p. 30.
100. Paul Brodwin, "Genetics, Identity, and the Anthropology of Essentialism," *Anthropological Quarterly* 75 (2002): 328.
101. Greely, "Genetic Genealogy," 225. See also 227; Ishmael Reed, "America's 'Black Only' Ethnicity," in Werner Sollors (ed.), *The Invention of Ethnicity* (New York: Oxford University Press, 1989), 227; Shriver and Kittles, "Genetic Ancestry," 615.
102. See Zerubavel, *The Fine Line*.
103. See, for example, Carol Stack, *All Our Kin* (New York: Basic Books, 1974), 54; David M. Schneider and Calvert B. Cottrell, *The American Kin Universe: A Genealogical Study* (Chicago: University of Chicago Press, 1975), 93; Schneider, *American Kinship*, 67.
104. See, for example, Craig T. Palmer and Lyle B. Steadman, "Human Kinship as a Descendant-Leaving Strategy: A Solution to an Evolutionary Puzzle," *Journal of Social and Evolutionary Systems* 20 (1997): 42–43; Maurice Bloch and Dan Sperber, "Kinship and Evolved Psychological Dispositions: The Mother's Brother Controversy Reconsidered," in Robert Parkin and Linda Stone (eds.), *Kinship and Family: An Anthropological Reader* (Malden, MA: Blackwell, 2004 [2002]), 447–48.
105. See, for example, Schusky, *Variation in Kinship*, 53–54; Circe Sturm, *Blood Politics: Race, Culture, and Identity in the Cherokee Nation of Oklahoma* (Berkeley: University of California Press, 2002), 32–33.
106. See, for example, Alfred R. Radcliffe-Brown, "The Study of Kinship Systems," in *Structure and Function in Primitive Society* (New York: Free Press, 1965 [1941]), 52; Fox, *Kinship and Marriage*, 167.
107. See, for example, Peter G. Hepper (ed.), *Kin Recognition* (Cambridge, UK: Cambridge University Press, 1991).
108. See also Pierre L. van den Berghe, *The Ethnic Phenomenon* (Westport, CT: Praeger, 1987 [1981]), 22, 26.
109. See also Mara Loveman, "Is 'Race' Essential?" *American Sociological Review* 64 (1999): 891–98; Jonathan Marks, "'We're Going to Tell These People Who They Really Are': Science and Relatedness," in Sarah Franklin and Susan

McKinnon (eds.), *Relative Values: Reconfiguring Kinship Studies* (Durham, NC: Duke University Press, 2001), 371; Rogers Brubaker, "Ethnicity without Groups," in *Ethnicity without Groups* (Cambridge, MA: Harvard University Press, 2004 [2002]), 7–27; Anthony D. Smith, in Atsuko Ichijo and Gordana Uzelac (eds.), *When Is the Nation? Towards an Understanding of Theories of Nationalism* (Abingdon, UK: Routledge, 2005), 122; Tony N. Frudakis, *Molecular Photofitting: Predicting Ancestry and Phenotype Using DNA* (Amsterdam: Elsevier, 2008), 159.

110. See also Zerubavel, *The Fine Line*, 116.
111. Catherine Nash, "Mapping Origins: Race and Relatedness in Population Genetics and Genetic Genealogy," in Paul Atkinson et al. (eds.), *New Genetics, New Identities* (London: Routledge, 2007), 84.
112. See also Steve Olson, *Mapping Human History: Discovering the Past through Our Genes* (Boston: Houghton Mifflin, 2002), 49–50; Troy Duster, "Deep Roots and Tangled Branches," *Chronicle of Higher Education*, February 3, 2006; Duana Fullwiley, "The Biologistical Construction of Race: 'Admixture' Technology and the New Genetic Medicine," *Social Studies of Science* 38 (2008): 701.
113. See also Kenneth M. Weiss and Brian W. Lambert, "Does History Matter?" *Evolutionary Anthropology* 19 (2010): 92–97.
114. Marvin Harris, *Patterns of Race in the Americas* (Westport, CT: Greenwood, 1980 [1964]), 55.
115. Frudakis, *Molecular Photofitting*, 35.
116. See also Zack, *Race and Mixed Race*, 73.
117. See, for example, http://www.ancestrybydna.com (accessed on May 23, 2010).
118. See also Abby L. Ferber, "Exploring the Social Construction of Race: Sociology and the Study of Interracial Relationships," in Naomi Zack (ed.), *American Mixed Race: The Culture of Microdiversity* (Lanham, MD: Rowman & Littlefield, 1995), 157, 160.
119. Nadia Abu El-Haj, "The Genetic Reinscription of Race," *Annual Review of Anthropology* 36 (2007): 288.
120. Frudakis, *Molecular Photofitting*, 14. See also p. 146.
121. See, for example, Kenneth M. Weiss and Jeffrey C. Long, "Non-Darwinian Estimation: My Ancestors, My Genes' Ancestors," *Genome Research* 19 (2009): 706–07; Weiss and Lambert, "Does History Matter?" 95. See also Duster, "Deep Roots and Tangled Branches."
122. Olson, *Mapping Human History*, 42. See also p. 49; Gísli Pálsson, "The Life of Family Trees and the Book of Icelanders," *Medical Anthropology* 21 (2002): 345.
123. See also Richard G. Klein, *The Human Career: Human Biological and Cultural Origins*, 2nd ed. (Chicago: University of Chicago Press, 1999), 3; Richard Dawkins, *The Ancestor's Tale: A Pilgrimage to the Dawn of Evolution* (Boston: Mariner Books, 2005), 309–10.

124. Willi Hennig, *Phylogenetic Systematics* (Urbana: University of Illinois Press, 1999 [1966]), 63. See also Zerubavel, *The Fine Line*, 61–80.

125. Dawkins, *The Ancestor's Tale*, 307–08.

126. Richard Dawkins, *The Blind Watchmaker: Why the Evidence of Evolution Reveals a Universe Without Design* (New York: W.W. Norton, 2006 [1986]), 373.

127. Dawkins, *The Ancestor's Tale*, 310.

128. See also Anderson, *Imagined Communities*; Bob Simpson, "Imagined Genetic Communities: Ethnicity and Essentialism in the Twenty-First Century," *Anthropology Today* 16, no. 3 (2000): 5.

Chapter 5

1. See also Robert R. Wilson, *Genealogy and History in the Biblical World* (New Haven, CT: Yale University Press, 1977).

2. Catherine Nash, *Of Irish Descent: Origin Stories, Genealogy, and the Politics of Belonging* (Syracuse, NY: Syracuse University Press, 2008), 45. See also pp. 17, 46.

3. See also Mary C. Waters, *Ethnic Options: Choosing Identities in America* (Berkeley: University of California Press, 1990); Wendy D. Roth and Biorn Ivemark, "'Not Everybody Knows That I'm Actually Black': The Effects of DNA Ancestry Testing on Racial and Ethnic Boundaries" (paper presented at the Annual Meeting of the American Sociological Association, Atlanta, 2010).

4. See, for example, Donald N. Levine, *Greater Ethiopia: The Evolution of a Multiethnic Society* (Chicago: University of Chicago Press, 2000 [1974]), 96–105; http://www.britannica.com/EBchecked/topic/194084/Ethiopia/37706/The-Zagwe-and-Solomonic-dynasties (accessed January 18, 2010); David P. Henige, *The Chronology of Oral Tradition: Quest for a Chimera* (Oxford: Clarendon Press, 1974), 115; Joseph Lennon, *Irish Orientalism: A Literary and Intellectual History* (Syracuse, NY: Syracuse University Press, 2004), 36. On genealogical appropriation, see Katherine Verdery, *National Ideology Under Socialism: Identity and Cultural Politics in Ceauşescu's Romania* (Berkeley: University of California Press, 1991), 138. See also pp. 156–66, 201.

5. See, for example, Tirso Suarez, "Hugo Chavez and Montezuma," http://vcrisis.com/index.php?content=letters/200605180840 (accessed on September 14, 2009); Neil MacDonald, "Alexander's 'Descendants' Boost Macedonian Identity," http://www.ft.com/cms/s/0/11034b1e-54ef-11dd-ae9c-000077b07658.html (accessed on December 2, 2008); Matthew Brunwasser, "Macedonia Dispute Has an Asian Flavor," http://www.nytimes.com/2008/10/01/world/asia/01iht-macedonia.1.16609558.html (accessed December 12, 2010).

6. See, for example, R. Howard Bloch, *Etymologies and Genealogies: A Literary Anthropology of the French Middle Ages* (Chicago: University of Chicago Press, 1983), 81–82; Preben M. Sørensen, "Social Institutions and Belief Systems of Medieval Iceland (c. 870–1400) and Their Relations to Literary Production," in Margaret Clunies Ross (ed.), *Old Icelandic Literature and Society* (Cambridge, UK: Cambridge University Press, 2000), 16–17; Diana Whaley, "A Useful Past: Historical Writing in Medieval Iceland," in *Old Icelandic Literature and Society*, 178; Judy Quinn, "From Orality to Literacy in Medieval Iceland," in *Old Icelandic Literature and Society*, 48–49; Daniel Rosenberg and Anthony Grafton, *Cartographies of Time: A History of the Timeline* (New York: Princeton Architectural Press, 2010), 49; *Fourth Book of the Chronicle of Fredegar with Its Continuations*, John M. Wallace-Hadrill (ed.) (London: Thomas Nelson, 1960), xi–xii, xx; Léon Poliakov, *The Aryan Myth: A History of Racist and Nationalistic Ideas in Europe* (New York: Basic Books, 1974), 18; Anthony D. Smith, *The Ethnic Origins of Nations* (Oxford: Basil Blackwell, 1986), 59; Matthew 1:6; Luke 3:31; Muhammad Ibn Ishaq, *The Life of Muhammad* (New York: Oxford University Press, 1997 [eighth century]), 3, 186. See also Poliakov, *The Aryan Myth*, 190ff; Heather Pringle, *The Master Plan: Himmler's Scholars and the Holocaust* (New York: Hyperion, 2006), 30–36; Lennon, *Irish Orientalism*, 5, 8–9, 26–27; David B. Goldstein, *Jacob's Legacy: A Genetic View of Jewish History* (New Haven, CT: Yale University Press, 2008), 88.

7. Bloch, *Etymologies and Genealogies*, 84. See also Alex Shoumatoff, *The Mountain of Names: A History of the Human Family* (New York: Simon and Schuster, 1985), 69, 78; David Lowenthal, *Possessed by the Past: The Heritage Crusade and the Spoils of History* (New York: Free Press, 1996), 173–87.

8. See, for example, David M. Schneider and Calvert B. Cottrell, *The American Kin Universe: A Genealogical Study* (Chicago: University of Chicago Press, 1975), 94. See also Hugh Baker, *Chinese Family and Kinship* (New York: Columbia University Press, 1979), 89.

9. See also Lowenthal, *Possessed by the Past*, 176.

10. See, for example, Bloch, *Etymologies and Genealogies*, 80.

11. Alex Haley, *Roots* (Garden City, NY: Doubleday, 1976), 1.

12. See, for example, http://www.monticello.org:8081/site/research-and-collections/seal-united-states (accessed on December 12, 2010); Patrick J. Geary, *The Myth of Nations: The Medieval Origins of Europe* (Princeton, NJ: Princeton University Press, 2002), 6–7.

13. http://www.britannica.com/EBchecked/topic/11626/Akihito (accessed January 10, 2010); http://www.kingabdullah.jo/main.php?main_page=0&lang_hmka1=1 (accessed July 8, 2008); http://news.bbc.co.uk/1/hi/world/africa/6411523.stm (accessed July 8, 2008). See also Shoumatoff, *The Mountain of Names*, 67, 72.

14. See, for example, Paul Wittek, *The Rise of the Ottoman Empire* (London: Royal Asiatic Society of Great Britain and Ireland, 1971 [1938]), 7–8; J. A. Barnes, "Genealogies," in A. L. Epstein (ed.), *The Craft of Social Anthropology* (London: Tavistock, 1967), 118; Poliakov, *The Aryan Myth*, 60; Henige, *The Chronology of Oral Tradition*, 25, 52; Lennon, *Irish Orientalism*, 7; Nash, *Of Irish Descent*, 1; Rosenberg and Grafton, *Cartographies of Time*, 49.

15. Poliakov, *The Aryan Myth*, 114.

16. Eviatar Zerubavel, *Time Maps: Collective Memory and the Social Shape of the Past* (Chicago: University of Chicago Press, 2003), 105–09.

17. See also Robert M. Taylor and Ralph J. Crandall, "Historians and Genealogists: An Emerging Community of Interest," in *Generations and Change: Genealogical Perspectives in Social History* (Macon, GA: Mercer University Press, 1986), 8–9.

18. See also Tim Ingold, *The Perception of the Environment: Essays on Livelihood, Dwelling, and Skill* (London: Routledge, 2000), 132.

19. See, for example, Wyndham Robertson and R. A. Brock, *Pocahontas, Alias Matoaka, and Her Descendants through Her Marriage at Jamestown, Virginia, in April, 1614, with John Rolfe, Gentleman* (Richmond, VA: J. W. Randolph & English, 1887).

20. See also Henige, *The Chronology of Oral Tradition*, 41; Liisa H. Malkki, *Purity and Exile: Violence, Memory, and National Cosmology among Hutu Refugees in Tanzania* (Chicago: University of Chicago Press, 1995), 59–61.

21. Michael T. Kaufman, "Two Distinct Peoples with Two Divergent Memories Battle over One Land," *New York Times*, April 4, 1999, International Section, p. 10; Noel Malcolm, *Kosovo: A Short History* (New York: HarperPerennial, 1999, updated edition), 22–23, 28–30. See also Zerubavel, *Time Maps*, 106–07.

22. Yael Zerubavel, *Recovered Roots: Collective Memory and the Making of Israeli National Tradition* (Chicago: University of Chicago Press, 1995); Shlomo Sand, *When and How the Jewish People Was Invented?* (Tel Aviv: Resling Publishing, 2008); Zerubavel, *Time Maps*, 106–09.

23. See, for example, Bernard Lewis, *History: Remembered, Recovered, Invented* (Princeton, NJ: Princeton University Press, 1975), 35–36. See also pp. 31–34, 37–41; David C. Gordon, *Self-Determination and History in the Third World* (Princeton, NJ: Princeton University Press, 1971), 90–91, 102–03; Hassan M. Fattah, "A Nation with a Long Memory, but a Truncated History," *New York Times*, January 10, 2007, p. A4; http://phoenicia.org/index.shtml (accessed on February 5, 2010).

24. See, for example, Ted Swedenburg, *Memories of Revolt: The 1936–1939 Rebellion and the Palestinian National Past* (Minneapolis: University of Minnesota Press, 1995), 80.

25. Matthew 1:16; Luke 3:23.

26. See also Engseng Ho, *The Graves of Tarim: Genealogy and Mobility Across the Indian Ocean* (Berkeley: University of California Press, 2006), 149–50, 179.

27. On genealogical purity, see also Marshall D. Johnson, *The Purpose of the Biblical Genealogies with Special Reference to the Setting of the Genealogies of Jesus* (London: Cambridge University Press, 1969), 87; Christine E. Hayes, *Gentile Impurities and Jewish Identities: Intermarriage and Conversion from the Bible to the Talmud* (New York: Oxford University Press, 2002); María E. Martínez, *Genealogical Fictions: Limpieza de Sangre, Religion, and Gender in Colonial Mexico* (Stanford, CA: Stanford University Press, 2008).

28. See, for example, Henige, *The Chronology of Oral Tradition*, 5, 30–31, 197.

29. See, for example, John Nolland, "Jechoniah and His Brothers (Matthew 1:11)," *Bulletin for Biblical Research* 7 (1997): 172; Floyd N. Jones, *The Chronology of the Old Testament*, 16th ed. (Green Forest, AR: Master Books, 2005), 38–39.

30. Henige, *The Chronology of Oral Tradition*, 30. On historical continuity, see Zerubavel, *Time Maps*, 37–54.

31. Zerubavel, *Time Maps*, 40–41. See also Bloch, *Etymologies and Genealogies*, 86.

32. Matthew 1:8. See also Paola Tartakoff, "Jewish Women and Apostasy in the Medieval Crown of Aragon, c. 1300–1391," *Jewish History* 24 (2010): 13.

33. See, for example, Henige, *The Chronology of Oral Tradition*, 24–25.

34. Genesis 11:10–26; Matthew 1:13–16. See also Johnson, *The Purpose of the Biblical Genealogies*, 78; Wilson, *Genealogy and History in the Biblical World*, 5.

35. W. Robertson Smith, *Kinship and Marriage in Early Arabia* (Cambridge, UK: Cambridge University Press, 1885), 10.

36. Joseph Blenkinsopp, *Sage, Priest, Prophet: Religious and Intellectual Leadership in Ancient Israel* (Louisville, KY: Westminster John Knox Press, 1995), 79, 84.

37. On historical discontinuity, see Zerubavel, *Time Maps*, 82–100.

38. See also Eviatar Zerubavel, *Social Mindscapes: An Invitation to Cognitive Sociology* (Cambridge, MA: Harvard University Press, 1997), 85; Zerubavel, *Time Maps*, 91–92.

39. See, for example, Karl A. Schleunes, *The Twisted Road to Auschwitz: Nazi Policy Toward German Jews 1933–1939* (Urbana: University of Illinois Press, 1970), 128–29.

40. See also Thomas H. Erikson, *Ethnicity and Nationalism*, 2nd ed. (London: Pluto Press, 2002 [1993]), 69.

41. Zerubavel, *Time Maps*, 73. See also p. 92.

42. See, for example, Amos Elon, *The Israelis: Founders and Sons* (New York: Bantam Books, 1971), 163–66; Oz Almog, *The Sabra: The Creation of the New Jew* (Berkeley: University of California Press, 2000 [1997]), 93–95.

43. See, for example, Y. Zerubavel, *Recovered Roots*.

44. Berl Katznelson, quoted in Doron Rosenblum, "Because Somebody Needs to Be an Israeli in Israel," *Ha'aretz*, April 29, 1998, Independence Day Supplement, 52.

45. Amnon Rubinstein, *To Be a Free People* (Tel-Aviv: Schocken, 1977), 103–04. See also Y. Zerubavel, *Recovered Roots*, xv.

46. Hannah Kwon, "'I'm So Glad Our Children Come from the Same Background': The Genealogical Construction of an 'Inter'-Marriage" (unpublished paper, Rutgers University, New Brunswick, NJ, 2009).

47. Jodi Rudoren, "Meet Our New Name," http://www.nytimes.com/2006/02/05/fashion/sundaystyles/05NAME.html?_R=1 (accessed on December 31, 2010).

48. See, for example, Rachelle Germana, "The Social Practice of Hyphenating: A Qualitative Study of Surname Hyphenation" (paper presented at the Annual Meeting of the Eastern Sociological Society, Baltimore, 2009).

49. See also Wayne Brekhus, *Peacocks, Chameleons, Centaurs: Gay Suburbia and the Grammar of Social Identity* (Chicago: University of Chicago Press, 2003), 74–95, 151–54.

50. Catherine Nash, "'They're Family!': Cultural Geographies of Relatedness in Popular Genealogy," in Sara Ahmed et al. (eds.), *Uprootings/Regroundings: Questions of Home and Migration* (Oxford: Berg, 2003), 187. See also Cookie W. Stephan, "Mixed-Heritage Individuals: Ethnic Identity and Trait Characteristics," in Maria P. P. Root (ed.), *Racially Mixed People in America* (Newbury Park: CA: SAGE, 1992), 52–53.

51. http://www.asianweek.com/101196/tigerwoods.html (accessed on October 20, 2007); http://www.lubbockonline.com/news/042397/woods.htm (accessed on October 15, 2007).

52. Peter Wade, "Hybridity Theory and Kinship Thinking," *Cultural Studies* 19 (2005): 602–21.

53. http://www.huffingtonpost.com/2008/03/18/obama-race-speech-read-th_n_92077.html (accessed on September 13, 2010); http://www.timesonline.co.uk/tol/news/world/us_and_americas/us_elections/article5111168.ece (accessed on January 24, 2010).

54. F. James Davis, *Who Is Black? One Nation's Definition* (University Park: Pennsylvania State University Press, 1991), 198. See also G. Reginald Daniel, *More Than Black? Multiracial Identity and the New Racial Order* (Philadelphia: Temple University Press, 2002), 145–51.

55. Poliakov, *The Aryan Myth*, 38–42.

56. http://www.banknotes.com/RO55.JPG (accessed on January 3, 2009). I would like to thank Carmen-Laura Lovin who first brought this bill to my attention.

57. See also Werner Sollors, *Neither Black Nor White Yet Both: Thematic Explorations of Interracial Literature* (Cambridge, MA: Harvard University Press, 1997), 116–25.

58. See, for example, Magnus Mörner, *Race Mixture in the History of Latin America* (Boston: Little, Brown, & Co., 1967), 58; Martínez, *Genealogical Fictions*, 142–44, 162–65.

59. See, for example, Speros Vryonis, *The Turkish State and History: Clio Meets the Grey Wolf* (Thessaloniki, Greece: Institute for Balkan Studies, 1991), 10, 63, 70–77; Pringle, *The Master Plan*, 109, 143, 355n48.

60. On the mental process of lumping, see Eviatar Zerubavel, "Lumping and Splitting: Notes on Social Classification," *Sociological Forum* 11 (1996): 421–33.

61. See, for example, Anthony D. Smith, "National Identity and Myths of Ethnic Descent," in *Myths and Memories of the Nation* (Oxford: Oxford University Press, 1999 [1984]), 64.

62. See also Edward E. Evans-Pritchard, "The Nuer of the Southern Sudan," in Robert Parkin and Linda Stone (eds.), *Kinship and Family: An Anthropological Reader* (Malden, MA: Blackwell, 2004 [1940]), 71.

63. See also Laura Bohannan, "A Genealogical Charter," *Africa* 22 (1952): 309; Meyer Fortes, "The Structure of Unilineal Descent Groups," in *Time and Social Structure and Other Essays* (London: Athlone Press, 1970 [1953]), 80.

64. See, for example, J. B. Bury, *A History of Greece to the Death of Alexander the Great*, 3rd ed. (London: Macmillan, 1951), 80.

65. Emrys Peters, "The Proliferation of Segments in the Lineage of the Bedouin of Cyrenaica," *Journal of the Royal Anthropological Institute of Great Britain and Ireland* 90 (1960): 29–30.

66. See Israel Finkelstein and Neil A. Silberman, *The Bible Unearthed: Archaeology's New Vision of Ancient Israel and the Origin of Its Sacred Texts* (New York: Free Press, 2001), 44, 47. See also John L. Martin, *Social Structures* (Princeton, NJ: Princeton University Press, 2009), 187.

67. Arlene Stein, "Trauma and Origins: Post-Holocaust Genealogists and the Work of Memory," *Qualitative Sociology* 32 (2009): 294. See also Kathryn Coe, *The Ancestress Hypothesis: Visual Art as Adaptation* (New Brunswick, NJ: Rutgers University Press, 2003), 12.

68. Poliakov, *The Aryan Myth*, 11.

69. James Bennet, "Hillary Clinton, in Morocco, Says NATO Attack Aims at Stopping Bloodshed," *New York Times*, March 31, 1999, p. A10.

70. Genesis 10.

71. William W. Howells, "Explaining Modern Man: Evolutionists versus Migrationists," *Journal of Human Evolution* 5 (1976): 477–95.

72. Gunnar Broberg, "*Homo sapiens*: Linnaeus's Classification of Man," in Tore Frängsmyr (ed.), *Linnaeus: The Man and His Work* (Berkeley: University of California Press, 1983), 170.

73. Arthur O. Lovejoy, *The Great Chain of Being: A Study of the History of an Idea* (Cambridge, MA: Harvard University Press, 1936), 234; Broberg, "*Homo sapiens*," 179; Poliakov, *The Aryan Myth*, 165; Ernst Mayr, *The Growth of Biological Thought: Diversity, Evolution, and Inheritance* (Cambridge, MA: Harvard University Press, 1982), 332; Monroe W. Strickberger, *Evolution*, 3rd ed. (Sudbury, MA: Jones & Bartlett, 2005), 10.

74. Thomas H. Huxley, *Evidence as to Man's Place in Nature* (Ann Arbor: University of Michigan Press, 2003 [1863]), 123, 125. See also pp. 97, 101, 112.
75. George H. Nuttall, *Blood Immunity and Blood Relationship: A Demonstration of Certain Blood-Relationships amongst Animals by Means of the Precipitin Test for Blood* (Cambridge, UK: Cambridge University Press, 1904), 1–4, 319. See also Ian Tattersall, *The Fossil Trail: How We Know What We Think We Know about Human Evolution* (New York: Oxford University Press, 1995), 122–23.
76. Ernst Haeckel, *Last Words on Evolution: A Popular Retrospect and Summary* (New York: Peter Eckler, 1905), 107.
77. Morris Goodman, "Serological Analysis of the Systematics of Recent Hominoids," *Human Biology* 35 (1963): 399–400; Morris Goodman, "Reconstructing Human Evolution from Proteins," in Steve Jones et al. (eds.), *The Cambridge Encyclopedia of Human Evolution* (Cambridge, UK: Cambridge University Press, 1992), 308. See also Jerold Lowenstein and Adrienne Zihlman, "The Invisible Ape," *New Scientist*, December 3, 1988, pp. 56–57; Vincent Sarich, "Immunological Evidence on Primates," in *The Cambridge Encyclopedia of Human Evolution*, 306; Jared Diamond, *The Third Chimpanzee: The Evolution and Future of the Human Animal* (New York: HarperCollins, 1992), 23; Donald Johanson and Blake Edgar, *From Lucy to Language* (New York: Simon and Schuster, 1996), 32; Paul R. Ehrlich, *Human Natures: Genes, Cultures, and the Human Prospect* (Washington, DC: Island Press, 2000), 69; Vincent Sarich and Frank Miele, *Race: The Reality of Human Differences* (Boulder, CO: Westview, 2004), 108.
78. "Initial Sequence of the Chimpanzee Genome and Comparison with the Human Genome," *Nature* 437 (September 1, 2005): 83.
79. Christopher Stringer and Robin McKie, *African Exodus: The Origins of Modern Humanity* (New York: Henry Holt, 1997 [1996]), 21; Raymond Corbey, *The Metaphysics of Apes: Negotiating the Animal-Human Boundary* (Cambridge, UK: Cambridge University Press, 2005), 146; Diamond, *The Third Chimpanzee*, 24. See also John Gribbin, "Human vs. Gorilla: The 1% Advantage," *Science Digest* 90 (August 1982): 73; Sarich, "Immunological Evidence on Primates," 304–05; John Gribbin and Jeremy Cherfas, *The First Chimpanzee: In Search of Human Origins* (London: Penguin, 2001), 125.
80. Vincent Sarich and Allan C. Wilson, "Immunological Time Scale for Hominid Evolution," *Science* 158 (1967): 1202; Lowenstein and Zihlman, "The Invisible Ape," 57–59; Goodman, "Reconstructing Human Evolution from Proteins," 308; Adrian E. Friday, "Human Evolution: The Evidence from DNA Sequencing," in Steve Jones et al. (eds.), *The Cambridge Encyclopedia of Human Evolution* (Cambridge, UK: Cambridge University Press, 1992), 320; Morris Goodman, "Epilogue: A Personal Account of the Origins of a New Paradigm," *Molecular Phylogenetics and Evolution* 5 (1996): 279; Sarich and Miele, *Race*, 112–14.

81. John Gribbin and Jeremy Cherfas, *The Monkey Puzzle: Reshaping the Evolutionary Tree* (New York: Pantheon, 1982), 29.

82. See, for example, Stephen J. Gould, *Wonderful Life: The Burgess Shale and the Nature of History* (New York: W.W. Norton, 1989), 30–35. See also p. 45; Charles Darwin, *The Descent of Man and Selection in Relation to Sex* (Amherst, NY: Prometheus, 1998 [1871]), 161; Peter J. Bowler, *Life's Splendid Drama: Evolutionary Biology and the Reconstruction of Life's Ancestry, 1860–1940* (Chicago: University of Chicago Press, 1996), 426; Gribbin and Cherfas, *The First Chimpanzee*, 45; Zerubavel, *Time Maps*, 21.

83. Simon Easteal and Genevieve Herbert, "Molecular Evidence from the Nuclear Genome for the Time Frame of Human Evolution," *Journal of Molecular Evolution* 44, Suppl. 1 (1997): S130.

84. Morris Goodman, "The Genomic Record of Humankind's Evolutionary Roots," *American Journal of Human Genetics* 64 (1999): 31.

85. See also Richard Dawkins, *The Blind Watchmaker: Why the Evidence of Evolution Reveals a Universe Without Design* (New York: W.W. Norton, 2006 [1986]), 375; Sarich and Miele, *Race*, 108, 118.

86. Stephen J. Gould, "If Kings Can Be Hermits, Then We Are All Monkeys' Uncles," in *Dinosaur in a Haystack: Reflections in Natural History* (New York: Harmony Books, 1995), 399. Compare also the figures on pp. 398 and 399 there. See also David A. Baum et al., "The Tree-Thinking Challenge," *Science* 310 (2005): 979–80.

87. Alan Mann and Mark Weiss, "Hominoid Phylogeny and Taxonomy: A Consideration of the Molecular and Fossil Evidence in an Historical Perspective," *Molecular Phylogenetics and Evolution* 5 (1996): 179.

88. Stringer and McKie, *African Exodus*, 20.

89. Goodman, "Epilogue: A Personal Account of the Origins of a New Paradigm," 271–72. See also Tattersall, *The Fossil Trail*, 123; Johanson and Edgar, *From Lucy to Language*, 40.

90. Morris Goodman and G. William Moore, "Immunodiffusion Systematics of the Primates: I. The Catarrhini," *Systematic Zoology* 20 (1971): 47, 61. See also Colin P. Groves, *A Theory of Human and Primate Evolution* (Oxford: Oxford University Press, 1989), 154–55. To acknowledge the fact that the chimpanzee and bonobo are genealogically closer to us than they are to the gorilla, however, some anthropologists have placed gorillas in a separate subfamily (rather than just a separate tribe) than humans, bonobos, and chimpanzees. See, for example, John H. Relethford, *Reflections of Our Past: How Human History Is Revealed in Our Genes* (Boulder, CO: Westview Press, 2003), 39–40; Bernard Wood and Brian G. Richmond, "Human Evolution: Taxonomy and Paleobiology," *Journal of Anatomy* 196 (2000): 21; Bernard Wood, *Human Evolution: A Very Short Introduction* (Oxford: Oxford University Press, 2005), 23.

91. See, for example, Marie-Claire King and Allan C. Wilson, "Our Close Cousin, the Chimpanzee," *New Scientist* 67 (July 3, 1975): 17; Elizabeth E. Watson et al., "*Homo* Genus: A Review of the Classification of Humans and the Great Apes," in Phillip V. Tobias et al. (eds.), *Humanity from African Naissance to Coming Millennia: Colloquia in Human Biology and Paleoanthropology* (Florence, Italy: Firenze University Press, 2001), 313. See also Gribbin and Cherfas, *The Monkey Puzzle*, 129.

92. Diamond, *The Third Chimpanzee*, 23–25; Harriet Ritvo, "Border Trouble: Shifting the Line between People and Other Animals," *Social Research* 62 (1995): 490; Goodman, "Epilogue: A Personal Account of the Origins of a New Paradigm," 269, 279, 281; Morris Goodman et al., "Toward a Phylogenetic Classification of Primates Based on DNA Evidence Complemented by Fossil Evidence," *Molecular Phylogenetics and Evolution* 9 (1998): 585, 594, 596; Goodman, "The Genomic Record of Humankind's Evolutionary Roots," 32–33; Derek E. Wildman et al., "Implications of Natural Selection in Shaping 99.4% Nonsynonymous DNA Identity between Humans and Chimpanzees: Enlarging Genus *Homo*," *Proceedings of the National Academy of Sciences of the United States of America* 100 (June 10, 2003): 7181–88. See also Mann and Weiss, "Hominoid Phylogeny and Taxonomy," 177–78.

93. Corbey, *The Metaphysics of Apes*, 146.

94. Linnaeus's letter to Johann Georg Gmelin, quoted in Corbey, *The Metaphysics of Apes*, 46. See also pp. 44–47.

95. See also Eviatar Zerubavel, *The Fine Line: Making Distinctions in Everyday Life* (Chicago: University of Chicago Press, 1993 [1991]), 63, 70, 79; Zerubavel, "Lumping and Splitting," 427–28.

96. Desmond Morris, *The Naked Ape* (New York: McGraw-Hill, 1967); Diamond, *The Third Chimpanzee*; Matt Cartmill and Fred H. Smith, *The Human Lineage* (Hoboken, NJ: Wiley-Blackwell, 2009).

97. On the latter, see also Germana, "The Social Practice of Hyphenating."

98. Tattersall, *The Fossil Trail*, 29; Corbey, *The Metaphysics of Apes*, 76–77.

99. Raymond A. Dart, "*Australopithecus Africanus*: The Man-Ape of South Africa," in W. Eric Meikle and Sue T. Parker (eds.), *Naming Our Ancestors: An Anthology of Hominid Taxonomy* (Prospect Heights, IL: Waveland Press, 1994 [1925]), 62. See also Michael Hammond, "The Expulsion of the Neanderthals from Human Ancestry: Marcellin Boule and the Social Context of Scientific Research," *Social Studies of Science* 12 (1982): 5.

100. Robin I. M. Dunbar, "What's in a Classification?" in Paola Cavalieri and Peter Singer (eds.), *The Great Ape Project: Equality beyond Humanity* (New York: St. Martin's Griffin, 1996 [1993]), 112. See also Richard Dawkins, "Gaps in the Mind," in *The Great Ape Project*, 82–87.

101. See also Dawkins's aptly titled essay "Gaps in the Mind."

102. See also Sollors, *Neither Black Nor White Yet Both*, 87.

103. See also Carol Bakhos, *Ishmael on the Border: Rabbinic Portrayals of the First Arab* (Albany: State University of New York Press, 2006), 75.

104. Milford Wolpoff and Rachel Caspari, *Race and Human Evolution* (Boulder, CO: Westview Press, 1997), 277.

105. Hammond, "The Expulsion of the Neanderthals from Human Ancestry." See also Peter J. Bowler, *The Invention of Progress: The Victorians and the Past* (Oxford: Basil Blackwell, 1989), 125. On the politics of polarization, see Zerubavel, *The Fine Line*, 46–47, 73; Asia Friedman, "Toward a Sociology of Perception: Sight, Sex, and Gender," *Cultural Sociology* 5 (2011): 187–206.

106. See, for example, Roger Lewin and Robert A. Foley, *Principles of Human Evolution*, 2nd ed. (Malden, MA: Blackwell, 2004), 293. See also Richard W. Wrangham, "Out of the Pan, Into the Fire: How Our Ancestors' Evolution Depended on What They Ate," in Frans B. M. de Waal (ed.), *Tree of Origin: What Primate Behavior Can Tell Us about Human Social Evolution* (Cambridge, MA: Harvard University Press, 2001), 122.

107. See, for example, Richard E. Green et al., "A Draft Sequence of the Neandertal Genome," *Science* 328 (May 7, 2010): 718, 721. See also Relethford, *Reflections of Our Past*, 84–99.

108. See, for example, Luigi L. Cavalli-Sforza and Francesco Cavalli-Sforza, *The Great Human Diasporas: The History of Diversity and Evolution* (Reading, MA: Addison-Wesley, 1995 [1993]), 50–55; Cartmill and Smith, *The Human Lineage*, 478. See also Corbey, *The Metaphysics of Apes*, 107.

109. See, for example, Richard G. Klein, *The Human Career: Human Biological and Cultural Origins*, 2nd ed. (Chicago: University of Chicago Press, 1999), 507; Bryan Sykes, *The Seven Daughters of Eve: The Science That Reveals Our Genetic Ancestry* (London: W.W. Norton, 2001), 125–26. See also Hammond, "The Expulsion of the Neanderthals from Human Ancestry"; Richard Lewontin, *Human Diversity* (New York: Scientific American Books, 1982), 164.

110. Gribbin and Cherfas, *The Monkey Puzzle*, 17; Gribbin and Cherfas, *The First Chimpanzee*, 152. See also Johanson and Edgar, *From Lucy to Language*, 33; Gribbin and Cherfas, *The First Chimpanzee*, 8.

111. Sarich, "Immunological Evidence on Primates," 305.

112. On the mental process of splitting, see Zerubavel, "Lumping and Splitting."

113. Geary, *The Myth of Nations*, 20–21; Peter J. Bowler, *Theories of Human Evolution: A Century of Debate, 1844–1944* (Baltimore: Johns Hopkins University Press, 1986), 112–30; Wolpoff and Caspari, *Race and Human Evolution*, 119–20.

114. Alys E. Weinbaum, *Wayward Reproductions: Genealogies of Race and Nation in Transatlantic Modern Thought* (Durham, NC: Duke University Press, 2004), 37.

115. See, for example, Martínez, *Genealogical Fictions*, 28, 43, 57, 62, 67–68.

116. Ibid., 52. On "stained" pedigrees, see also pp. 47, 63, 69.

117. Ibid., 53.

118. See, for example, Bowler, *The Invention of Progress*, 122; Michael Bradley, *The Iceman Inheritance: Prehistoric Sources of Western Man's Racism, Sexism, and Aggression* (New York: Kayode Publications, 1991 [1978]), 104. See also Stephen Howe, *Afrocentrism: Mythical Pasts and Imagined Homes* (London: Verso, 1998), 73–74, 227, 271.

119. See, for example, William Stanton, *The Leopard's Spots: Scientific Attitudes Toward Race in America 1815–59* (Chicago: University of Chicago Press, 1960), 15–16, 50; George W. Stocking, "French Anthropology in 1800," in *Race, Culture, and Evolution: Essays in the History of Anthropology* (New York: Free Press, 1968 [1964]), 39; George W. Stocking, "The Persistence of Polygenist Thought in Post-Darwinian Anthropology," in *Race, Culture, and Evolution*, 44–45, 57, 63, 68; Theodore D. McCown and Kenneth A. R. Kennedy (eds.), *Climbing Man's Family Tree: A Collection of Major Writings on Human Phylogeny, 1699 to 1971* (Englewood Cliffs, NJ: Prentice-Hall, 1972), 32; Stephen J. Gould, *The Mismeasure of Man*, rev. ed. (New York: W.W. Norton, 1996 [1981]), 71–104; Nancy Stepan, *The Idea of Race in Science: Great Britain 1800–1960* (Hamden, CT: Archon Books, 1982), 29, 106–08; Donald K. Grayson, *The Establishment of Human Antiquity* (New York: Academic Press, 1983), 147–64; Bowler, *Theories of Human Evolution*, 55–58, 140–41; Bowler, *The Invention of Progress*, 107, 119; Clive Gamble, *Timewalkers: The Prehistory of Global Colonization* (Cambridge, MA: Harvard University Press, 1994), 25; Benjamin Braude, "The Sons of Noah and the Construction of Ethnic and Geographical Identities in the Medieval and Early Modern Periods," *The William and Mary Quarterly*, 3d ser., 54 (1997): 103–42.

120. See also Bowler, *Theories of Human Evolution*, 55.

121. See, for example, Carleton S. Coon, *The Origin of Races* (New York: Alfred A. Knopf, 1962), 4.

122. See, for example, Franz Weidenreich, "Facts and Speculations Concerning the Origin of *Homo sapiens*," in Theodore D. McCown and Kenneth A. R. Kennedy (eds.), *Climbing Man's Family Tree: A Collection of Major Writings on Human Phylogeny, 1699 to 1971* (Englewood Cliffs, NJ: Prentice-Hall, 1972 [1947]), 351–53; Coon, *The Origin of Races*, 371–481, 657; Alan G. Thorne and Milford H. Wolpoff, "Regional Continuity in Australasian Pleistocene Hominid Evolution," *American Journal of Physical Anthropology* 55 (1981): 337, 341–42; Milford H. Wolpoff et al., "Modern Human Origins," *Science* 241 (1988): 772–73; Alan G. Thorne and Milford H. Wolpoff, "The Multiregional Evolution of Humans," *Scientific American* 266 (April 1992): 76–83. See also Tattersall, *The Fossil Trail*, 214–16; Alan R. Templeton, "Out of Africa Again and Again," *Nature* 416 (March 7, 2002): 45–51; Lewin and Foley, *Principles of Human Evolution*, 372–73; Claudio Tuniz et al., *The Bone Readers: Atoms, Genes, and the Politics of Australia's Deep Past* (Crows Nest, Australia: Allen & Unwin, 2009), 145, 160.

123. See also Stepan, *The Idea of Race in Science*, 106; Bowler, *Theories of Human Evolution*, 127–28, 131; Bowler, *The Invention of Progress*, 120.

124. Arthur de Gobineau, *The Inequality of Human Races* (New York: Howard Fertig, 1967 [1854]), 137. See also Wolpoff and Caspari, *Race and Human Evolution*, 84.

125. Nat Brandt, *Harlem at War: The Black Experience in WWII* (Syracuse, NY: Syracuse University Press, 1996), 133.

126. See also Wolpoff and Caspari, *Race and Human Evolution*, 59.

127. Stanton, *The Leopard's Spots*, 107, 142; Stocking, "French Anthropology in 1800," 39; Stocking, "The Persistence of Polygenist Thought in Post-Darwinian Anthropology," 44–45; McCown and Kennedy, *Climbing Man's Family Tree*, 32; Poliakov, *The Aryan Myth*, 234; Richard H. Popkin, "The Pre-Adamite Theory in the Renaissance," in Edward P. Mahoney (ed.), *Philosophy and Humanism: Renaissance Essays in Honor of Paul Oskar Kristeller* (New York: Columbia University Press, 1976), 57–58, 66–69; Grayson, *The Establishment of Human Antiquity*, 140, 148; Bowler, *The Invention of Progress*, 107; Braude, "The Sons of Noah"; Sarich and Miele, *Race*, 62–63; Philip Almond, "Adam, Pre-Adamites, and Extra-Terrestrial Beings in Early Modern Europe," *Journal of Religious History* 30 (2006): 165–68; David N. Livingstone, *Adam's Ancestors: Race, Religion, and the Politics of Human Origins* (Baltimore: Johns Hopkins University Press, 2008).

128. Stocking, "The Persistence of Polygenist Thought in Post-Darwinian Anthropology," 61. See also Bowler, *Theories of Human Evolution*, 140.

129. Ernst Haeckel, *The History of Creation: On the Development of the Earth and Its Inhabitants by the Action of Natural Causes*, Vol. 2 (New York: D. Appleton, 1876), 305–06.

130. Hermann Klaatsch, *The Evolution and Progress of Mankind* (New York: Frederick A. Stokes, 1923), 107.

131. Carl Vogt, *Lectures on Man: His Place in Creation and in the History of the Earth* (London: Longman, Green, Longman, and Roberts, 1864), 465–67. See also Klaatsch, *The Evolution and Progress of Mankind*, 105–06, 269–84; Stocking, "The Persistence of Polygenist Thought in Post-Darwinian Anthropology," 57, 63, 68; Poliakov, *The Aryan Myth*, 279; Stepan, *The Idea of Race in Science*, 106–08; Bowler, *Theories of Human Evolution*, 58, 135–37, 141; Bowler, *The Invention of Progress*, 119; Wolpoff and Caspari, *Race and Human Evolution*, 125–26, 130, 142, 151.

132. See also Robert J. O'Hara, "Telling the Tree: Narrative Representation and the Study of Evolutionary History," *Biology and Philosophy* 7 (1992): 148.

133. *Ancestors: Webster's Quotations, Facts, and Phrases* (San Diego, CA: ICON Group International, 2008), 2.

134. See, for example, Ronald D. Lambert, "Reclaiming the Ancestral Past: Narrative, Rhetoric, and the 'Convict Stain,'" *Journal of Sociology* 38 (2002): 115–16.

135. See, for example, Virginia R. Domínguez, *White by Definition: Social Classification in Creole Louisiana* (New Brunswick, NJ: Rutgers University Press, 1986), 193–97, 203; France W. Twine, *Racism in a Racial Democracy: The Maintenance of White Supremacy in Brazil* (New Brunswick, NJ: Rutgers University Press, 1998), 122–33. See also Mara Loveman and Jeronimo O. Muniz, "How Puerto Rico Became White: Boundary Dynamics and Intercensus Racial Reclassification," *American Sociological Review* 72 (2007): 915–39.

136. Marvin Harris, *Patterns of Race in the Americas* (Westport, CT: Greenwood, 1980 [1964]), 56. See also Davis, *Who Is Black?* 5; Naomi Zack, "Life After Race," in *American Mixed Race: The Culture of Microdiversity* (Lanham, MD: Rowman & Littlefield, 1995), xvii; Stephen Satris, "What Are They?" in *American Mixed Race*, 59.

137. Alex Haley, *The Autobiography of Malcolm X* (New York: Ballantine, 1999 [1964]), 5. See also Davis, *Who Is Black?* 5.

138. Winthrop D. Jordan, *White over Black: American Attitudes toward the Negro, 1550–1812* (New York: W.W. Norton, 1977), 178; Davis, *Who Is Black?* 39–42, 48, 62, 79; Zack, "Life After Race," xvii; David A. Hollinger, "Amalgamation and Hypodescent: The Question of Ethnoracial Mixture in the History of the United States," *American Historical Review* 108 (2003): 1369.

139. On the inverse relations between purity and ambiguity, see Zerubavel, *The Fine Line*, 33–60.

140. Jordan, *White over Black*, 178; Joel Williamson, *New People: Miscegenation and Mulattoes in the United States* (New York: Free Press, 1980), 74, 114; Jennifer L. Hochschild and Brenna M. Powell, "United States Census 1850–1930: Mulattoes, Half-Breeds, Mixed Parentage, Hindoos, and the Mexican Race," *Studies in American Political Development* 22 (2008): 70–71.

141. Patrick Wolfe, "Land, Labor, and Difference: Elementary Structures of Race," *American Historical Review* 106 (2001): 893.

142. See also Daniel, *More Than Black?* xi, 3.

143. Williamson, *New People*, 97. See also Robert E. Park, "The Nature of Race Relations," in *Race and Culture: Essays in the Sociology of Contemporary Man* (Glencoe, IL: Free Press, 1950 [1939]), 112; Charles S. Mangum, *The Legal Status of the Negro* (Chapel Hill: University of North Carolina Press, 1940), 6; Domínguez, *White by Definition*, 270–71; Davis, *Who Is Black?* 5.

144. Mangum, *The Legal Status of the Negro*, 7, 9; Pauli Murray, *States' Laws on Race and Color* (Cincinnati, OH: Woman's Division of Christian Service, 1950), 22, 39. See also Gilbert T. Stephenson, *Race Distinctions in American Law* (New York: AMS Press, 1969 [1910]), 16.

145. Ian Haney López, *White by Law: The Legal Construction of Race*, rev. ed. (New York: New York University Press, 2006), 20.

146. Mireya Navarro, "Who Are We? New Dialogue on Mixed Race," *New York Times*, March 31, 2008, p. A15.

Chapter 6

1. See, for example, Richard D. Alford, *Naming and Identity: A Cross-Cultural Study of Personal Naming Practices* (New Haven, CT: HRAF Press, 1988), 90–94; Hildred Geertz and Clifford Geertz, "Teknonymy in Bali: Parenthood, Age-Grading and Genealogical Amnesia," *Journal of the Royal Anthropological Institute of Great Britain and Ireland* 94 (1964), no. 2: 94–108.
2. Leading American eugenicist Charles Davenport, in Daniel J. Kevles, *In the Name of Eugenics: Genetics and the Uses of Human Heredity* (Cambridge, MA: Harvard University Press, 1995 [1985]), 47. See also p. 48.
3. See also Auksuolė Čepaitienė, "Imagining Assisted Reproductive Technologies: Family, Kinship, and 'Local Thinking' in Lithuania," in Jeanette Edwards and Carles Salazar (eds.), *European Kinship in the Age of Biotechnology* (New York: Berghahn Books, 2009), 34–39.
4. See also Steven Pinker, *How the Mind Works* (New York: W.W. Norton, 1997), 436.
5. See also George P. Murdock, *Social Structure* (New York: Macmillan, 1949), 296–97; Claude Lévi-Strauss, *The Elementary Structures of Kinship* (Boston: Beacon, 1969 [1949]).
6. David A. Hollinger, *Postethnic America: Beyond Multiculturalism* (New York: Basic Books, 1995).
7. J. Hector St. John de Crèvecoeur, *Letters from an American Farmer* (New York: Fox, Duffield & Co., 1904 [1782]), 55.
8. Emerson, quoted in Stuart P. Sherman, "Introduction," in *Essays and Poems of Emerson* (New York: Harcourt, Brace, & Co., 1921 [1845]), xxxiv. See also Milton M. Gordon, *Assimilation in American Life: The Role of Race, Religion, and National Origins* (New York: Oxford University Press, 1964), 115–19; Werner Sollors, *Beyond Ethnicity: Consent and Descent in American Culture* (New York: Oxford University Press, 1986), 94–96, 100.
9. Israel Zangwill, *The Melting-Pot* (New York: Macmillan, 1932 [1909]). See also Sollors, *Beyond Ethnicity*, 66–101.
10. See, for example, Aisha Khan, *Callaloo Nation: Metaphors of Race and Religious Identity among South Asians in Trinidad* (Durham, NC: Duke University Press, 2004).
11. Viranjini Munasinghe, *Callaloo or Tossed Salad? East Indians and the Cultural Politics of Identity in Trinidad* (Ithaca, NY: Cornell University Press, 2001), 21–22.
12. Ibid., 22.
13. See Eviatar Zerubavel, *The Fine Line: Making Distinctions in Everyday Life* (Chicago: University of Chicago Press, 1993 [1991]), 103–05.
14. Sollors, *Beyond Ethnicity*, 72.
15. See also Richard D. Alba, "Assimilation's Quiet Tide," *Public Interest* 119 (Spring 1995): 13.

16. Gordon, *Assimilation in American Life*, 81. See also Pierre L. van den Berghe, *The Ethnic Phenomenon* (Westport, CT: Praeger, 1987 [1981]), 216; Paul R. Spickard, *Mixed Blood: Intermarriage and Ethnic Identity in Twentieth-Century America* (Madison: University of Wisconsin Press, 1989), 368; Zerubavel, *The Fine Line*, 51; Pierre L. van den Berghe, "Ethnies and Nations: Genealogy Indeed," in Atsuko Ichijo and Gordana Uzelac (eds.), *When Is the Nation? Towards an Understanding of Theories of Nationalism* (Abingdon, UK: Routledge, 2005), 115.

17. Simon Marcson, "A Theory of Intermarriage and Assimilation," *Social Forces* 29 (1950–51): 75.

18. Zerubavel, *The Fine Line*.

19. Michael Novak, *Unmeltable Ethnics: Politics and Culture in American Life* (New Brunswick, NJ: Transaction, 1996 [1972]).

20. See, for example, Madison Grant, *The Passing of the Great Race, or the Racial Basis of European History* (New York: Charles Scribner's Sons, 1918 [1916]), 263.

21. See, for example, E. David Cronon, *Black Moses: The Story of Marcus Garvey and the Universal Negro Improvement Association* (Madison: University of Wisconsin Press, 1969 [1955]), 191–93.

22. See, for example, Winthrop D. Jordan, *White over Black: American Attitudes toward the Negro, 1550–1812* (New York: W.W. Norton, 1977), 170; Virginia R. Domínguez, *White by Definition: Social Classification in Creole Louisiana* (New Brunswick, NJ: Rutgers University Press, 1986), 153; Cynthia L. Nakashima, "An Invisible Monster: The Creation and Denial of Mixed-Race People in America," in Maria P. P. Root (ed.), *Racially Mixed People in America* (Newbury Park, CA: SAGE, 1992), 165–71.

23. Léon Poliakov, *The Aryan Myth: A History of Racist and Nationalistic Ideas in Europe* (New York: Basic Books, 1974), 282.

24. Ibid.

25. Michael Burleigh and Wolfgang Wipperman, *The Racial State: Germany 1933–1945* (Cambridge, UK: Cambridge University Press, 1991), 37.

26. Ibid., 42; Felicity J. Rash, *The Language of Violence: Adolph Hitler's Mein Kampf* (New York: Peter Lang, 2006), 49.

27. David Lowenthal, *Possessed by the Past: The Heritage Crusade and the Spoils of History* (New York: Free Press, 1996), 209; Nancy Foner, *In a New Land: A Comparative View of Immigration* (New York: New York University Press, 2005), 15.

28. Grant, *The Passing of the Great Race*, 15.

29. See also Joel Williamson, *New People: Miscegenation and Mulattoes in the United States* (New York: Free Press, 1980), 52.

30. See also María E. Martínez, *Genealogical Fictions: Limpieza de Sangre, Religion, and Gender in Colonial Mexico* (Stanford, CA: Stanford University Press, 2008), 55.

31. See, for example, Williamson, *New People*, 138; F. James Davis, *Who Is Black? One Nation's Definition* (University Park: Pennsylvania State University Press, 1991), 39, 48, 62, 79; Lowenthal, *Possessed by the Past*, 208.

32. See, for example, Christine E. Hayes, *Gentile Impurities and Jewish Identities: Intermarriage and Conversion from the Bible to the Talmud* (New York: Oxford University Press, 2002); Martínez, *Genealogical Fictions*.

33. Guido Bolaffi et al. (eds.), *Dictionary of Race, Ethnicity, and Culture* (Thousand Oaks, CA: SAGE, 2003), 182–83.

34. See, for example, Hayes, *Gentile Impurities and Jewish Identities*, 28, 69, 71, 90–91; Zygmunt Bauman, *Liquid Times: Living in An Age of Uncertainty* (Cambridge, UK: Polity Press, 2007), 86–92.

35. Sollors, *Beyond Ethnicity*, 224. On the relations between purity and separateness, see also Zerubavel, *The Fine Line*, 33–60.

36. Prescott F. Hall, quoted in Lothrop Stoddard, *The Rising Tide of Color Against White World-Supremacy* (New York: Charles Scribner's Sons, 1921), 259–60.

37. See, for example, Matt Cartmill and Fred H. Smith, *The Human Lineage* (Hoboken, NJ: Wiley-Blackwell, 2009), 39.

38. See, for example, Steve Olson, *Mapping Human History: Discovering the Past through Our Genes* (Boston: Houghton Mifflin, 2002), 115.

39. Deuteronomy 7:3; Ezra 9:12; Nehemiah 13:25. See also Hayes, *Gentile Impurities and Jewish Identities*; Patrick J. Geary, *The Myth of Nations: The Medieval Origins of Europe* (Princeton, NJ: Princeton University Press, 2002), 53.

40. *The Babylonian Talmud*, Kiddushin 68b.

41. See, for example, Werner Sollors, *Neither Black Nor White Yet Both* (Cambridge, MA: Harvard University Press, 1997), 397, 407; Jennifer Heuer, "The One-Drop Rule in Reverse? Interracial Marriages in Napoleonic and Restoration France," *Law and History Review* 27 (2009): 515–48; Karl A. Schleunes, *The Twisted Road to Auschwitz: Nazi Policy Toward German Jews 1933–1939* (Urbana: University of Illinois Press, 1970), 125, 108.

42. See, for example, Spickard, *Mixed Blood*, 286; Naomi Zack, *Race and Mixed Race* (Philadelphia: Temple University Press, 1993), 78–79; Sollors, *Neither Black Nor White Yet Both*, 396; Frank W. Sweet, *Legal History of the Color Line: The Rise and Triumph of the One-Drop Rule* (Palm Coast, FL: Backintyme, 2005), 121.

43. On reproductive isolation and speciation, see, for example, George G. Simpson, *Principles of Animal Taxonomy* (New York: Columbia University Press, 1961), 150; Ernst Mayr, *The Growth of Biological Thought: Diversity, Evolution, and Inheritance* (Cambridge, MA: Harvard University Press, 1982), 273–75; Marc Ereshefsky, *The Poverty of the Linnaean Hierarchy: A Philosophical Study of Biological Taxonomy* (Cambridge, UK: Cambridge University Press, 2001), 82.

44. Richard Dawkins, *The Ancestor's Tale: A Pilgrimage to the Dawn of Evolution* (Boston: Mariner Books, 2005), 411–12. See also Olson, *Mapping Human History*, 134.

45. See, for example, Cartmill and Smith, *The Human Lineage*, 38–39. See also John C. Avise, "Phylogeography: Retrospect and Prospect." *Journal of Biogeography* 36 (2009): 5.

46. Dawkins, *The Ancestor's Tale*, 399; Stephen R. L. Clark, "Apes and the Idea of Kindred," in Paola Cavalieri and Peter Singer (eds.), *The Great Ape Project: Equality beyond Humanity* (New York: St. Martin's Griffin, 1996 [1993]), 117.

47. See, for example, Cartmill and Smith, *The Human Lineage*, 478–79.

48. See, for example, Peter Read, "The Stolen Generations: The Removal of Aboriginal Children in New South Wales 1883 to 1969," in http://www.daa.nsw.gov.au/publications/StolenGenerations.pdf (accessed on April 7, 2010); Doreen Mellor and Anna Haebich (eds.), *Many Voices: Reflections on Experiences of Indigenous Child Separation* (Canberra, Australia: National Library of Australia, 2002).

49. See, for example, Davis, *Who Is Black?* 129; Betty J. Lifton, *Journey of the Adopted Self: A Quest for Wholeness* (New York: Basic Books, 1994), 84.

50. See, for example, Ruth Seifert, "The Second Front: The Logic of Sexual Violence in Wars," in Manfred B. Steger and Nancy S. Lind (eds.), *Violence and Its Alternatives: An Interdisciplinary Reader* (New York: St. Martin's Press, 1999), 151; R. Charli Carpenter, "Surfacing Children: Limitations of Genocidal Rape Discourse," *Human Rights Quarterly* 22 (2000): 441–44; Yaschica Williams and Janine Bower, "Media Images of Wartime Sexual Violence: Ethnic Cleansing in Rwanda and the Former Yugoslavia," in Drew Humphries (ed.), *Women, Violence, and the Media: Readings in Feminist Criminology* (Lebanon, NH: University Press of New England, 2009), 161.

51. See, for example, Kevles, *In the Name of Eugenics*, 93–94; Stefan Kühl, *The Nazi Connection: Eugenics, American Racism, and German National Socialism* (New York: Oxford University Press, 1994); Edwin Black, *War Against the Weak: Eugenics and America's Campaign to Create a Master Race* (New York: Four Walls Eight Windows, 2003); http://en.wikipedia.org/wiki/Compulsory_sterilization (accessed on April 8, 2010).

52. Black, *War Against the Weak*, 406.

Chapter 7

1. Spencer Wells, *The Journey of Man: A Genetic Odyssey* (Princeton, NJ: Princeton University Press, 2002), 193–94. See also Spencer Wells, *Deep Ancestry: Inside the Genographic Project* (Washington, DC: National Geographic, 2006), 30–31.

2. See, for example, David A. Hollinger, *Postethnic America: Beyond Multiculturalism* (New York: Basic Books, 1995).

3. David C. Mountain and Jeanne K. Guelke, "Genetics, Genealogy, and Geography," in Dallen J. Timothy and Jeanne K. Guelke (eds.), *Geography and Genealogy: Locating Personal Pasts* (Aldershot, UK: Ashgate, 2008), 161.

4. Werner Sollors, *Beyond Ethnicity: Consent and Descent in American Culture* (New York: Oxford University Press, 1986), 4. See also Hollinger, *Postethnic America*, 134.

5. Neha Gondal, "Genealogy, Personal Networks, and Community Structure: The Modern Phenomenon of the Shrinking Family" (paper presented at the Annual Meeting of the American Sociological Association, San Francisco, 2009).

6. See, for example, Andrew J. Cherlin, *The Marriage-Go-Round: The State of Marriage and the Family in America Today* (New York: Alfred A. Knopf, 2009), 15, 17.

7. See, for example, Martine Segalen, "The Shift in Kinship Studies in France: The Case of Grandparenting," in Sarah Franklin and Susan McKinnon (eds.), *Relative Values: Reconfiguring Kinship Studies* (Durham: NC: Duke University Press, 2001), 246, 259; Marilyn Strathern, *Kinship, Law, and the Unexpected: Relatives Are Always a Surprise* (Cambridge, UK: Cambridge University Press, 2005), 26–27. See also Monica McGoldrick et al., *Genograms: Assessment and Intervention*, 2nd ed. (New York: W.W. Norton, 1999).

8. See also Bob Simpson, "Bringing the 'Unclear' Family into Focus: Divorce and Re-Marriage in Contemporary Britain," *Man* 29 (1994): 831–51; Strathern, *Kinship, Law, and the Unexpected*, 22.

9. Helena Ragoné, "Surrogate Motherhood and American Kinship," in Robert Parkin and Linda Stone (eds.), *Kinship and Family: An Anthropological Reader* (Malden, MA: Blackwell, 2004 [1994]), 342–61; Susan M. Kahn, *Reproducing Jews: A Cultural Account of Assisted Conception in Israel* (Durham, NC: Duke University Press, 2000), 112; Charis Thompson, "Strategic Naturalizing: Kinship in an Infertility Clinic," in Sarah Franklin and Susan McKinnon (eds.), *Relative Values: Reconfiguring Kinship Studies* (Durham, NC: Duke University Press, 2001), 178; Anne Cadoret, "The Contribution of Homoparental Families to the Current Debate on Kinship," in Jeanette Edwards and Carles Salazar (eds.), *European Kinship in the Age of Biotechnology* (New York: Berghahn Books, 2009), 79–96; Amrita Pande, "'It May Be Her Eggs But It's My Blood': Surrogates and Everyday Forms of Kinship in India," *Qualitative Sociology* 32 (2009): 380.

10. Kahn, *Reproducing Jews*, 138. See also pp. 128–33.

11. See, for example, Mark Henderson, "DNA Swap Could Cure Inherited Diseases," http://www.timesonline.co.uk/tol/news/science/article6811080.ece (accessed on April 10, 2010).

12. Adam Kolber, "Fractional Parents," http://kolber.typepad.com/ethics_law_blog/2009/09/fractional-parents.html (accessed on April 10, 2010).

13. See also Jeanette Edwards, "Incorporating Incest: Gamete, Body, and Relation in Assisted Conception," *Journal of the Royal Anthropological Institute* 10 (2004): 764, 766.

14. See, for example, Thompson, "Strategic Naturalizing," 185–87; Charis Thompson, *Making Parents: The Ontological Choreography of Reproductive Technologies* (Cambridge, MA: MIT Press, 2005), 161–63.
15. See, for example, Kahn, *Reproducing Jews*, 138; John Gribbin and Jeremy Cherfas, *The First Chimpanzee: In Search of Human Origins* (London: Penguin, 2001), 247–48.
16. See also Sarah Franklin, *Dolly Mixtures: The Remaking of Genealogy* (Durham, NC: Duke University Press, 2007), 26, 28.
17. See, for example, http://www.donorsiblingregistry.com (accessed on September 20, 2010); Janet L. Dolgin, "Biological Evaluations: Blood, Genes, and Family," *Akron Law Review* 41 (2008): 348, 350, 384–88.
18. See, for example, Carol Stack, *All Our Kin* (New York: Basic Books, 1974); David M. Schneider, *A Critique of the Study of Kinship* (Ann Arbor: University of Michigan Press, 1984); Janet Carsten (ed.), *Cultures of Relatedness: New Approaches to the Study of Kinship* (Cambridge, UK: Cambridge University Press, 2000).
19. See, for example, Jack Goody, "Adoption in Cross-Cultural Perspective," *Comparative Studies in Society and History* 11 (1969): 55–78; Judith S. Modell, *Kinship with Strangers: Adoption and Interpretations of Kinship in American Culture* (Berkeley: University of California Press, 1994), 225–38; Signe Howell, "Self-Conscious Kinship: Some Contested Values in Norwegian Transnational Adoption," in Sarah Franklin and Susan McKinnon (eds.), *Relative Values: Reconfiguring Kinship Studies* (Durham, NC: Duke University Press, 2001), 207–08; Signe Howell, "Kinning: The Creation of Life Trajectories in Transnational Adoptive Families," *Journal of the Royal Anthropological Institute* 9 (2003): 465, 468, 472, 481; Signe Howell, *The Kinning of Foreigners: Transnational Adoption in a Global Perspective* (New York: Berghahn Books, 2006).
20. J. A. Barnes, "Genealogies," in A. L. Epstein (ed.), *The Craft of Social Anthropology* (London: Tavistock, 1967), 102.
21. See, for example, http://www.dznewmember.org/lessons_for_a_lifetime/sisterhood.html (accessed on September 6, 2009). See also Jennifer Lugris, "The Organization and Social Role of Family Trees in Greek Organizations" (unpublished paper, Rutgers University, New Brunswick, NJ, 2007).
22. Yael Zerubavel, "Antiquity and the Renewal Paradigm: Strategies of Representation and Mnemonic Practices in Israeli Culture," in Doron Mendels (ed.), *On Memory: An Interdisciplinary Approach* (Bern, Switzerland: Peter Lang, 2007), 344.
23. Max Weber, *Economy and Society: An Outline of Interpretive Sociology* (Berkeley: University of California Press, 1978 [1925]), 248–49; 1135–41.
24. See, for example, http://broadwayworld.com/article/Principal_Clarinet_Stanley_Drucker_To_Make_Final_NY_Philharmonic (accessed on August 15, 2009); *Newsweek*, July 20, 2009, p. 68.

25. http://www.sunnipath.com/Academy/Online/Information/philosophy.aspx (accessed on June 29, 2008). See also Alex Shoumatoff, *The Mountain of Names: A History of the Human Family* (New York: Simon and Schuster, 1985), 55, 72; Andrew Shryock, *Nationalism and the Genealogical Imagination: Oral History and Textual Authority in Tribal Jordan* (Berkeley: University of California Press, 1997), 6.

26. See, for example, http://en.wikipedia.org/wiki/academic_genealogy (accessed on May 26, 2010).

27. See, for example, Donald N. Levine, *Visions of the Sociological Tradition* (Chicago: University of Chicago Press, 1995), 131, 246, 264. See also Randall Collins, *The Sociology of Philosophies: A Global Theory of Intellectual Change* (Cambridge, MA: Harvard University Press, 1998).

28. On musical pedigrees, see also David Lowenthal, *Possessed by the Past: The Heritage Crusade and the Spoils of History* (New York: Free Press, 1996), 33; Shryock, *Nationalism and the Genealogical Imagination*, 313.

29. See, for example, Marc Shell, *The End of Kinship: "Measure for Measure," Incest, and the Ideal of Universal Siblinghood* (Baltimore: Johns Hopkins University Press, 1995 [1988]), 10–16; A. Marina Iossifides, "Sisters in Christ: Metaphors of Kinship among Greek Nuns," in Peter Loizos and Evthymios Papataxiarchis (eds.), *Contested Identities: Gender and Kinship in Modern Greece* (Princeton, NJ: Princeton University Press, 1991), 135–55; Danièle Hervieu-Léger, *Religion as a Chain of Memory* (New Brunswick, NJ: Rutgers University Press, 2000 [1993]), 150–56; Sara Corbett, "The Holy Grail of the Unconscious," *New York Times Magazine*, September 20, 2009, p. 48.

30. See, for example, http://genealogy.math.ndsu.nodak.edu/index.php (accessed on June 23, 2008); Marcel J. Harmon et al., "Reconstructing the Flow of Information across Time and Space: A Phylogenetic Analysis of Ceramic Traditions from Prehispanic Western and Northern Mexico and the American Southwest," in Carl P. Lipo et al. (eds.), *Mapping Our Ancestors: Phylogenetic Approaches in Anthropology and Prehistory* (New Brunswick, NJ: AldineTransaction, 2006), 209–10; Astrit Schmidt-Burkhardt, *Stammbäume der Kunst: Zur Genealogie der Avantgarde* (Berlin: Akademie Verlag, 2005), 286.

31. Interview with Ted Koppel on the August 15, 2006 PBS program *Frontline*. http://www.pbs.org/wgbh/pages/frontline/newswar/interviews/koppel.html (accessed on July 8, 2009).

32. See also Ilya Tëmkin and Niles Eldredge, "Phylogenetics and Material Culture Evolution," *Current Anthropology* 48 (2007): 146–53 on the history of the psaltery and the cornet.

33. See, for example, Banister Fletcher, *A History of Architecture on the Comparative Method for Students, Craftsmen, and Amateurs*, 16th ed. (New York: Charles Scribner's Sons, 1958), iii.

34. See, for example, Pieter van Reenen and Margot van Mulken (eds.), *Studies in Stemmatology* (Amsterdam: John Benjamins Publishing Co., 1996); Joshua M.

Baker, "Everything in Its Right Place: The Sociocognitive Categorization of Music" (unpublished senior thesis, Rutgers University, New Brunswick, NJ, 2010). See also Norman I. Platnick and H. Don Cameron, "Cladistic Methods in Textual, Linguistic, and Phylogenetic Analysis," *Systematic Zoology* 26 (1977): 380–85; Niles Eldredge, "Biological and Material Cultural Evolution: Are There Any True Parallels?" in François Tonneau and Nicholas S. Thompson (eds.), *Perspectives in Ethology* (New York: Plenum, 2000), 113–53; Carlo Ginzburg, "Family Resemblances and Family Trees: Two Cognitive Metaphors," *Critical Inquiry* 30 (2004): 550; Niles Eldredge, "Foreword," in Carl P. Lipo et al. (eds.), *Mapping Our Ancestors: Phylogenetic Approaches in Anthropology and Prehistory* (New Brunswick, NJ: AldineTransaction, 2006), xiii; R. Lee Lyman and Michael J. O'Brien, "Seriation and Cladistics: The Difference between Anagenetic and Cladogenetic Evolution," in *Mapping Our Ancestors*, 81–87; Harmon et al., "Reconstructing the Flow of Information across Time and Space"; Peter Jordan and Thomas Mace, "Tracking Culture-Historical Lineages: Can 'Descent with Modification' Be Linked to 'Association by Descent'?" in *Mapping Our Ancestors*, 149–67.

35. See W. Keith Percival, "Biological Analogy in the Study of Language before the Advent of Comparative Grammar," in Henry M. Hoenigswald and Linda F. Wiener (eds.), *Biological Metaphor and Cladistic Classification: An Interdisciplinary Perspective* (Philadelphia: University of Pennsylvania Press, 1987), 21.

36. Rulon S. Wells, "The Life and Growth of Language: Metaphors in Biology and Linguistics," in Henry M. Hoenigswald and Linda F. Wiener (eds.), *Biological Metaphor and Cladistic Classification: An Interdisciplinary Perspective* (Philadelphia: University of Pennsylvania Press, 1987), 51; Konrad Koerner, "On Schleicher and Trees," in *Biological Metaphor and Cladistic Classification*, 112; Stephen G. Alter, *Darwinism and the Linguistic Image: Language, Race, and Natural Theology in the Nineteenth Century* (Baltimore: Johns Hopkins University Press, 1999), 111; John van Wyhe, "The Descent of Words: Evolutionary Thinking 1780–1880," *Endeavour* 29 (September 2005): 95. See also August Schleicher, "Darwinism Tested by the Science of Language," in Konrad Koerner (ed.), *Linguistics and Evolutionary Theory* (Amsterdam: John Benjamins, 1983 [1863]), 35–37, 71. But see Percival, "Biological Analogy in the Study of Language," 26.

37. See also Morris Swadesh, "What Is Glottochronology?" in *The Origin and Diversification of Language* (Chicago: Aldine, 1971 [1960]), 271–76; Colin Renfrew, *Archaeology and Language: The Puzzle of Indo-European Origins* (New York: Cambridge University Press, 1987), 101, 113–15, 118.

38. Yael Zerubavel, "Trans-Historical Encounters in the Land of Israel: On Symbolic Bridges, National Memory, and the Literary Imagination," *Jewish Social Studies* 11 (2005): 115–35.

39. Plate 16 in Amatzia Baram, *Culture, History, and Ideology in the Formation of Ba'thist Iraq, 1968–89* (New York: St. Martin's Press, 1991). See also plate 7b.

40. http://www.templemountfaithful.org; http://www.templeinstitute.org/creation_timeline_1.htm (accessed on December 16, 2007).

41. http://www.archons.org/pdf/IHT_12-27-06.pdf (accessed on December 26, 2009), also published in the *New York Times*, December 21, 2006, p. A25.

42. See also Robert E. Park and Ernest W. Burgess, *Introduction to the Science of Sociology* (Chicago: University of Chicago Press, 1969 [1921]), 360–61, 365; Eviatar Zerubavel, *Social Mindscapes: An Invitation to Cognitive Sociology* (Cambridge, MA: Harvard University Press, 1997), 92.

43. www.cathedralsofcalifornia.com/?m=200709&paged=2 (accessed on February 16, 2010).

44. For a history of this and other splits within the Irish Republican Army, see, for example, http://en.wikipedia.org/wiki/List_of_organisations_known_as_the_Irish_Republican_Army (accessed on December 29, 2009).

45. http://www.orthodoxonline.com/tree.htm (accessed on September 23, 2007).

BIBLIOGRAPHY

Abu El-Haj, Nadia. "The Genetic Reinscription of Race." *Annual Review of Anthropology* 36 (2007): 283–300.

African American Lives. PBS Home Video. 2006.

African American Lives 2. PBS Home Video. 2008.

Alba, Richard D. *Ethnic Identity: The Transformation of White America.* New Haven, CT: Yale University Press, 1990.

———. "Assimilation's Quiet Tide." *Public Interest* 119 (Spring 1995): 3–18.

Alba, Richard, and Victor Nee. "Rethinking Assimilation Theory for a New Era of Immigration." *International Migration Review* 31 (1997): 826–74.

Alford, Richard D. *Naming and Identity: A Cross-Cultural Study of Personal Naming Practices.* New Haven, CT: HRAF Press, 1988.

Almog, Oz. *The Sabra: The Creation of the New Jew.* Berkeley: University of California Press, 2000 [1997].

Almond, Philip. "Adam, Pre-Adamites, and Extra-Terrestrial Beings in Early Modern Europe." *Journal of Religious History* 30 (2006): 163–74.

Alter, Stephen G. *Darwinism and the Linguistic Image: Language, Race, and Natural Theology in the Nineteenth Century.* Baltimore: Johns Hopkins University Press, 1999.

Ancestors: Webster's Quotations, Facts, and Phrases. San Diego, CA: ICON Group International, 2008.

Anderson, Benedict. *Imagined Communities: Reflections on the Origin and Spread of Nationalism.* London: Verso, 1983.

Angier, Natalie. "Do Races Differ? Not Really, Genes Show." *New York Times,* August 22, 2000, pp. F1–6.

Appiah, Anthony. "The Uncompleted Argument: DuBois and the Illusion of Race." In *"Race," Writing, and Difference,* edited by Henry L. Gates Jr., pp. 21–37. Chicago: University of Chicago Press, 1986.

Atkinson, Quentin D., and Russell D. Gray. "Are Accurate Dates an Intractable Problem for Historical Linguistics?" In *Mapping Our Ancestors: Phylogenetic Approaches in Anthropology and Prehistory,* edited by Carl P. Lipo et al., pp. 269–96. New Brunswick, NJ: AldineTransaction, 2006.

Avise, John C. "Phylogeography: Retrospect and Prospect." *Journal of Biogeography* 36 (2009): 3–15.

Ayala, Francisco J. "The Myth of Eve: Molecular Biology and Human Origins." *Science* 270 (December 22, 1995): 1930–36.

Ayoub, Millicent R. "The Family Reunion." *Ethnology* 5 (1966): 415–33.

Babylonian Talmud, The. London: The Soncino Press, 1948.

Baker, Hugh. *Chinese Family and Kinship.* New York: Columbia University Press, 1979.

Baker, Joshua M. "Everything in Its Right Place: The Sociocognitive Categorization of Music." Unpublished senior thesis, Rutgers University, New Brunswick, NJ, 2010.

Bakhos, Carol. *Ishmael on the Border: Rabbinic Portrayals of the First Arab.* Albany: State University of New York Press, 2006.

Bamford, Sandra. "Conceiving Relatedness: Non-Substantial Relations Among the Kamea of Papua New Guinea." *Journal of the Royal Anthropological Institute (New Series)* 10 (2004): 287–306.

Baram, Amatzia. *Culture, History, and Ideology in the Formation of Ba'thist Iraq, 1968–89.* New York: St. Martin's Press, 1991.

Barnes, J. A. "Genealogies." In *The Craft of Social Anthropology,* edited by A. L. Epstein, pp. 101–28. London: Tavistock, 1967.

Bassett, Mary T. "The Pursuit of Equity in Health: Reflections on Race and Public Health Data in Southern Africa." *American Journal of Public Health* 90 (2000): 1690–93.

Basu, Paul. *Highland Homecomings: Genealogy and Heritage Tourism in the Scottish Diaspora.* Abingdon, UK: Routledge, 2007.

Baum, David A., et al. "The Tree-Thinking Challenge." *Science* 310 (2005): 979–80.

Bauman, Zygmunt. *Liquid Times: Living in an Age of Uncertainty.* Cambridge, UK: Polity Press, 2007.

Beecher, Michael D. "Successes and Failures of Parent-Offspring Recognition in Animals." In *Kin Recognition,* edited by Peter G. Hepper, pp. 94–124. Cambridge, UK: Cambridge University Press, 1991.

Begley, Sharon. "Beyond Stones and Bones." *Newsweek,* March 19, 2007.

Bennet, James. "Hillary Clinton, in Morocco, Says NATO Attack Aims at Stopping Bloodshed." *New York Times,* March 31, 1999, p. A10.

Bentley, Nancy. "The Fourth Dimension: Kinlessness and African American Narrative." *Critical Inquiry* 35 (Winter 2009): 270–92.

Berger, Peter L., and Thomas Luckmann. *The Social Construction of Reality: A Treatise in the Sociology of Knowledge.* Garden City, NY: Doubleday Anchor, 1967 [1966].

Bernstein, Irwin. "The Correlation Between Kinship and Behavior in Non-Human Primates." In *Kin Recognition,* edited by Peter G. Hepper, pp. 6–29. Cambridge, UK: Cambridge University Press, 1991.

Bigelow, R. S. "Classification and Phylogeny." *Systematic Zoology* 7, no. 2 (1958): 49–59.

Black, Edwin. *War Against the Weak: Eugenics and America's Campaign to Create a Master Race.* New York: Four Walls Eight Windows, 2003.

Blenkinsopp, Joseph. *Sage, Priest, Prophet: Religious and Intellectual Leadership in Ancient Israel.* Louisville, KY: Westminster John Knox Press, 1995.

Bloch, Maurice, and Dan Sperber. "Kinship and Evolved Psychological Dispositions: The Mother's Brother Controversy Reconsidered." In *Kinship and Family: An Anthropological Reader,* edited by Robert Parkin and Linda Stone, pp. 438–55. Malden, MA: Blackwell, 2004 [2002].

Bloch, R. Howard. *Etymologies and Genealogies: A Literary Anthropology of the French Middle Ages.* Chicago: University of Chicago Press, 1983.

Bohannan, Laura. "A Genealogical Charter." *Africa* 22 (1952): 301–15.

Bohannan, Paul. *Social Anthropology.* New York: Holt, Rinehart and Winston, 1963.

Bolaffi, Guido, et al. (eds.). *Dictionary of Race, Ethnicity, and Culture.* Thousand Oaks, CA: SAGE, 2003.

Bolnick, Deborah A. "Individual Ancestry Inference and the Reification of Race as a Biological Phenomenon." In *Revisiting Race in a Genomic Age,* edited by Barbara A. Koenig et al., pp. 70–85. New Brunswick, NJ: Rutgers University Press, 2008.

Bouquet, Mary. "Family Trees and Their Affinities: The Visual Imperative of the Genealogical Diagram." *Journal of the Royal Anthropological Institute,* n.s, 2 (1996): 43–66.

Bowler, Peter J. *Theories of Human Evolution: A Century of Debate, 1844–1944.* Baltimore: Johns Hopkins University Press, 1986.

———. *The Invention of Progress: The Victorians and the Past.* Oxford: Basil Blackwell, 1989.

———. *Life's Splendid Drama: Evolutionary Biology and the Reconstruction of Life's Ancestry, 1860–1940.* Chicago: University of Chicago Press, 1996.

Bradley, Michael. *The Iceman Inheritance: Prehistoric Sources of Western Man's Racism, Sexism, and Aggression.* New York: Kayode Publications, 1991 [1978].

Brandt, Nat. *Harlem at War: The Black Experience in WWII.* Syracuse, NY: Syracuse University Press, 1996.

Braude, Benjamin. "The Sons of Noah and the Construction of Ethnic and Geographical Identities in the Medieval and Early Modern Periods." *The William and Mary Quarterly,* 3d ser., 54 (1997): 103–42.

Brekhus, Wayne. "Social Marking and the Mental Coloring of Identity: Sexual Identity Construction and Maintenance in the United States." *Sociological Forum* 11 (1996): 497–522.

———. *Peacocks, Chameleons, Centaurs: Gay Suburbia and the Grammar of Social Identity*. Chicago: University of Chicago Press, 2003.

Brekhus, Wayne, et al. "On the Contributions of Cognitive Sociology to the Sociological Study of Race." *Sociology Compass* 4 (2010): 61–76.

Breuil, Henri. "The Discovery of the Antiquity of Man: Some of the Evidence." *Journal of the Royal Anthropological Institute of Great Britain and Ireland* 75 (1945): 21–31.

Broberg, Gunnar. "*Homo sapiens*: Linnaeus's Classification of Man." In *Linnaeus: The Man and His Work,* edited by Tore Frängsmyr, pp. 156–94. Berkeley: University of California Press, 1983.

Brodwin, Paul. "Genetics, Identity, and the Anthropology of Essentialism." *Anthropological Quarterly* 75 (2002): 323–30.

Brubaker, Rogers. *Citizenship and Nationhood in France and Germany*. Cambridge, MA: Harvard University Press, 1992.

———. "Ethnicity without Groups." In *Ethnicity without Groups,* pp. 7–27. Cambridge, MA: Harvard University Press, 2004 [2002].

———. "Ethnicity, Race, and Nationalism." *Annual Review of Sociology* 35 (2009): 21–42.

Brunwasser, Matthew. "Macedonia Dispute Has an Asian Flavor." http://www.nytimes.com/2008/10/01/world/asia/01iht-macedonia.1.16609558.html.

Burkhardt, Richard W. *The Spirit of System: Lamarck and Evolutionary Biology*. Cambridge, MA: Harvard University Press, 1977.

Burleigh, Michael, and Wolfgang Wipperman. *The Racial State: Germany 1933–1945*. Cambridge, UK: Cambridge University Press, 1991.

Bury, J. B. *A History of Greece to the Death of Alexander the Great*. 3rd Edition. London: Macmillan, 1951.

Cadoret, Anne. "The Contribution of Homoparental Families to the Current Debate on Kinship." In *European Kinship in the Age of Biotechnology,* edited by Jeanette Edwards and Carles Salazar, pp. 79–96. New York: Berghahn Books, 2009.

Caldwell, Richard S. *Hesiod's Theogony*. Newburyport, MA: Focus Classical Library, 1987.

Calhoun, Craig. "Nationalism and Ethnicity." *Annual Review of Sociology* 19 (1993): 211–39.

Cann, Rebecca L., et al. "Mitochondrial DNA and Human Evolution." *Nature* 325 (1987): 31–36.

Cannings, C., and E. A. Thompson. *Genealogical and Genetic Structure*. Cambridge, UK: Cambridge University Press, 1981.

Carpenter, R. Charli. "Surfacing Children: Limitations of Genocidal Rape Discourse." *Human Rights Quarterly* 22 (2000): 428–77.

Carsten, Janet. "The Substance of Kinship and the Heat of the Hearth: Feeding, Personhood, and Relatedness among Malays in Pulau Langkawi." In *Kinship and Family: An Anthropological Reader,* edited by Robert Parkin and Linda Stone, pp. 309–27. Malden, MA: Blackwell, 2004 [1995].

———— (ed.). *Cultures of Relatedness: New Approaches to the Study of Kinship.* Cambridge, UK: Cambridge University Press, 2000.

Cartmill, Matt, and Fred H. Smith. *The Human Lineage.* Hoboken, NJ: Wiley-Blackwell, 2009.

Castronovo, Russ. *Fathering the Nation: American Genealogies of Slavery and Freedom.* Berkeley: University of California Press, 1995.

Cavalli-Sforza, Luigi L. *Genes, Peoples, and Languages.* New York: North Point Press, 2000.

Cavalli-Sforza, Luigi L., and Francesco Cavalli-Sforza. *The Great Human Diasporas: The History of Diversity and Evolution.* Reading, MA: Addison-Wesley, 1995 [1993].

Cavalli-Sforza, Luigi L., et al. *The History and Geography of Human Genes.* Abridged ed. Princeton, NJ: Princeton University Press, 1996.

Čepaitienė, Auksuolė. "Imagining Assisted Reproductive Technologies: Family, Kinship, and 'Local Thinking' in Lithuania." In *European Kinship in the Age of Biotechnology,* edited by Jeanette Edwards and Carles Salazar, pp. 29–44. New York: Berghahn Books, 2009.

Cerulo, Karen A. *Never Saw It Coming: Cultural Challenges to Envisioning the Worst.* Chicago: University of Chicago Press, 2006.

————. "Nonhumans in Social Interaction." *Annual Review of Sociology* 35 (2009): 531–52.

Cherlin, Andrew J. *The Marriage-Go-Round: The State of Marriage and the Family in America Today.* New York: Alfred A. Knopf, 2009.

Clark, Stephen R. L. "Apes and the Idea of Kindred." In *The Great Ape Project: Equality beyond Humanity,* edited by Paola Cavalieri and Peter Singer, pp. 113–25. New York: St. Martin's Griffin, 1996 [1993].

Clarke, Morgan. "The Modernity of Milk Kinship." *Social Anthropology* 15 (2007): 287–304.

Clogg, Richard. *A Concise History of Greece.* 2nd ed. Cambridge, UK: Cambridge University Press, 2002 [1992].

Coe, Kathryn. *The Ancestress Hypothesis: Visual Art as Adaptation.* New Brunswick, NJ: Rutgers University Press, 2003.

Cohen, Shaye J. D. "The Matrilineal Principle in Historical Perspective." *Judaism* 34 (Winter 1985): 5–13.

Collins, Patricia H. "It's All in the Family: Intersections of Gender, Race, and Nation." *Hypatia* 13 (Summer 1998): 62–82.

Collins, Randall. *The Sociology of Philosophies: A Global Theory of Intellectual Change.* Cambridge, MA: Harvard University Press, 1998.

Conniff, Richard. "The Family Tree, Pruned." *Smithsonian* 38 (July 2007): 90–97.

Cooley, Charles H. *Human Nature and the Social Order.* New York: Schocken, 1964 [1922].

Coon, Carleton S. *The Origin of Races.* New York: Alfred A. Knopf, 1962.

Corbett, Sara. "The Holy Grail of the Unconscious." *New York Times Magazine,* September 20, 2009, pp. 34–65.

Corbey, Raymond. *The Metaphysics of Apes: Negotiating the Animal-Human Boundary.* Cambridge, UK: Cambridge University Press, 2005.

Cose, Ellis. "It Was Always Headed Here." *Newsweek,* March 31, 2008, p. 33.

Crèvecoeur, J. Hector St. John de. *Letters from an American Farmer.* New York: Fox, Duffield & Co., 1904 [1782].

Cronon, E. David. *Black Moses: The Story of Marcus Garvey and the Universal Negro Improvement Association.* Madison: University of Wisconsin Press, 1969 [1955].

Daly, Martin, and Margo I. Wilson. "Whom Are Newborn Babies Said to Resemble?" *Ethology and Sociobiology* 3 (1982): 69–78.

Daniel, G. Reginald. *More Than Black? Multiracial Identity and the New Racial Order.* Philadelphia: Temple University Press, 2002.

Dart, Raymond A. "*Australopithecus Africanus*: The Man-Ape of South Africa." In *Naming Our Ancestors: An Anthology of Hominid Taxonomy,* edited by W. Eric Meikle and Sue T. Parker, pp. 53–70. Prospect Heights, IL: Waveland Press, 1994 [1925].

Darwin, Charles. *On the Origin of Species.* New York: Sterling, 2008 [1859].

———. *The Descent of Man and Selection in Relation to Sex.* Amherst, NY: Prometheus, 1998 [1871].

Davis, F. James. *Who Is Black? One Nation's Definition.* University Park: Pennsylvania State University Press, 1991.

Dawkins, Richard. *The Blind Watchmaker: Why the Evidence of Evolution Reveals a Universe Without Design.* New York: W.W. Norton, 2006 [1986].

———. "Gaps in the Mind." In *The Great Ape Project: Equality beyond Humanity,* edited by Paola Cavalieri and Peter Singer, pp. 80–87. New York: St. Martin's Griffin, 1996 [1993].

———. *River out of Eden: A Darwinian View of Life.* New York: Basic Books, 1995.

———. *The Ancestor's Tale: A Pilgrimage to the Dawn of Evolution.* Boston: Mariner Books, 2005.

Delaney, Carol. *The Seed and the Soil: Gender and Cosmology in Turkish Village Society.* Berkeley: University of California Press, 1991.

———. "Father State, Motherland, and the Birth of Modern Turkey." In *Naturalizing Power: Essays in Feminist Cultural Analysis,* edited by Sylvia Yanagisako and Carol Delaney, pp. 177–99. New York: Routledge, 1995.

———. "Cutting the Ties That Bind: The Sacrifice of Abraham and Patriarchal Kinship." In *Relative Values: Reconfiguring Kinship Studies,* edited by Sarah Franklin and Susan McKinnon, pp. 445–67. Durham, NC: Duke University Press, 2001.

Deleuze, Gilles, and Felix Guattari. *A Thousand Plateaus: Capitalism and Schizophrenia.* Minneapolis: University of Minnesota Press, 1987.

Diamond, Jared. *The Third Chimpanzee: The Evolution and Future of the Human Animal.* New York: HarperCollins, 1992.

Dolgin, Janet L. "Biological Evaluations: Blood, Genes, and Family." *Akron Law Review* 41 (2008): 347–98.

Domínguez, Virginia R. *White by Definition: Social Classification in Creole Louisiana.* New Brunswick, NJ: Rutgers University Press, 1986.

Dunbar, Robin I. M. "What's in a Classification?" In *The Great Ape Project: Equality beyond Humanity,* edited by Paola Cavalieri and Peter Singer, pp. 109–12. New York: St. Martin's Griffin, 1996 [1993].

Durkheim, Emile. *The Division of Labor in Society.* New York: Free Press, 1984 [1893].

Duster, Troy. "Deep Roots and Tangled Branches." *Chronicle of Higher Education,* February 3, 2006.

Easteal, Simon, and Genevieve Herbert. "Molecular Evidence from the Nuclear Genome for the Time Frame of Human Evolution." *Journal of Molecular Evolution* 44, Suppl. 1 (1997): S121–S132.

Edwards, Jeanette. "Incorporating Incest: Gamete, Body, and Relation in Assisted Conception." *Journal of the Royal Anthropological Institute* 10 (2004): 755–74.

Ehrlich, Paul R. *Human Natures: Genes, Cultures, and the Human Prospect.* Washington, DC: Island Press, 2000.

Eldredge, Niles. "Biological and Material Cultural Evolution: Are There Any True Parallels?" In *Perspectives in Ethology,* edited by François Tonneau and Nicholas S. Thompson, pp. 113–53. New York: Plenum, 2000.

———. "Foreword." In *Mapping Our Ancestors: Phylogenetic Approaches in Anthropology and Prehistory,* edited by Carl P. Lipo, et al., pp. xiii–xvi. New Brunswick, NJ: AldineTransaction, 2006.

Eldredge, Niles, and Joel Cracraft. *Phylogenetic Patterns and the Evolutionary Process: Method and Theory in Comparative Biology.* New York: Columbia University Press, 1980.

Elliott, Carl, and Paul Brodwin. "Identity and Genetic Ancestry Tracing." *British Medical Journal* 325 (2002): 1469–71.

Elliott, Michael A. "Telling the Difference: Nineteenth-Century Legal Narratives of Racial Taxonomy." *Law and Social Inquiry* 24 (1999): 611–36.

Elon, Amos. *The Israelis: Founders and Sons.* New York: Bantam Books, 1971.

Ereshefsky, Marc. *The Poverty of the Linnaean Hierarchy: A Philosophical Study of Biological Taxonomy.* Cambridge, UK: Cambridge University Press, 2001.

Erikson, Thomas H. *Ethnicity and Nationalism.* 2nd ed. London: Pluto Press, 2002 [1993].

Evans-Pritchard, Edward E. *The Nuer: A Description of the Modes of Livelihood and Political Institutions of a Nilotic People.* London: Oxford University Press, 1940.

———. "The Nuer of the Southern Sudan." In *Kinship and Family: An Anthropological Reader,* edited by Robert Parkin and Linda Stone, pp. 64–78. Malden, MA: Blackwell, 2004 [1940].

Faces of America. PBS Home Video, 2010.

Faison, Seth. "Qufu Journal: Not Equal to Confucius, but Friends to His Memory." *New York Times,* October 10, 1997.

Farber, Bernard. *Conceptions of Kinship.* New York: Elsevier, 1981.

Fattah, Hassan M. "A Nation with a Long Memory, but a Truncated History." *New York Times,* January 10, 2007, p. A4.

Faubion, James D., and Jennifer A. Hamilton. "Sumptuary Kinship." *Anthropological Quarterly* 80 (2007): 533–59.

Ferber, Abby L. "Exploring the Social Construction of Race: Sociology and the Study of Interracial Relationships." In *American Mixed Race: The Culture of Microdiversity,* edited by Naomi Zack, pp. 155–67. Lanham, MD: Rowman & Littlefield, 1995.

Fields, Barbara J. "Ideology and Race in American History." In *Region, Race, and Reconstruction: Essays in Honor of C. Vann Woodward,* edited by J. Morgan Kousser and James M. McPherson, pp. 143–77. New York: Oxford University Press, 1982.

Finkelstein, Israel, and Neil A. Silberman. *The Bible Unearthed: Archaeology's New Vision of Ancient Israel and the Origin of Its Sacred Texts.* New York: Free Press, 2001.

Finkler, Kaja. "The Kin in the Gene: The Medicalization of Family and Kinship in American Society." *Current Anthropology* 42 (2001): 235–49.

Fishbane, Michael. *Biblical Interpretation in Ancient Israel.* Oxford: Oxford University Press, 1985.

Fletcher, Banister. *A History of Architecture on the Comparative Method for Students, Craftsmen, and Amateurs.* 16th ed. New York: Charles Scribner's Sons, 1958.

Foner, Nancy. *In a New Land: A Comparative View of Immigration.* New York: New York University Press, 2005.

Fortes, Meyer. "The Significance of Descent in Tale Social Structure." In *Time and Social Structure and Other Essays,* pp. 33–66. London: Athlone Press, 1970 [1943–44].

———. "The Structure of Unilineal Descent Groups." In *Time and Social Structure and Other Essays,* pp. 67–95. London: Athlone Press, 1970 [1953].

———. "Descent, Filiation, and Affinity." In *Time and Social Structure and Other Essays,* pp. 96–121. London: Athlone Press, 1970 [1959].

Foster, Johanna E. "Feminist Theory and the Politics of Ambiguity: A Comparative Analysis of the Multiracial Movement, the Intersex Movement and the Disability Rights Movement as Contemporary Struggles over Social Classification in the United States." PhD diss., Rutgers University, New Brunswick, NJ, 2000.

Fourth Book of the Chronicle of Fredegar with Its Continuations. Edited by John. M. Wallace-Hadrill. London: Thomas Nelson, 1960.

Fox, Robin. *Kinship and Marriage: An Anthropological Perspective.* Cambridge, UK: Cambridge University Press, 1983 [1967].

———. *The Tory Islanders: A People of the Celtic Fringe.* Cambridge, UK: Cambridge University Press, 1978.

Franklin, Sarah. *Dolly Mixtures: The Remaking of Genealogy.* Durham, NC: Duke University Press, 2007.

Freedman, Maurice. *Lineage Organization in Southeastern China*. London: Athlone Press, 1965 [1958].

———. *Chinese Lineage and Society: Fukien and Kwangtung*. London: Athlone Press, 1966.

Freeman, Harold P. "Commentary on the Meaning of Race in Science and Society." *Cancer Epidemiology, Biomarkers and Prevention* 12 (March 2003): 232s–236s.

Freeman, J. D. "On the Concept of the Kindred." In *Kinship and Social Organization*, edited by Paul Bohannan and John Middleton, pp. 255–72. Garden City, NY: American Museum of Natural History, 1968 [1961].

Friday, Adrian E. "Human Evolution: The Evidence from DNA Sequencing." In *The Cambridge Encyclopedia of Human Evolution*, edited by Steve Jones, et al., pp. 316–21. Cambridge, UK: Cambridge University Press, 1992.

Friedberg, Avraham S. *Zikhronot le-Veit David*. Ramat Gan, Israel: Masada, 1958 [1893–1904]. [In Hebrew.]

Friedman, Asia. "Toward a Sociology of Perception: Sight, Sex, and Gender." *Cultural Sociology* 5 (2011): 187–206.

Frudakis, Tony N. *Molecular Photofitting: Predicting Ancestry and Phenotype Using DNA*. Amsterdam: Elsevier, 2008.

Fullwiley, Duana. "The Biologistical Construction of Race: 'Admixture' Technology and the New Genetic Medicine." *Social Studies of Science* 38 (2008): 695–735.

Gamble, Clive. *Timewalkers: The Prehistory of Global Colonization*. Cambridge, MA: Harvard University Press, 1994.

Gardner, Martin. "Did Adam and Eve Have Navels?" In *Did Adam and Eve Have Navels? Debunking Pseudoscience*, pp. 7–14. New York: W.W. Norton, 2001 [1998].

Garroutte, Eva M. "The Racial Formation of American Indians: Negotiating Legitimate Identities within Tribal and Federal Law." *American Indian Quarterly* 25 (2001): 224–39.

Gates, Henry L. Jr. "Family Matters: When Science Clashes with Ancestral Lore." *The New Yorker*, December 1, 2008, pp. 34–38.

———. *In Search of Our Roots: How 19 Extraordinary African Americans Reclaimed Their Past*. New York: Crown Publishers, 2009.

Geary, Patrick J. *The Myth of Nations: The Medieval Origins of Europe*. Princeton, NJ: Princeton University Press, 2002.

Geertz, Hildred, and Clifford Geertz. "Teknonymy in Bali: Parenthood, Age-Grading and Genealogical Amnesia." *Journal of the Royal Anthropological Institute of Great Britain and Ireland* 94, no. 2 (1964): 94–108.

Gellner, Ernest. "Reply: Do Nations Have Navels?" *Nations and Nationalism* 2 (1996): 366–70.

Germana, Rachelle. "The Social Practice of Hyphenating: A Qualitative Study of Surname Hyphenation." Paper presented at the Annual Meeting of the Eastern Sociological Society, Baltimore, 2009.

Gershoni, Israel, and James P. Jankowski. *Egypt, Islam, and the Arabs: The Search for Egyptian Nationhood, 1900–1930*. New York: Oxford University Press, 1986.

Gibbons, Ann. "The Mystery of Humanity's Missing Mutations." *Science* 267 (January 6, 1995): 35–36.

Gillis, John R. *A World of Their Own Making: Myth, Ritual, and the Quest for Family Values*. New York: Basic Books, 1996.

Ginzburg, Carlo. "Family Resemblances and Family Trees: Two Cognitive Metaphors." *Critical Inquiry* 30 (2004): 537–56.

Gobineau, Arthur de. *The Inequality of Human Races*. New York: Howard Fertig, 1967 [1854].

Goldberg, Carey. "DNA Offers Link to Black History." *New York Times*, August 28, 2000, p. A10.

Goldberg, David T. *The Racial State*. Malden, MA: Blackwell, 2002.

Goldstein, David B. *Jacob's Legacy: A Genetic View of Jewish History*. New Haven, CT: Yale University Press, 2008.

Gondal, Neha. "Genealogy, Personal Networks, and Community Structure: The Modern Phenomenon of the Shrinking Family." Paper presented at the Annual Meeting of the American Sociological Association, San Francisco, 2009.

Goodman, Morris. "Serological Analysis of the Systematics of Recent Hominoids." *Human Biology* 35 (1963): 377–436.

———. "Reconstructing Human Evolution from Proteins." In *The Cambridge Encyclopedia of Human Evolution*, edited by Steve Jones, et al., pp. 307–12. Cambridge, UK: Cambridge University Press, 1992.

———. "Epilogue: A Personal Account of the Origins of a New Paradigm." *Molecular Phylogenetics and Evolution* 5 (1996): 269–85.

———. "The Genomic Record of Humankind's Evolutionary Roots." *American Journal of Human Genetics* 64 (1999): 31–39.

Goodman, Morris, and G. William Moore. "Immunodiffusion Systematics of the Primates: I. The Catarrhini." *Systematic Zoology* 20 (1971): 19–62.

Goodman, Morris, et al. "Toward a Phylogenetic Classification of Primates Based on DNA Evidence Complemented by Fossil Evidence." *Molecular Phylogenetics and Evolution* 9 (1998): 585–98.

Goody, Jack. "Adoption in Cross-Cultural Perspective." *Comparative Studies in Society and History* 11 (1969): 55–78.

———. *The Development of the Family and Marriage in Europe*. Cambridge, UK: Cambridge University Press, 1983.

Gordon, David C. *Self-Determination and History in the Third World*. Princeton, NJ: Princeton University Press, 1971.

Gordon, Milton M. *Assimilation in American Life: The Role of Race, Religion, and National Origins*. New York: Oxford University Press, 1964.

Gould, Stephen J. "Bushes and Ladders in Human Evolution." In *Ever Since Darwin: Reflections in Natural History,* pp. 56–62. New York: W.W. Norton, 1979 [1976].

———. *Ontogeny and Phylogeny.* Cambridge, MA: Harvard University Press, 1977.

———. *The Mismeasure of Man.* Rev. ed. New York: W.W. Norton, 1996 [1981].

———. "Evolution and the Triumph of Homology, or Why History Matters." *American Scientist* 74 (February 1986): 60–69.

———. *Time's Arrow, Time's Cycle: Myth and Metaphor in the Discovery of Geological Time.* Cambridge, MA: Harvard University Press, 1987.

———. *Wonderful Life: The Burgess Shale and the Nature of History.* New York: W.W. Norton, 1989.

———. "If Kings Can Be Hermits, Then We Are All Monkeys' Uncles." In *Dinosaur in a Haystack: Reflections in Natural History,* pp. 388–400. New York: Harmony Books, 1995.

Grant, Madison. *The Passing of the Great Race, or the Racial Basis of European History.* New York: Charles Scribner's Sons, 1918 [1916].

Grayson, Donald K. *The Establishment of Human Antiquity.* New York: Academic Press, 1983.

Greely, Henry T. "Genetic Genealogy: Genetics Meets the Marketplace." In *Revisiting Race in a Genomic Age,* edited by Barbara A. Koenig, et al., pp. 215–34. New Brunswick, NJ: Rutgers University Press, 2008.

Green, Richard E., et al. "A Draft Sequence of the Neandertal Genome." *Science* 328 (May 7, 2010): 710–22.

Greene, John C. *The Death of Adam: Evolution and Its Impact on Western Thought.* Ames: Iowa State University Press, 1959.

Gribbin, John. "Human vs. Gorilla: The 1% Advantage." *Science Digest* 90 (August 1982): 73–77.

Gribbin, John, and Jeremy Cherfas. *The Monkey Puzzle: Reshaping the Evolutionary Tree.* New York: Pantheon, 1982.

———. *The First Chimpanzee: In Search of Human Origins.* London: Penguin, 2001.

Gricar, Julie M. "How Thick Is Blood? The Social Construction and Cultural Configuration of Kinship." PhD diss., Columbia University, New York, 1991.

Groves, Colin P. *A Theory of Human and Primate Evolution.* Oxford: Oxford University Press, 1989.

Gruber, Jacob W. "Brixham Cave and the Antiquity of Man." In *Context and Meaning in Cultural Anthropology,* edited by Melford E. Spiro, pp. 373–402. New York: Free Press, 1965.

Guare, John. *Six Degrees of Separation.* New York: Random House, 1990.

Gyekye, Kwame. *Tradition and Modernity: Philosophical Reflections on the African Experience.* New York: Oxford University Press, 1997.

Hackstaff, Karla B. "Who Are We? Genealogists Negotiating Ethno-Racial Identities." *Qualitative Sociology* 32 (2009): 173–94.

Haeckel, Ernst. *Anthropogenie oder Entwickelungsgeschichte des Menschen*. Leipzig: Wilhelm Engelmann, 1874.

———. *The Evolution of Man: A Popular Exposition of the Principal Points of Human Ontogeny and Phylogeny*. New York: D. Appleton, 1879 [1874].

———. *The History of Creation: On the Development of the Earth and Its Inhabitants by the Action of Natural Causes*. New York: D. Appleton, 1876.

———. *Last Words on Evolution: A Popular Retrospect and Summary*. New York: Peter Eckler, 1905.

Haley, Alex. *The Autobiography of Malcolm X*. New York: Ballantine, 1999 [1964].

———. *Roots*. Garden City, NY: Doubleday, 1976.

Halpin, Zuleyma T. "Kin Recognition Cues of Vertebrates." In *Kin Recognition*, edited by Peter G. Hepper, pp. 220–58. Cambridge, UK: Cambridge University Press, 1991.

Hamilton, Jennifer A. "The Case of the Genetic Ancestor: DNA Ancestry Testing, Legal Subjectivity and Race in America." Paper presented at the DNA, Race, and History Conference, Rutgers University, New Brunswick, NJ, April 2008.

Hammer, Michael F. "A Recent Common Ancestry for Human Y Chromosomes." *Nature* 378 (1995): 376–78.

Hammond, Michael. "The Expulsion of the Neanderthals from Human Ancestry: Marcellin Boule and the Social Context of Scientific Research." *Social Studies of Science* 12 (1982): 1–36.

Haney López, Ian. *White by Law: The Legal Construction of Race*. Rev. ed. New York: New York University Press, 2006.

Hareven, Tamara K. "The Search for Generational Memory: Tribal Rites in Industrial Society." *Daedalus* 107 (Fall 1978): 137–49.

Harmon, Marcel J., et al. "Reconstructing the Flow of Information across Time and Space: A Phylogenetic Analysis of Ceramic Traditions from Prehispanic Western and Northern Mexico and the American Southwest." In *Mapping Our Ancestors: Phylogenetic Approaches in Anthropology and Prehistory*, edited by Carl P. Lipo, et al., pp. 209–29. New Brunswick, NJ: AldineTransaction, 2006.

Harris, Marvin. *Patterns of Race in the Americas*. Westport, CT: Greenwood, 1980 [1964].

Hayes, Christine E. *Gentile Impurities and Jewish Identities: Intermarriage and Conversion from the Bible to the Talmud*. New York: Oxford University Press, 2002.

Henderson, Mark. "DNA Swap Could Cure Inherited Diseases." http://www.timesonline.co.uk/tol/news/science/article6811080.ece.

Henige, David P. *The Chronology of Oral Tradition: Quest for a Chimera*. Oxford: Clarendon Press, 1974.

Hennig, Willi. *Phylogenetic Systematics*. Urbana: University of Illinois Press, 1999 [1966].

Hepper, Peter G. (ed.). *Kin Recognition*. Cambridge, UK: Cambridge University Press, 1991.

Hervieu-Léger, Danièle. *Religion as a Chain of Memory.* New Brunswick, NJ: Rutgers University Press, 2000 [1993].

Heuer, Jennifer. "The One-Drop Rule in Reverse? Interracial Marriages in Napoleonic and Restoration France." *Law and History Review* 27 (2009): 515–48.

Ho, Engseng. *The Graves of Tarim: Genealogy and Mobility Across the Indian Ocean.* Berkeley: University of California Press, 2006.

Hochschild, Jennifer L., and Brenna M. Powell. "United States Census 1850–1930: Mulattoes, Half-Breeds, Mixed Parentage, Hindoos, and the Mexican Race." *Studies in American Political Development* 22 (2008): 59–96.

Hollinger, David A. *Postethnic America: Beyond Multiculturalism.* New York: Basic Books, 1995.

———. "National Culture and Communities of Descent." *Reviews in American History* 26 (1998): 312–28.

———. "Amalgamation and Hypodescent: The Question of Ethnoracial Mixture in the History of the United States." *American Historical Review* 108 (2003): 1363–90.

Hornblower, Margot, et al. "Roots Mania." *Time,* April 19, 1999, pp. 54–67.

Howe, Stephen. *Afrocentrism: Mythical Pasts and Imagined Homes.* London: Verso, 1998.

Howell, Signe. "Self-Conscious Kinship: Some Contested Values in Norwegian Transnational Adoption." In *Relative Values: Reconfiguring Kinship Studies,* edited by Sarah Franklin and Susan McKinnon, pp. 203–23. Durham, NC: Duke University Press, 2001.

———. "Kinning: The Creation of Life Trajectories in Transnational Adoptive Families." *Journal of the Royal Anthropological Institute* 9 (2003): 465–84.

———. *The Kinning of Foreigners: Transnational Adoption in a Global Perspective.* New York: Berghahn Books, 2006.

Howells, William W. "Explaining Modern Man: Evolutionists versus Migrationists." *Journal of Human Evolution* 5 (1976): 477–95.

Hurston, Zora N. *Dust Tracks on a Road: An Autobiography.* 2nd ed. Urbana: University of Illinois Press, 1984 [1942].

Huxley, Julian. "The Three Types of Evolutionary Process." *Nature* 180 (1957): 454–55.

Huxley, Thomas H. *Evidence as to Man's Place in Nature.* Ann Arbor: University of Michigan Press, 2003 [1863].

Ibn Ishaq, Muhammad. *The Life of Muhammad.* New York: Oxford University Press, 1997 [eighth century].

Ichijo, Atsuko, and Gordana Uzelac (eds.). *When Is the Nation? Towards an Understanding of Theories of Nationalism.* Abingdon, UK: Routledge, 2005.

Ignatieff, Michael. *Blood and Belonging: Journeys into the New Nationalism.* New York: Farrar, Straus, and Giroux, 1994 [1993].

Ingold, Tim. *The Perception of the Environment: Essays on Livelihood, Dwelling, and Skill.* London: Routledge, 2000.

———. *Lines: A Brief History*. London: Routledge, 2007.

"Initial Sequence of the Chimpanzee Genome and Comparison with the Human Genome." *Nature* 437 (September 1, 2005): 69–87.

Iossifides, A. Marina. "Sisters in Christ: Metaphors of Kinship among Greek Nuns." In *Contested Identities: Gender and Kinship in Modern Greece,* edited by Peter Loizos and Evthymios Papataxiarchis, pp. 135–55. Princeton, NJ: Princeton University Press, 1991.

Jaisson, Pierre. "Kinship and Fellowship in Ants and Social Wasps." In *Kin Recognition,* edited by Peter G. Hepper, pp. 60–93. Cambridge, UK: Cambridge University Press, 1991.

Jay, Nancy. *Throughout Your Generations Forever: Sacrifice, Religion, and Paternity.* Chicago: University of Chicago Press, 1992.

Johanson, Donald, and Blake Edgar. *From Lucy to Language.* New York: Simon and Schuster, 1996.

Johnson, Marshall D. *The Purpose of the Biblical Genealogies with Special Reference to the Setting of the Genealogies of Jesus.* London: Cambridge University Press, 1969.

Jones, Floyd N. *The Chronology of the Old Testament.* 16th ed. Green Forest, AR: Master Books, 2005.

Jordan, Peter, and Thomas Mace. "Tracking Culture-Historical Lineages: Can 'Descent with Modification' Be Linked to 'Association by Descent'?" In *Mapping Our Ancestors: Phylogenetic Approaches in Anthropology and Prehistory,* edited by Carl P. Lipo, et al., pp. 149–67. New Brunswick, NJ: AldineTransaction, 2006.

Jordan, Winthrop D. *White over Black: American Attitudes toward the Negro, 1550–1812.* New York: W.W. Norton, 1977.

Journey of Man. PBS Home Video, 2003.

Jukes, Thomas H. "Random Walking." *Journal of Molecular Evolution* 34 (1992): 469–70.

Kahn, Susan M. *Reproducing Jews: A Cultural Account of Assisted Conception in Israel.* Durham, NC: Duke University Press, 2000.

Kallen, Horace M. "Democracy versus the Melting-Pot: A Study of American Nationality." *The Nation,* February 25, 1915. http://www.expo98.msu.edu/people/Kallen.htm.

Kaufman, Michael T. "Two Distinct Peoples with Two Divergent Memories Battle over One Land." *New York Times,* April 4, 1999, International Section, p.10.

Kendall, Henry. *The Kinship of Men: An Argument from Pedigrees, or Genealogy Viewed as a Science.* Boston: Cupples and Hurd, 1888.

Kevles, Daniel J. *In the Name of Eugenics: Genetics and the Uses of Human Heredity.* Cambridge, MA: Harvard University Press, 1995 [1985].

Keyes, Charles E. "Towards a New Formulation of the Concept of Ethnic Group." *Ethnicity* 3 (1976): 202–13.

Khan, Aisha. *Callaloo Nation: Metaphors of Race and Religious Identity among South Asians in Trinidad.* Durham, NC: Duke University Press, 2004.

King, Marie-Claire, and Allan C. Wilson. "Our Close Cousin, the Chimpanzee." *New Scientist* 67 (July 3, 1975): 16–18.

Klaatsch, Hermann. *The Evolution and Progress of Mankind.* New York: Frederick A. Stokes, 1923.

Klapisch-Zuber, Christiane. "The Genesis of the Family Tree." In *I Tatti Studies: Essays in the Renaissance,* Vol. 4, pp. 105–29. Florence, Italy: Villa I Tatti, 1991.

Klein, Richard G. *The Human Career: Human Biological and Cultural Origins.* 2nd ed. Chicago: University of Chicago Press, 1999.

Koerner, Konrad. "On Schleicher and Trees." In *Biological Metaphor and Cladistic Classification: An Interdisciplinary Perspective,* edited by Henry M. Hoenigswald and Linda F. Wiener, pp. 109–13. Philadelphia: University of Pennsylvania Press, 1987.

Kolber, Adam. "Fractional Parents." http://kolber.typepad.com/ethics_law_blog/2009/09/fractional-parents.html.

Kühl, Stefan. *The Nazi Connection: Eugenics, American Racism, and German National Socialism.* New York: Oxford University Press, 1994.

Kwon, Hannah. "'I'm So Glad Our Children Come from the Same Background': The Genealogical Construction of an 'Inter'-Marriage." Unpublished paper, Rutgers University, New Brunswick, NJ, 2009.

Lamarck, Jean-Baptiste. *Zoological Philosophy: An Exposition with Regard to the Natural History of Animals.* New York: Hafner, 1963 [1809].

Lambert, Ronald D. "Reclaiming the Ancestral Past: Narrative, Rhetoric, and the 'Convict Stain.'" *Journal of Sociology* 38 (2002): 111–27.

Lawrence, Cecile A. "Racelessness." In *American Mixed Race: The Culture of Microdiversity,* edited by Naomi Zack, pp. 25–37. Lanham, MD: Rowman & Littlefield, 1995.

Leach, Edmund. "On Certain Unconsidered Aspects of Double Descent Systems." *Man* 62 (1962): 130–34.

Lee, Catherine. "'Race' and 'Ethnicity' in Biomedical Research: How Do Scientists Construct and Explain Differences in Health?" *Social Science and Medicine* 30 (2009): 1–8.

Lefaucheur, Nadine. "Fatherless Children and Accouchement Sous X, From Marriage to Demarriage: A Paradigmatic Approach." *Journal of Family History* 28 (2003): 161–81.

Lennon, Joseph. *Irish Orientalism: A Literary and Intellectual History.* Syracuse, NY: Syracuse University Press, 2004.

Levine, Donald N. *Greater Ethiopia: The Evolution of a Multiethnic Society.* Chicago: University of Chicago Press, 2000 [1974].

———. *Visions of the Sociological Tradition.* Chicago: University of Chicago Press, 1995.

Lévi-Strauss, Claude. *The Elementary Structures of Kinship.* Boston: Beacon, 1969 [1949].

Levner, Israel B. *Kol Agadot Yisrael.* Tel-Aviv: Achiasaf, 1982 [1902]. [In Hebrew.]

Lewin, Roger, and Robert A. Foley. *Principles of Human Evolution.* 2nd ed. Malden, MA: Blackwell, 2004.

Lewis, Bernard. *History: Remembered, Recovered, Invented.* Princeton, NJ: Princeton University Press, 1975.

Lewontin, Richard. *Human Diversity.* New York: Scientific American Books, 1982.

Li, Jun Z., et al. "Worldwide Human Relationships Inferred from Genome-Wide Patterns of Variation." *Science* 319 (2008): 1100–04.

Lieberson, Stanley, and Mary C. Waters. *From Many Strands: Ethnic and Racial Groups in Contemporary America.* New York: Russell Sage Foundation, 1988.

Lifton, Betty J. *Journey of the Adopted Self: A Quest for Wholeness.* New York: Basic Books, 1994.

Linke, Uli. *Blood and Nation: The European Aesthetics of Race.* Philadelphia: University of Pennsylvania Press, 1999.

Livingstone, David N. *Adam's Ancestors: Race, Religion, and the Politics of Human Origins.* Baltimore: Johns Hopkins University Press, 2008.

Lovejoy, Arthur O. *The Great Chain of Being: A Study of the History of an Idea.* Cambridge, MA: Harvard University Press, 1936.

Loveman, Mara. "Is 'Race' Essential?" *American Sociological Review* 64 (1999): 891–98.

Loveman, Mara, and Jeronimo O. Muniz. "How Puerto Rico Became White: Boundary Dynamics and Intercensus Racial Reclassification." *American Sociological Review* 72 (2007): 915–39.

Lowenstein, Jerold, and Adrienne Zihlman. "The Invisible Ape." *New Scientist,* December 3, 1988, pp. 56–59.

Lowenthal, David. *Possessed by the Past: The Heritage Crusade and the Spoils of History.* New York: Free Press, 1996.

Lugris, Jennifer. "The Organization and Social Role of Family Trees in Greek Organizations." Unpublished paper, Rutgers University, New Brunswick, NJ, 2007.

Lyell, Charles. *Geological Evidences of the Antiquity of Man.* London: John Murray, 1863.

Lyman, R. Lee, and Michael J. O'Brien. "Seriation and Cladistics: The Difference between Anagenetic and Cladogenetic Evolution." In *Mapping Our Ancestors: Phylogenetic Approaches in Anthropology and Prehistory,* edited by Carl P. Lipo, et al., pp. 65–88. New Brunswick, NJ: AldineTransaction, 2006.

MacDonald, Neil. "Alexander's 'Descendants' Boost Macedonian Identity." http://www.ft.com/cms/s/0/11034b1e-54ef-11dd-ae9c-000077b07658.html.

Malcolm, Noel. *Kosovo: A Short History.* Updated ed. New York: HarperPerennial, 1999.

Malkki, Liisa H. "National Geographic: The Rooting of Peoples and the Territorialization of National Identity Among Scholars and Refugees." *Cultural Anthropology* 7 (1992): 24–44.

———. *Purity and Exile: Violence, Memory, and National Cosmology among Hutu Refugees in Tanzania.* Chicago: University of Chicago Press, 1995.

Mangum, Charles S. *The Legal Status of the Negro*. Chapel Hill: University of North Carolina Press, 1940.

Mann, Alan, and Mark Weiss. "Hominoid Phylogeny and Taxonomy: A Consideration of the Molecular and Fossil Evidence in an Historical Perspective." *Molecular Phylogenetics and Evolution* 5 (1996): 169–81.

Marcson, Simon. "A Theory of Intermarriage and Assimilation." *Social Forces* 29 (1950–51): 75–78.

Marks, Jonathan. "'We're Going to Tell These People Who They Really Are': Science and Relatedness." In *Relative Values: Reconfiguring Kinship Studies*, edited by Sarah Franklin and Susan McKinnon, pp. 355–83. Durham, NC: Duke University Press, 2001.

———. *What It Means to Be 98% Chimpanzee: Apes, People, and Their Genes*. Berkeley: University of California Press, 2002.

———. "Race: Past, Present, and Future." In *Revisiting Race in a Genomic Age*, edited by Barbara A. Koenig, et al., pp. 21–38. New Brunswick, NJ: Rutgers University Press, 2008.

Martin, John L. *Social Structures*. Princeton, NJ: Princeton University Press, 2009.

Martínez, María E. *Genealogical Fictions: Limpieza de Sangre, Religion, and Gender in Colonial Mexico*. Stanford, CA: Stanford University Press, 2008.

Mason, Jennifer. "Tangible Affinities and the Real Life Fascination of Kinship." *Sociology* 42 (2008): 29–45.

Mayr, Ernst. *The Growth of Biological Thought: Diversity, Evolution, and Inheritance*. Cambridge, MA: Harvard University Press, 1982.

———. "Darwin's Five Theories of Evolution." In *The Darwinian Heritage*, edited by David Kohn, pp. 755–72. Princeton, NJ: Princeton University Press, 1985.

McCown, Theodore D., and Kenneth A. R. Kennedy (eds.). *Climbing Man's Family Tree: A Collection of Major Writings on Human Phylogeny, 1699 to 1971*. Englewood Cliffs, NJ: Prentice-Hall, 1972.

McGoldrick, Monica, et al. *Genograms: Assessment and Intervention*. 2nd ed. New York: W.W. Norton, 1999.

Mead, Margaret. *Sex and Temperament in Three Primitive Societies*. New York: William Morrow, 1935.

Mellor, Doreen, and Anna Haebich (eds.). *Many Voices: Reflections on Experiences of Indigenous Child Separation*. Canberra, Australia: National Library of Australia, 2002.

Meyer, Melissa L. *Thicker Than Water: The Origins of Blood as Symbol and Ritual*. New York: Routledge, 2005.

Milgram, Stanley. "The Small World Problem." In *The Individual in a Social World: Essays and Experiments*, 2nd ed., pp. 259–75. New York: McGraw-Hill, 1992 [1967].

Modell, Judith S. *Kinship with Strangers: Adoption and Interpretations of Kinship in American Culture*. Berkeley: University of California Press, 1994.

Moretti, Franco. *Graphs, Maps, Trees: Abstract Models for a Literary History.* London: Verso, 2005.

Morgan, Gregory J. "Emile Zuckerkandl, Linus Pauling, and the Molecular Evolutionary Clock, 1959–1965." *Journal of the History of Biology* 31 (1998): 155–78.

Morgan, Lewis H. *Systems of Consanguinity and Affinity of the Human Family.* Lincoln: University of Nebraska Press, 1997 [1871].

Mörner, Magnus. *Race Mixture in the History of Latin America.* Boston: Little, Brown, & Co., 1967.

Morris, Desmond. *The Naked Ape.* New York: McGraw-Hill, 1967.

Mountain, David C., and Jeanne K. Guelke. "Genetics, Genealogy, and Geography." In *Geography and Genealogy: Locating Personal Pasts,* edited by Dallen J. Timothy and Jeanne K. Guelke, pp. 153–73. Aldershot, UK: Ashgate, 2008.

Mullaney, Jamie L. "Making It 'Count': Mental Weighing and Identity Attribution." *Symbolic Interaction* 22 (1999): 269–83.

Munasinghe, Viranjini. *Callaloo or Tossed Salad? East Indians and the Cultural Politics of Identity in Trinidad.* Ithaca, NY: Cornell University Press, 2001.

Murchie, Guy. *The Seven Mysteries of Life: An Exploration in Science and Philosophy.* New York: Mariner Books, 1999 [1978].

Murdock, George P. *Social Structure.* New York: Macmillan, 1949.

———. "Cognatic Forms of Social Organization." In *Kinship and Social Organization,* edited by Paul Bohannan and John Middleton, pp. 236–53. Garden City, NY: American Museum of Natural History, 1968 [1960].

Murray, Pauli. *States' Laws on Race and Color.* Cincinnati, OH: Woman's Division of Christian Service, 1950.

Nagel, Joane. "Constructing Ethnicity: Creating and Recreating Ethnic Identity and Culture." *Social Problems* 41 (1994): 152–76.

Nakashima, Cynthia L. "An Invisible Monster: The Creation and Denial of Mixed-Race People in America." In *Racially Mixed People in America,* edited by Maria P. P. Root, pp. 162–78. Newbury Park, CA: SAGE, 1992.

Nash, Catherine. "Genealogical Identities." *Environment and Planning D: Society and Space* 20 (2002): 27–52.

———. "'They're Family!': Cultural Geographies of Relatedness in Popular Genealogy." In *Uprootings/Regroundings: Questions of Home and Migration,* edited by Sara Ahmed, et al., pp. 179–203. Oxford: Berg, 2003.

———. "Genetic Kinship." *Cultural Studies* 18, no. 1 (2004): 1–33.

———. "Mapping Origins: Race and Relatedness in Population Genetics and Genetic Genealogy." In *New Genetics, New Identities,* edited by Paul Atkinson, et al., pp. 77–100. London: Routledge, 2007.

———. *Of Irish Descent: Origin Stories, Genealogy, and the Politics of Belonging.* Syracuse, NY: Syracuse University Press, 2008.

Navarro, Mireya. "Who Are We? New Dialogue on Mixed Race." *New York Times,* March 31, 2008, pp. A1, 15.

Nelkin, Dorothy, and Susan Lindee. *The DNA Mystique: The Gene as a Cultural Icon.* New York: W.H. Freeman, 1995.

Nelson, Alondra. "Bio Science: Genetic Genealogy Testing and the Pursuit of African Ancestry." *Social Studies of Science* 38 (2008): 759–83.

———. "The Factness of Diaspora: The Social Sources of Genetic Genealogy." In *Revisiting Race in a Genomic Age,* edited by Barbara A. Koenig, et al., pp. 253–68. New Brunswick, NJ: Rutgers University Press, 2008.

Neville, Gwen K. *Kinship and Pilgrimage: Rituals of Reunion in American Protestant Culture.* New York: Oxford University Press, 1987.

Nolland, John. "Jechoniah and His Brothers (Matthew 1:11)." *Bulletin for Biblical Research* 7 (1997): 169–78.

Novak, Michael. *Unmeltable Ethnics: Politics and Culture in American Life.* New Brunswick, NJ: Transaction, 1996 [1972].

Nugent, Colleen. "Children's Surnames, Moral Dilemmas: Accounting for the Predominance of Fathers' Surnames for Children." *Gender and Society* 24 (2010): 499–525.

Nuttall, George H. *Blood Immunity and Blood Relationship: A Demonstration of Certain Blood-Relationships amongst Animals by Means of the Precipitin Test for Blood.* Cambridge, UK: Cambridge University Press, 1904.

O'Hara, Robert J. "Telling the Tree: Narrative Representation and the Study of Evolutionary History." *Biology and Philosophy* 7 (1992): 135–60.

Olson, Steve. *Mapping Human History: Discovering the Past through Our Genes.* Boston: Houghton Mifflin, 2002.

Oppenheimer, Jane M. "Haeckel's Variations on Darwin." In *Biological Metaphor and Cladistic Classification: An Interdisciplinary Perspective,* edited by Henry M. Hoenigswald and Linda F. Wiener, pp. 123–35. Philadelphia: University of Pennsylvania Press, 1987.

Owusu-Bempah, Kwame. *Children and Separation: Socio-Genealogical Connectedness Perspective.* London: Routledge, 2007.

Padawer, Ruth. "Losing Fatherhood." *New York Times Magazine,* November 22, 2009, pp. 38–62.

Palmer, Craig T., and Lyle B. Steadman. "Human Kinship as a Descendant-Leaving Strategy: A Solution to an Evolutionary Puzzle." *Journal of Social and Evolutionary Systems* 20 (1997): 39–51.

Pálsson, Gísli. "The Life of Family Trees and the Book of Icelanders." *Medical Anthropology* 21 (2002): 337–67.

Pande, Amrita. "'It May Be Her Eggs But It's My Blood': Surrogates and Everyday Forms of Kinship in India." *Qualitative Sociology* 32 (2009): 379–97.

Park, Robert E. "The Nature of Race Relations." In *Race and Culture: Essays in the Sociology of Contemporary Man,* pp. 81–116. Glencoe, IL: Free Press, 1950 [1939].

Park, Robert E., and Ernest W. Burgess. *Introduction to the Science of Sociology.* Abridged ed. Chicago: University of Chicago Press, 1969 [1921].

Parkes, Peter. "Fosterage, Kinship, and Legend: When Milk Was Thicker Than Blood?" *Comparative Studies in Society and History* 46 (2004): 587–615.

———. "Milk Kinship in Islam: Substance, Structure, History." *Social Anthropology* 13 (2005): 307–29.

Patterson, Orlando. *The Ordeal of Integration: Progress and Resentment in America's "Racial" Crisis.* New York: Basic Civitas, 1997.

Percival, W. Keith. "Biological Analogy in the Study of Language before the Advent of Comparative Grammar." In *Biological Metaphor and Cladistic Classification: An Interdisciplinary Perspective,* edited by Henry M. Hoenigswald and Linda F. Wiener, pp. 3–38. Philadelphia: University of Pennsylvania Press, 1987.

Peters, Emrys. "The Proliferation of Segments in the Lineage of the Bedouin of Cyrenaica." *Journal of the Royal Anthropological Institute of Great Britain and Ireland* 90 (1960): 29–53.

Pinker, Steven. *How the Mind Works.* New York: W.W. Norton, 1997.

———. "Strangled by Roots: The Genealogy Craze in America." *New Republic,* August 6, 2007, pp. 32–35.

———. "My Genome, My Self." *New York Times Magazine,* January 11, 2009, pp. 24–50.

Platnick, Norman I., and H. Don Cameron. "Cladistic Methods in Textual, Linguistic, and Phylogenetic Analysis." *Systematic Zoology* 26 (1977): 380–85.

Polacco, Patricia. *Pink and Say.* New York: Philomel Books, 1994.

Poliakov, Léon. *The Aryan Myth: A History of Racist and Nationalistic Ideas in Europe.* New York: Basic Books, 1974.

Pool, Ithiel de Sola, and Manfred Kochen. "Contacts and Influence." In *The Small World,* edited by Manfred Kochen, pp. 3–51. Norwood, NJ: Ablex, 1989 [1978].

Popkin, Richard H. "The Pre-Adamite Theory in the Renaissance." In *Philosophy and Humanism: Renaissance Essays in Honor of Paul Oskar Kristeller,* edited by Edward P. Mahoney, pp. 50–69. New York: Columbia University Press, 1976.

Preece, Jennifer Jackson. *Minority Rights: Between Diversity and Community.* Cambridge, UK: Polity Press, 2005.

Pringle, Heather. *The Master Plan: Himmler's Scholars and the Holocaust.* New York: Hyperion, 2006.

Quinn, Judy. "From Orality to Literacy in Medieval Iceland." In *Old Icelandic Literature and Society,* edited by Margaret Clunies Ross, pp. 30–60. Cambridge, UK: Cambridge University Press, 2000.

Radcliffe-Brown, Alfred R. "Patrilineal and Matrilineal Succession." In *Structure and Function in Primitive Society,* pp. 32–48. New York: Free Press, 1965 [1935].

———. "The Study of Kinship Systems." In *Structure and Function in Primitive Society,* pp. 49–89. New York: Free Press, 1965 [1941].

Ragoné, Helena. "Surrogate Motherhood and American Kinship." In *Kinship and Family: An Anthropological Reader,* edited by Robert Parkin and Linda Stone, pp. 342–61. Malden, MA: Blackwell, 2004 [1994].

Rash, Felicity J. *The Language of Violence: Adolph Hitler's Mein Kampf.* New York: Peter Lang, 2006.

Read, Dwight W. "What Is Kinship?" In *The Cultural Analysis of Kinship: The Legacy of David M. Schneider,* edited by Richard Feinberg and Martin Ottenheimer, pp. 78–117. Urbana: University of Illinois Press, 2001.

Read, Peter. "The Stolen Generations: The Removal of Aboriginal Children in New South Wales 1883 to 1969." http://www.daa.nsw.gov.au/publications/Stolen-Generations.pdf.

Reed, Ishmael. "America's 'Black Only' Ethnicity." In *The Invention of Ethnicity,* edited by Werner Sollors, pp. 226–29. New York: Oxford University Press, 1989.

Relethford, John H. *Reflections of Our Past: How Human History Is Revealed in Our Genes.* Boulder, CO: Westview Press, 2003.

Renfrew, Colin. *Archaeology and Language: The Puzzle of Indo-European Origins.* New York: Cambridge University Press, 1987.

Richards, Robert J. *The Meaning of Evolution: The Morphological Construction and Ideological Reconstruction of Darwin's Theory.* Chicago: University of Chicago Press, 1992.

Ridley, Mark. *Evolution and Classification: The Reformation of Cladism.* London: Longman, 1986.

———. "The Search for LUCA." *Natural History* 109, no. 9 (November 2000): 82–85.

Ritvo, Harriet. "Border Trouble: Shifting the Line between People and Other Animals." *Social Research* 62 (1995): 481–500.

Robertson, Wyndham, and R. A. Brock. *Pocahontas, Alias Matoaka, and Her Descendants through Her Marriage at Jamestown, Virginia, in April, 1614, with John Rolfe, Gentleman.* Richmond, VA: J.W. Randolph & English, 1887.

Rogers, Alan R., and Lynn B. Jorde. "Genetic Evidence on Modern Human Origins." *Human Biology* 67 (1995): 1–36.

Rosenberg, Daniel, and Anthony Grafton. *Cartographies of Time: A History of the Timeline.* New York: Princeton Architectural Press, 2010.

Rosenblum, Doron. "Because Somebody Needs to Be an Israeli in Israel." *Ha'aretz,* April 29, 1998, Independence Day Supplement. [In Hebrew.]

Roth, Wendy D., and Biorn Ivemark. "'Not Everybody Knows That I'm Actually Black': The Effects of DNA Ancestry Testing on Racial and Ethnic Boundaries." Paper presented at the Annual Meeting of the American Sociological Association, Atlanta, 2010.

Rothman, Barbara K. *Recreating Motherhood.* New Brunswick, NJ: Rutgers University Press, 2000 [1989].

Rubinstein, Amnon. *To Be a Free People.* Tel-Aviv: Schocken, 1977. [In Hebrew.]

Rudoren, Jodi. "Meet Our New Name." http://www.nytimes.com/2006/02/05/fashion/sundaystyles/05NAME.html?_R=1

Ruvolo, Maryellen, et al. "Mitochondrial COII Sequences and Modern Human Origins." *Molecular Biology and Evolution* 10 (1993): 1115–35.

Sand, Shlomo. *When and How the Jewish People Was Invented?* Tel Aviv: Resling Publishing, 2008. [In Hebrew.]

Sants, H. J. "Genealogical Bewilderment in Children with Substitute Parents." *British Journal of Medical Psychology* 37 (1964): 133–41.

Sarich, Vincent. "Immunological Evidence on Primates." In *The Cambridge Encyclopedia of Human Evolution*, edited by Steve Jones, et al., pp. 303–06. Cambridge, UK: Cambridge University Press, 1992.

Sarich, Vincent, and Frank Miele. *Race: The Reality of Human Differences*. Boulder, CO: Westview Press, 2004.

Sarich, Vincent, and Allan C. Wilson. "Immunological Time Scale for Hominid Evolution." *Science* 158 (1967): 1200–03.

Satris, Stephen. "What Are They?" In *American Mixed Race: The Culture of Microdiversity*, edited by Naomi Zack, pp. 53–60. Lanham, MD: Rowman & Littlefield, 1995.

Schleicher, August. "Darwinism Tested by the Science of Language." In *Linguistics and Evolutionary Theory*, edited by Konrad Koerner, pp. 13–69. Amsterdam: John Benjamins, 1983 [1863].

Schleunes, Karl A. *The Twisted Road to Auschwitz: Nazi Policy Toward German Jews 1933–1939*. Urbana: University of Illinois Press, 1970.

Schmidt-Burkhardt, Astrit. *Stammbäume der Kunst: Zur Genealogie der Avantgarde*. Berlin: Akademie Verlag, 2005.

Schmitt, Raymond L. "Symbolic Immortality in Ordinary Contexts: Impediments to the Nuclear Era." *Omega* 13 (1982–83): 95–116.

Schneider, David M. *American Kinship: A Cultural Account*. Englewood Cliffs, NJ: Prentice-Hall, 1980.

———. *A Critique of the Study of Kinship*. Ann Arbor: University of Michigan Press, 1984.

Schneider, David M., and Calvert B. Cottrell. *The American Kin Universe: A Genealogical Study*. Chicago: University of Chicago Press, 1975.

Schusky, Ernest L. *Variation in Kinship*. New York: Holt, Rinehart, and Winston, 1974.

Schutz, Alfred, and Thomas Luckmann. *The Structures of the Life-World*. Evanston, IL: Northwestern University Press, 1973.

Seabrook, John. "The Tree of Me." In *Flash of Genius and Other True Stories of Invention*, pp. 111–37. New York: St. Martin's Griffin, 2008 [2001].

Segalen, Martine. "The Shift in Kinship Studies in France: The Case of Grandparenting." In *Relative Values: Reconfiguring Kinship Studies*, edited by Sarah Franklin and Susan McKinnon, pp. 246–73. Durham: NC: Duke University Press, 2001.

Seifert, Ruth. "The Second Front: The Logic of Sexual Violence in Wars." In *Violence and Its Alternatives: An Interdisciplinary Reader*, edited by Manfred B. Steger and Nancy S. Lind, pp. 145–53. New York: St. Martin's Press, 1999.

Shell, Marc. *The End of Kinship: "Measure for Measure," Incest, and the Ideal of Universal Siblinghood*. Baltimore: Johns Hopkins University Press, 1995 [1988].

Sherman, Stuart P. "Introduction." In *Essays and Poems of Emerson*, pp. vii–xlv. New York: Harcourt, Brace, & Co., 1921.

Shils, Edward. *Tradition*. Chicago: University of Chicago Press, 1981.

Shoumatoff, Alex. *The Mountain of Names: A History of the Human Family*. New York: Simon and Schuster, 1985.

Shriver, Mark D., and Rick A. Kittles. "Genetic Ancestry and the Search for Personalized Genetic Histories." *Nature Review: Genetics* 5 (2004): 611–18.

Shryock, Andrew. *Nationalism and the Genealogical Imagination: Oral History and Textual Authority in Tribal Jordan*. Berkeley: University of California Press, 1997.

Shulevitz, Judith. "Roots and Branches." *The Book: An Online Review at the New Republic*, April 2, 2010.

Simpson, Bob. "Bringing the 'Unclear' Family into Focus: Divorce and Re-Marriage in Contemporary Britain." *Man* 29 (1994): 831–51.

———. "Imagined Genetic Communities: Ethnicity and Essentialism in the Twenty-First Century." *Anthropology Today* 16, no. 3 (2000): 3–6.

Simpson, George G. *Principles of Animal Taxonomy*. New York: Columbia University Press, 1961.

Simpson, Ruth. "I Was There: Establishing Ownership of Historical Moments." Paper presented at the Annual Meeting of the American Sociological Association, Los Angeles, 1994.

Smail, Daniel L. *On Deep History and the Brain*. Berkeley: University of California Press, 2008.

Smith, Anthony D. "National Identity and Myths of Ethnic Descent." In *Myths and Memories of the Nation*, pp. 57–95. Oxford: Oxford University Press, 1999 [1984].

———. *The Ethnic Origins of Nations*. Oxford: Basil Blackwell, 1986.

———. *The Antiquity of Nations*. Cambridge, UK: Polity, 2004.

———. "The Genealogy of Nations: An Ethno-Symbolic Approach." In *When Is the Nation? Towards an Understanding of Theories of Nationalism*, edited by Atsuko Ichijo and Gordana Uzelac, pp. 94–112. Abingdon, UK: Routledge, 2005.

Smith, W. Robertson. *Kinship and Marriage in Early Arabia*. Cambridge, UK: Cambridge University Press, 1885.

Sollors, Werner. *Beyond Ethnicity: Consent and Descent in American Culture*. New York: Oxford University Press, 1986.

———. *Neither Black Nor White Yet Both: Thematic Explorations of Interracial Literature*. Cambridge, MA: Harvard University Press, 1997.

Sørensen, Preben M. "Social Institutions and Belief Systems of Medieval Iceland (c. 870–1400) and Their Relations to Literary Production." In *Old Icelandic Literature and Society*, edited by Margaret Clunies Ross, pp. 8–29. Cambridge, UK: Cambridge University Press, 2000.

Sorokin, Pitirim A. *Social and Cultural Dynamics,* Vol. 4: *Basic Problems, Principles, and Methods.* New York: Bedminster Press, 1941.

Spickard, Paul R. *Mixed Blood: Intermarriage and Ethnic Identity in Twentieth-Century America.* Madison: University of Wisconsin Press, 1989.

———. "The Illogic of American Racial Categories." In *Racially Mixed People in America,* edited by Maria P. P. Root, pp. 12–23. Newbury Park: CA: SAGE, 1992.

Spiegel, Gabrielle M. "Genealogy: Form and Function in Medieval Historical Narrative." *History and Theory* 22 (1983): 43–53.

Spillers, Hortense J. "Mama's Baby, Papa's Maybe: An American Grammar Book." *Diacritics* 17 (Summer 1987): 65–81.

Spruhan, Paul. "A Legal History of Blood Quantum in Federal Indian Law to 1935." *South Dakota Law Review* 51 (2006): 1–50.

Stack, Carol. *All Our Kin.* New York: Basic Books, 1974.

Stanton, William. *The Leopard's Spots: Scientific Attitudes Toward Race in America 1815–59.* Chicago: University of Chicago Press, 1960.

Steichen, Edward. *The Family of Man.* New York: Museum of Modern Art, 1955.

Stein, Arlene. "Trauma and Origins: Post-Holocaust Genealogists and the Work of Memory." *Qualitative Sociology* 32 (2009): 293–309.

Stepan, Nancy. *The Idea of Race in Science: Great Britain 1800–1960.* Hamden, CT: Archon Books, 1982.

Stephan, Cookie W. "Mixed-Heritage Individuals: Ethnic Identity and Trait Characteristics." In *Racially Mixed People in America,* edited by Maria P. P. Root, pp. 50–63. Newbury Park: CA: SAGE, 1992.

Stephenson, Gilbert T. *Race Distinctions in American Law.* New York: AMS Press, 1969 [1910].

Stocking, George W. "French Anthropology in 1800." In *Race, Culture, and Evolution: Essays in the History of Anthropology,* pp. 15–41. New York: Free Press, 1968 [1964].

———. "The Persistence of Polygenist Thought in Post-Darwinian Anthropology." In *Race, Culture, and Evolution: Essays in the History of Anthropology,* pp. 44–68. New York: Free Press, 1968.

Stoddard, Lothrop. *The Rising Tide of Color Against White World-Supremacy.* New York: Charles Scribner's Sons, 1921.

Strathern, Marilyn. *Kinship, Law, and the Unexpected: Relatives Are Always a Surprise.* Cambridge, UK: Cambridge University Press, 2005.

Streisand, Betsy. "Who's Your Daddy?" http://health.usnews.com/usnews/health/articles/060213/13donor.

Strickberger, Monroe W. *Evolution.* 3rd ed. Sudbury, MA: Jones & Bartlett, 2005.

Stringer, Christopher, and Robin McKie. *African Exodus: The Origins of Modern Humanity.* New York: Henry Holt, 1997 [1996].

Strong, Pauline T., and Barrik van Winkle. "'Indian Blood': Reflections on the Reckoning and Refiguring of Native North American Identity." *Cultural Anthropology* 11 (1996): 547–76.

Sturm, Circe. *Blood Politics: Race, Culture, and Identity in the Cherokee Nation of Oklahoma*. Berkeley: University of California Press, 2002.

Suarez, Tirso. "Hugo Chavez and Montezuma." http://vcrisis.com/index.php?content=letters/200605180840.

Swadesh, Morris. "What Is Glottochronology?" In *The Origin and Diversification of Language*, pp. 271–84. Chicago: Aldine, 1971 [1960].

Swedenburg, Ted. *Memories of Revolt: The 1936–1939 Rebellion and the Palestinian National Past*. Minneapolis: University of Minnesota Press, 1995.

Sweet, Frank W. *Legal History of the Color Line: The Rise and Triumph of the One-Drop Rule*. Palm Coast, FL: Backintyme, 2005.

Sykes, Bryan. *The Seven Daughters of Eve: The Science That Reveals Our Genetic Ancestry*. London: W.W. Norton, 2001.

———. *Saxons, Vikings, and Celts: The Genetic Roots of Britain and Ireland*. New York: W.W. Norton, 2006.

Tartakoff, Paola. "Jewish Women and Apostasy in the Medieval Crown of Aragon, c. 1300–1391." *Jewish History* 24 (2010): 7–32.

Tattersall, Ian. *The Fossil Trail: How We Know What We Think We Know about Human Evolution*. New York: Oxford University Press, 1995.

———. "Once We Were Not Alone." *Scientific American* 282 (January 2000): 56–62.

Taylor, Rex. "John Doe, Jr.: A Study of His Distribution in Space, Time, and the Social Structure." *Social Forces* 53 (1974): 11–21.

Taylor, Robert M. "Summoning the Wandering Tribes: Genealogy and Family Reunions in American History." *Journal of Social History* 16 (Winter 1982): 21–37.

Taylor, Robert M., and Ralph J. Crandall. "Historians and Genealogists: An Emerging Community of Interest." In *Generations and Change: Genealogical Perspectives in Social History*, pp. 3–27. Macon, GA: Mercer University Press, 1986.

Tëmkin, Ilya, and Niles Eldredge. "Phylogenetics and Material Culture Evolution." *Current Anthropology* 48 (2007): 146–53.

Templeton, Alan R. "Out of Africa Again and Again." *Nature* 416 (March 7, 2002): 45–51.

Thomas, Northcote W. *Kinship Organisations and Group Marriage in Australia*. New York: Humanities Press, 1966 [1906].

Thompson, Charis. "Strategic Naturalizing: Kinship in an Infertility Clinic." In *Relative Values: Reconfiguring Kinship Studies*, edited by Sarah Franklin and Susan McKinnon, pp. 175–202. Durham, NC: Duke University Press, 2001.

———. *Making Parents: The Ontological Choreography of Reproductive Technologies*. Cambridge, MA: MIT Press, 2005.

Thorne, Alan G., and Milford H. Wolpoff. "Regional Continuity in Australasian Pleistocene Hominid Evolution." *American Journal of Physical Anthropology* 55 (1981): 337–49.

———. "The Multiregional Evolution of Humans." *Scientific American* 266 (April 1992): 76–83.

Timothy, Dallen J. "Genealogical Mobility: Tourism and the Search for a Personal Past." In *Geography and Genealogy: Locating Personal Pasts*, edited by Dallen J. Timothy and Jeanne K. Guelke, pp. 115–35. Aldershot, UK: Ashgate, 2008.

Tönnies, Ferdinand. *Community and Society*. New York: Harper Torchbooks, 1963 [1887].

Trautmann, Thomas R. "The Revolution in Ethnological Time." *Man* 27 (1992): 379–97.

Triseliotis, John. *In Search of Origins: The Experiences of Adopted People*. London: Routledge and Kegan Paul, 1973.

Tuniz, Claudio, et al. *The Bone Readers: Atoms, Genes, and the Politics of Australia's Deep Past*. Crows Nest, Australia: Allen & Unwin, 2009.

Turner, A. J., and A. Coyle. "What Does It Mean to Be a Donor Offspring? The Identity Experiences of Adults Conceived by Donor Insemination and the Implications for Counseling and Therapy." *Human Reproduction* 15 (2000): 2041–51.

Tutton, Richard. "'They Want to Know Where They Came from': Population Genetics, Identity, and Family Genealogy." *New Genetics and Society* 23 (2004): 105–20.

Twain, Mark. *Pudd'nhead Wilson*. Mineola, NY: Dover, 1999 [1894].

Twine, France W. *Racism in a Racial Democracy: The Maintenance of White Supremacy in Brazil*. New Brunswick, NJ: Rutgers University Press, 1998.

Tyler, Katharine. "The Genealogical Imagination: The Inheritance of Interracial Identities." *The Sociological Review* 53 (2005): 476–94.

Valentine, James W. *On the Origin of Phyla*. Chicago: University of Chicago Press, 2004.

van den Berghe, Pierre L. *Man in Society: A Biosocial View*. New York: Elsevier, 1975.

———. *The Ethnic Phenomenon*. Westport, CT: Praeger, 1987 [1981].

———. "Ethnies and Nations: Genealogy Indeed." In *When Is the Nation? Towards an Understanding of Theories of Nationalism*, edited by Atsuko Ichijo and Gordana Uzelac, pp. 113–18. Abingdon, UK: Routledge, 2005.

van Reenen, Pieter, and Margot van Mulken (eds.). *Studies in Stemmatology*. Amsterdam: John Benjamins Publishing Co., 1996.

van Wyhe, John. "The Descent of Words: Evolutionary Thinking 1780–1880." *Endeavour* 29 (September 2005): 94–100.

Verdery, Katherine. *National Ideology Under Socialism: Identity and Cultural Politics in Ceauşescu's Romania*. Berkeley: University of California Press, 1991.

———. *What Was Socialism, and What Comes Next?* Princeton, NJ: Princeton University Press, 1996.

———. *The Political Lives of Dead Bodies: Reburial and Postsocialist Change*. New York: Columbia University Press, 1999.

Vogt, Carl. *Lectures on Man: His Place in Creation and in the History of the Earth*. London: Longman, Green, Longman, and Roberts, 1864.

Vryonis, Speros Jr. *The Turkish State and History: Clio Meets the Grey Wolf.* Thessaloniki, Greece: Institute for Balkan Studies, 1991.

Wachter, Kenneth W. "Ancestors at the Norman Conquest." In *Genealogical Demography,* edited by Bennett Dyke and Warren T. Morrill, pp. 85–93. New York: Academic Press, 1980 [1978].

Wade, Nicholas. *Before the Dawn: Recovering the Lost History of Our Ancestors.* New York: Penguin, 2006.

Wade, Peter. "Hybridity Theory and Kinship Thinking." *Cultural Studies* 19 (2005): 602–21.

Wagner, Anthony. "Bridges to Antiquity." In *Pedigree and Progress: Essays in the Genealogical Interpretation of History,* pp. 50–75. London: Phillimore, 1975.

Waldinger, Roger, and Mehdi Bozorgmehr. "The Making of a Multicultural Metropolis." In *Ethnic Los Angeles,* pp. 3–37. New York: Russell Sage Foundation, 1996.

Waldman, Bruce. "Kin Recognition in Amphibians." In *Kin Recognition,* edited by Peter G. Hepper, pp. 162–219. Cambridge, UK: Cambridge University Press, 1991.

Warner, W. Lloyd. *The Living and the Dead: A Study of the Symbolic Life of Americans.* New Haven, CT: Yale University Press, 1959.

Washington, Booker T. *The Future of the American Negro.* Boston: Small, Maynard, and Co., 1900.

Waters, Mary C. *Ethnic Options: Choosing Identities in America.* Berkeley: University of California Press, 1990.

Watson, Arthur. *The Early Iconography of the Tree of Jesse.* London: Oxford University Press, 1934.

Watson, Elizabeth E., et al. "*Homo* Genus: A Review of the Classification of Humans and the Great Apes." In *Humanity from African Naissance to Coming Millennia: Colloquia in Human Biology and Paleoanthropology,* edited by Phillip V. Tobias, et al., pp. 307–18. Florence, Italy: Firenze University Press, 2001.

Watson, Julia. "Ordering the Family: Genealogy as Autobiographical Pedigree." In *Getting a Life: Everyday Uses of Autobiography,* edited by Sidonie Smith and Julia Watson, pp. 297–323. Minneapolis: University of Minnesota Press, 1996.

Weber, Max. *Economy and Society: An Outline of Interpretive Sociology.* Berkeley: University of California Press, 1978 [1925].

Weidenreich, Franz. "Facts and Speculations Concerning the Origin of *Homo sapiens.*" In *Climbing Man's Family Tree: A Collection of Major Writings on Human Phylogeny, 1699 to 1971,* edited by Theodore D. McCown and Kenneth A. R. Kennedy, pp. 336–53. Englewood Cliffs, NJ: Prentice-Hall, 1972 [1947].

Weinbaum, Alys E. *Wayward Reproductions: Genealogies of Race and Nation in Transatlantic Modern Thought.* Durham, NC: Duke University Press, 2004.

Weiss, Kenneth M., and Brian W. Lambert. "Does History Matter?" *Evolutionary Anthropology* 19 (2010): 92–97.

Weiss, Kenneth M., and Jeffrey C. Long. "Non-Darwinian Estimation: My Ancestors, My Genes' Ancestors." *Genome Research* 19 (2009): 703–10.

Wells, Rulon S. "The Life and Growth of Language: Metaphors in Biology and Linguistics." In *Biological Metaphor and Cladistic Classification: An Interdisciplinary Perspective*, edited by Henry M. Hoenigswald and Linda F. Wiener, pp. 39–80. Philadelphia: University of Pennsylvania Press, 1987.

Wells, Spencer. *The Journey of Man: A Genetic Odyssey*. Princeton, NJ: Princeton University Press, 2002.

——. *Deep Ancestry: Inside the Genographic Project*. Washington, DC: National Geographic, 2006.

Whaley, Diana. "A Useful Past: Historical Writing in Medieval Iceland." In *Old Icelandic Literature and Society*, edited by Margaret Clunies Ross, pp. 161–202. Cambridge, UK: Cambridge University Press, 2000.

Wildman, Derek E., et al. "Implications of Natural Selection in Shaping 99.4% Nonsynonymous DNA Identity between Humans and Chimpanzees: Enlarging Genus *Homo*." *Proceedings of the National Academy of Sciences of the United States of America* 100 (June 10, 2003): 7181–88.

Wilkins, David E. *American Indian Politics and the American Political System*. 2nd ed. Lanham, MD: Rowman & Littlefield, 2007.

Wilkins, Ernest H. "The Genealogy of the Genealogy Trees of the *Genealogia Deorum*." *Modern Philology* 23 (1925): 61–65.

Williams, Brackette F. "A Class Act: Anthropology and the Race to Nation Across Ethnic Terrain." *Annual Review of Anthropology* 18 (1989): 401–44.

Williams, Yaschica, and Janine Bower. "Media Images of Wartime Sexual Violence: Ethnic Cleansing in Rwanda and the Former Yugoslavia." In *Women, Violence, and the Media: Readings in Feminist Criminology*, edited by Drew Humphries, pp. 156–74. Lebanon, NH: University Press of New England, 2009.

Williamson, Joel. *New People: Miscegenation and Mulattoes in the United States*. New York: Free Press, 1980.

Wilson, Allan C., and Rebecca L. Cann. "The Recent African Genesis of Humans." *Scientific American* 266 (April 1992): 68–73.

Wilson, Robert R. *Genealogy and History in the Biblical World*. New Haven, CT: Yale University Press, 1977.

Wilson, Terry P. "Blood Quantum: Native American Mixed Bloods." In *Racially Mixed People in America*, edited by Maria P. P. Root, pp. 108–25. Newbury Park, CA: SAGE, 1992.

Wimmer, Andreas. "The Making and Unmaking of Ethnic Boundaries: A Multilevel Process Theory." *American Journal of Sociology* 113 (2008): 970–1022.

Winston, Cynthia, and Rick A. Kittles. "Psychological and Ethical Issues Related to Identity and Inferring Ancestry of African Americans." In *Biological Anthropology and Ethics: From Repatriation to Genetic Identity*, edited by Trudy R. Turner, pp. 209–30. Albany: State University of New York Press, 2005.

Wittek, Paul. *The Rise of the Ottoman Empire*. London: Royal Asiatic Society of Great Britain and Ireland, 1971 [1938].

Woese, Carl. "The Universal Ancestor." *Proceedings of the National Academy of Sciences of the United States of America* 95 (1998): 6854–59.

Wolfe, Patrick. "Land, Labor, and Difference: Elementary Structures of Race." *American Historical Review* 106 (2001): 866–905.

Wolpoff, Milford, and Rachel Caspari. *Race and Human Evolution*. Boulder, CO: Westview Press, 1997.

Wolpoff, Milford H., et al. "Modern Human Origins." *Science* 241 (1988): 772–73.

Wood, Bernard. *Human Evolution: A Very Short Introduction*. Oxford: Oxford University Press, 2005.

Wood, Bernard, and Mark Collard. "The Human Genus." *Science* 284 (April 2, 1999): 65–71.

Wood, Bernard, and Brian G. Richmond. "Human Evolution: Taxonomy and Paleobiology." *Journal of Anatomy* 196 (2000): 19–60.

Wrangham, Richard W. "Out of the Pan, Into the Fire: How Our Ancestors' Evolution Depended on What They Ate." In *Tree of Origin: What Primate Behavior Can Tell Us about Human Social Evolution*, edited by Frans B. M. de Waal, pp. 121–43. Cambridge, MA: Harvard University Press, 2001.

Zack, Naomi. *Race and Mixed Race*. Philadelphia: Temple University Press, 1993.

———. "Life After Race." In *American Mixed Race: The Culture of Microdiversity*, pp. 297–307. Lanham, MD: Rowman & Littlefield, 1995.

Zangwill, Israel. *The Melting-Pot*. New York: Macmillan, 1932 [1909].

Zerubavel, Eviatar. *The Seven-Day Circle: The History and Meaning of the Week*. Chicago: University of Chicago Press, 1989 [1985].

———. *The Fine Line: Making Distinctions in Everyday Life*. Chicago: University of Chicago Press, 1993 [1991].

———. "The Rigid, the Fuzzy, and the Flexible: Notes on the Mental Sculpting of Academic Identity." *Social Research* 62 (1995): 1093–1106.

———. "Lumping and Splitting: Notes on Social Classification." *Sociological Forum* 11 (1996): 421–33.

———. *Social Mindscapes: An Invitation to Cognitive Sociology*. Cambridge, MA: Harvard University Press, 1997.

———. *Time Maps: Collective Memory and the Social Shape of the Past*. Chicago: University of Chicago Press, 2003.

———. "The Social Marking of the Past: Toward a Socio-Semiotics of Memory." In *Matters of Culture: Cultural Sociology in Practice*, edited by Roger Friedland and John Mohr, pp. 184–95. Cambridge, UK: Cambridge University Press, 2004.

———. "Generally Speaking: The Logic and Mechanics of Social Pattern Analysis." *Sociological Forum* 22 (2007): 131–45.

Zerubavel, Yael. *Recovered Roots: Collective Memory and the Making of Israeli National Tradition*. Chicago: University of Chicago Press, 1995.

―――. "Trans-Historical Encounters in the Land of Israel: On Symbolic Bridges, National Memory, and the Literary Imagination," *Jewish Social Studies* 11 (2005): 115–35.

―――. "Antiquity and the Renewal Paradigm: Strategies of Representation and Mnemonic Practices in Israeli Culture." In *On Memory: An Interdisciplinary Approach*, edited by Doron Mendels, pp. 331–48. Bern, Switzerland: Peter Lang, 2007.

Zimmer, Carl. *Smithsonian Intimate Guide to Human Origins*. New York: HarperCollins, 2005.

AUTHOR INDEX

Abu El-Haj, Nadia, 160
Alba, Richard D., 149, 153, 174
Alford, Richard D., 139, 151, 174
Almog, Oz, 164
Almond, Philip, 172
Alter, Stephen G., 145, 147, 181
Anderson, Benedict, 138, 150, 153, 161
Angier, Natalie, 149
Appiah, Anthony, 155, 159
Atkinson, Quentin D., 138
Avise, John C., 148, 177
Ayala, Francisco J., 154
Ayoub, Millicent R., 158

Baker, Hugh, 20, 136, 139, 144, 162
Baker, Joshua M., 181
Bakhos, Carol, 170
Bamford, Sandra, 158
Barnes, J. A., 115, 141, 163, 179
Bassett, Mary T., 157
Basu, Paul, 135
Baum, David A., 168
Bauman, Zygmunt, 176
Beecher, Michael D., 144
Begley, Sharon, 143
Bennet, James, 166
Bentley, Nancy, 135

Berger, Peter L., 138
Bernstein, Irwin, 144
Bigelow, R. S., 147, 151
Black, Edwin, 153, 177
Blenkinsopp, Joseph, 164
Bloch, Maurice, 159
Bloch, R. Howard, 139, 140, 162, 164
Bohannan, Laura, 166
Bohannan, Paul, 158
Bolaffi, Guido, 176
Bolnick, Deborah A., 134
Bouquet, Mary, 143, 147
Bower, Janine, 177
Bowler, Peter J., 137, 142, 145, 146, 147, 168, 170, 171, 172
Bozorgmehr, Mehdi, 153
Bradley, Michael, 171
Brandt, Nat, 172
Braude, Benjamin, 171, 172
Brekhus, Wayne, 155, 156, 165
Breuil, Henri, 141, 142
Broberg, Gunnar, 166
Brock, R. A., 163
Brodwin, Paul, 159
Brubaker, Rogers, 150, 160
Brunwasser, Matthew, 161
Burgess, Ernest W., 182

Burkhardt, Richard W., 142
Burleigh, Michael, 175
Bury, J. B., 166

Cadoret, Anne, 178
Caldwell, Richard S., 133
Calhoun, Craig, 153
Cameron, H. Don, 181
Cann, Rebecca L., 148, 149
Cannings, C., 144, 152
Carpenter, R. Charli, 177
Carsten, Janet, 155, 179
Cartmill, Matt, 93, 147, 151, 169, 170, 176, 177
Caspari, Rachel, 143, 146, 151, 170, 172
Castronovo, Russ, 136
Cavalli-Sforza, Francesco, 138, 146, 148, 149, 170
Cavalli-Sforza, Luigi L., 138, 146, 148, 149, 170
Čepaitienė, Auksuolė, 174
Cerulo, Karen A., 138, 155
Cherfas, Jeremy, 167, 168, 169, 170, 179
Cherlin, Andrew J., 178
Clark, Stephen R. L., 177
Clarke, Morgan, 155
Clogg, Richard, 133
Coe, Kathryn, 138, 166
Cohen, Shaye J. D., 158
Collard, Mark, 143
Collins, Patricia H., 150, 153
Collins, Randall, 139, 180
Conniff, Richard, 157
Cooley, Charles H., 11, 137
Coon, Carleton S., 171
Corbett, Sara, 180
Corbey, Raymond, 142, 147, 167, 169, 170
Cose, Ellis, 53, 157
Cottrell, Calvert B., 144, 159, 162
Coyle, A., 136
Cracraft, Joel, 137, 146, 147
Crandall, Ralph J., 133, 163
Crèvecoeur, J. Hector St. John de, 108, 174
Cronon, E. David, 175

Daly, Martin, 156
Daniel, G. Reginald, 154, 165, 173
Dart, Raymond A., 169
Darwin, Charles, 137, 145, 147, 151, 168
Davenport, Charles, 174
Davis, F. James, 154, 165, 173, 176, 177
Dawkins, Richard, 49, 75, 139, 141, 145, 149, 151, 160, 161, 168, 169, 176, 177
Delaney, Carol, 150, 153, 155, 156
Deleuze, Gilles, 152
Diamond, Jared, 93, 148, 167, 169
Dolgin, Janet L., 179
Domínguez, Virginia R., 140, 154, 158, 173, 175
Dunbar, Robin I. M., 94, 169
Durkheim, Emile, 143
Duster, Troy, 160

Easteal, Simon, 168
Edgar, Blake, 140, 147, 149, 167, 168, 170
Edwards, Jeanette, 178
Ehrlich, Paul R., 167
Eldredge, Niles, 137, 146, 147, 180, 181
Elliott, Carl, 159
Elliott, Michael A., 154
Elon, Amos, 164
Emerson, Ralph W., 108, 174
Ereshefsky, Marc, 137, 146, 147, 151, 176
Erikson, Thomas H., 164
Evans-Pritchard, Edward E., 138, 144, 149, 151, 166

Faison, Seth, 141
Farber, Bernard, 144, 155
Fattah, Hassan M., 163
Faubion, James D., 136, 152
Ferber, Abby L., 160
Fields, Barbara J., 157
Finkelstein, Israel, 166
Finkler, Kaja, 134
Fletcher, Banister, 180
Foley, Robert A., 146, 148, 170, 171
Foner, Nancy, 175
Fortes, Meyer, 138, 149, 151, 155, 166
Foster, Johanna E., 158
Fox, Robin, 3, 138, 140, 149, 157, 158, 159
Franklin, Sarah, 179

AUTHOR INDEX

Freedman, Maurice, 141, 144, 151
Freeman, Harold P., 157
Freeman, J. D., 157, 158
Friday, Adrian E., 167
Friedberg, Avraham S., 22, 140
Friedman, Asia, 158, 170
Frudakis, Tony N., 134, 148, 149, 160
Fullwiley, Duana, 160

Gamble, Clive, 171
Gardner, Martin, 136
Garroutte, Eva M., 135
Gates, Henry L. Jr., 134, 135, 136, 137, 139, 140
Geary, Patrick J., 154, 162, 170, 176
Geertz, Clifford, 158, 174
Geertz, Hildred, 158, 174
Gellner, Ernest, 136
Germana, Rachelle, 165, 169
Gershoni, Israel, 150, 153
Gibbons, Ann, 148, 149
Gillis, John R., 134
Ginzburg, Carlo, 181
Gobineau, Arthur de, 100, 172
Goldberg, Carey, 136
Goldberg, David T., 154, 156
Goldstein, David B., 162
Gondal, Neha, 178
Goodman, Morris, 90, 138, 167, 168, 169
Goody, Jack, 155, 179
Gordon, David C., 163
Gordon, Milton M., 174, 175
Gould, Stephen J., 141, 146, 147, 151, 168, 171
Grafton, Anthony, 139, 162, 163
Grant, Madison, 105, 110, 111, 175
Gray, Russell D., 138
Grayson, Donald K., 27, 141, 142, 171, 172
Greely, Henry T., 71, 134, 156, 159
Green, Richard E., 170
Greene, John C., 142, 146
Gribbin, John, 167, 168, 169, 170, 179
Gricar, Julie M., 158
Groves, Colin P., 168
Gruber, Jacob W., 141, 142
Guare, John, 22, 140
Guattari, Felix, 152

Guelke, Jeanne K., 135, 178
Gyekye, Kwame, 150

Hackstaff, Karla B., 134, 135
Haebich, Anna, 177
Haeckel, Ernst, 88, 145, 146, 147, 167, 172
Haley, Alex, 162, 173
Hall, Prescott, F., 176
Halpin, Zuleyma T., 144
Hamilton, Jennifer A., 134, 136, 152
Hammer, Michael F., 149
Hammond, Michael, 143, 169, 170
Haney López, Ian, 173
Hareven, Tamara K., 134, 140
Harmon, Marcel J., 180, 181
Harris, Marvin, 160, 173
Hayes, Christine E., 164, 176
Henderson, Mark, 178
Henige, David P., 138, 140, 154, 161, 163, 164
Hennig, Willi, 49, 147, 151, 161
Hepper, Peter G., 159
Herbert, Genevieve, 168
Hervieu-Léger, Danièle, 180
Heuer, Jennifer, 176
Ho, Engseng, 140, 163
Hochschild, Jennifer L., 173
Hoffmann, Léon-François, 156
Hollinger, David A., 145, 150, 153, 173, 174, 177, 178
Hornblower, Margot, 133, 134
Howe, Stephen, 154, 171
Howell, Signe, 135, 179
Howells, William W., 166
Hurston, Zora N., 7, 137
Huxley, Julian, 146
Huxley, Thomas H., 28, 88, 142, 167

Ibn Ishaq, Muhammad, 162
Ignatieff, Michael, 56, 150, 153
Ingold, Tim, 139, 140, 144, 163
Iossifides, A. Marina, 180
Ivemark, Biorn, 161

Jaisson, Pierre, 144
Jankowski, James P., 150, 153
Jay, Nancy, 144, 156

215

Johanson, Donald, 140, 147, 149, 167, 168, 170
Johnson, Marshall D., 140, 141, 164
Jones, Floyd N., 142, 164
Jordan, Peter, 181
Jordan, Winthrop D., 156, 173, 175
Jorde, Lynn B., 149
Jukes, Thomas H., 142

Kahn, Susan M., 158, 178, 179
Kallen, Horace M., 54, 152
Katznelson, Berl, 83, 164
Kaufman, Michael T., 163
Kendall, Henry, 139, 154, 157
Kennedy, Kenneth A. R., 171, 172
Kevles, Daniel J., 174, 177
Keyes, Charles E., 151
Khan, Aisha, 174
King, Marie-Claire, 169
Kittles, Rick A., 134, 136, 137, 148, 159
Klaatsch, Hermann, 101, 172
Klapisch-Zuber, Christiane, 144
Klein, Richard G., 50, 143, 147, 151, 160, 170
Kochen, Manfred, 139
Koerner, Konrad, 146, 181
Kolber, Adam, 178
Kühl, Stefan, 177
Kwon, Hannah, 165

Lamarck, Jean-Baptiste, 29, 30, 142, 146
Lambert, Brian W., 160
Lambert, Ronald D., 141, 172
Lawrence, Cecile A., 156
Leach, Edmund, 158
Lee, Catherine, 150
Lefaucheur, Nadine, 136
Lennon, Joseph, 161, 162, 163
Levine, Donald N., 161, 180
Lévi-Strauss, Claude, 174
Levner, Israel B., 141
Lewin, Roger, 146, 148, 170, 171
Lewis, Bernard, 163
Lewontin, Richard, 140, 149, 170
Li, Jun Z., 148
Lieberson, Stanley, 153
Lifton, Betty J., 136, 153, 177

Lindee, Susan, 152, 153
Linke, Uli, 143
Livingstone, David N., 172
Long, Jeffrey C., 160
Lovejoy, Arthur O., 142, 166
Loveman, Mara, 159, 173
Lowenstein, Jerold, 167
Lowenthal, David, 156, 158, 162, 175, 176, 180
Luckmann, Thomas, 138, 139
Lugris, Jennifer, 179
Lyell, Charles, 142
Lyman, R. Lee, 146, 181

MacDonald, Neil, 161
Mace, Thomas, 181
Malcolm, Noel, 163
Malkki, Liisa H., 152, 163
Mangum, Charles S., 173
Mann, Alan, 168, 169
Marcson, Simon, 175
Marks, Jonathan, 154, 155, 159
Martin, John L., 166
Martínez, María E., 141, 155, 164, 165, 170, 175, 176
Mason, Jennifer, 152
Mayr, Ernst, 142, 143, 145, 146, 147, 151, 166, 176
McCown, Theodore D., 171, 172
McGoldrick, Monica, 178
McKie, Robin, 149, 167, 168
Mead, Margaret, 139
Mellor, Doreen, 177
Meyer, Melissa L., 152, 157
Miele, Frank, 167, 168, 172
Milgram, Stanley, 139, 140
Modell, Judith S., 136, 139, 152, 179
Moore, G. William, 168
Moretti, Franco, 146, 147
Morgan, Gregory J., 148
Morgan, Lewis H., 143, 144, 152, 155
Mörner, Magnus, 165
Morris, Desmond, 93, 169
Mountain, David C., 135, 178
Mullaney, Jamie L., 155
Munasinghe, Viranjini, 109, 174
Muniz, Jeronimo O., 173

Murchie, Guy, 139, 145
Murdock, George P., 157, 158, 174
Murray, Pauli, 173

Nagel, Joane, 153
Nakashima, Cynthia L., 175
Nash, Catherine, 135, 150, 151, 152, 153,
    154, 156, 158, 160, 161, 163, 165
Navarro, Mireya, 173
Nee, Victor, 153
Nelkin, Dorothy, 152, 153
Nelson, Alondra, 133, 134, 136
Neville, Gwen K., 149, 157
Nolland, John, 164
Novak, Michael, 175
Nugent, Colleen, 156
Nuttall, George H., 167

O'Brien, Michael J., 146, 181
O'Hara, Robert J., 147, 172
Olson, Steve, 148, 160, 176
Oppenheimer, Jane M., 147
Owusu-Bempah, Kwame, 135, 136

Padawer, Ruth, 156
Palmer, Craig T., 144, 159
Pálsson, Gísli, 141, 160
Pande, Amrita, 178
Park, Robert E., 173, 182
Parkes, Peter, 155
Patterson, Orlando, 153
Percival, W. Keith, 146, 181
Peters, Emrys, 166
Pinker, Steven, 70, 157, 159, 174
Platnick, Norman I., 181
Polacco, Patricia, 140
Poliakov, Léon, 162, 163, 165, 166, 172, 175
Pool, Ithiel de Sola, 139
Popkin, Richard H., 172
Powell, Brenna M., 173
Preece, Jennifer Jackson, 154
Pringle, Heather, 154, 162, 166

Quinn, Judy, 162

Radcliffe-Brown, Alfred R., 145, 158, 159
Ragoné, Helena, 178

Rash, Felicity J., 175
Read, Dwight W., 141
Read, Peter, 177
Reed, Ishmael, 159
Relethford, John H., 148, 157, 168, 170
Renfrew, Colin, 181
Richards, Robert J., 145, 146, 147
Richmond, Brian G., 168
Ridley, Mark, 142, 145, 151
Ritvo, Harriet, 169
Robertson, Wyndham, 163
Rogers, Alan R., 149
Rosenberg, Daniel, 139, 162, 163
Rosenblum, Doron, 164
Roth, Wendy D., 161
Rothman, Barbara K., 55, 152, 155,
    156, 158
Rubinstein, Amnon, 165
Rudoren, Jodi, 165
Ruvolo, Maryellen, 148

Sand, Shlomo, 163
Sants, H. J., 136, 137
Sarich, Vincent, 98, 167, 168, 170, 172
Satris, Stephen, 156, 173
Schleicher, August, 181
Schleunes, Karl A., 164, 176
Schmidt-Burkhardt, Astrit, 180
Schmitt, Raymond L., 138
Schneider, David M., 31, 54, 144, 152, 154,
    159, 162, 179
Schusky, Ernest L., 144, 158, 159
Schutz, Alfred, 138, 139
Seabrook, John, 156
Segalen, Martine, 178
Seifert, Ruth, 177
Shell, Marc, 156, 180
Sherman, Stuart P., 174
Shils, Edward, 140
Shoumatoff, Alex, 136, 140, 141, 144, 145,
    158, 162, 180
Shriver, Mark D., 134, 137, 148, 159
Shryock, Andrew, 137, 180
Shulevitz, Judith, 137
Silberman, Neil A., 166
Simpson, Bob, 161, 178
Simpson, George G., 143, 147, 151, 176

Simpson, Ruth, 140
Smail, Daniel L., 142,
Smith, Anthony D., 47, 136, 149, 150, 160, 162, 166
Smith, Fred H., 93, 147, 151, 169, 170, 176, 177
Smith, W. Robertson, 164
Sollors, Werner, 109, 152, 154, 155, 156, 165, 169, 174, 176, 178
Sørensen, Preben M., 162
Sorokin, Pitirim A., 140
Sperber, Dan, 159
Spickard, Paul R., 156, 159, 175, 176
Spiegel, Gabrielle M., 139, 140
Spillers, Hortense J., 135
Spruhan, Paul, 134
Stack, Carol, 159, 179
Stanton, William, 171, 172
Steadman, Lyle B., 145, 159
Steichen, Edward, 145
Stein, Arlene, 135, 166
Stepan, Nancy, 171, 172
Stephan, Cookie W., 165
Stephenson, Gilbert T., 156, 173
Stocking, George W., 171, 172
Stoddard, Lothrop, 176
Strathern, Marilyn, 178
Streisand, Betsy, 136
Strickberger, Monroe W., 166
Stringer, Christopher, 149, 167, 168
Strong, Pauline T., 135, 154, 157
Sturm, Circe, 135, 159
Suarez, Tirso, 161
Swadesh, Morris, 181
Swedenburg, Ted, 163
Sweet, Frank W., 154, 155, 157, 176
Sykes, Bryan, 21, 53, 134, 140, 148, 152, 156, 170

Tartakoff, Paola, 164
Tattersall, Ian, 143, 145, 167, 168, 169, 171
Taylor, Rex, 139
Taylor, Robert M., 133, 163
Tëmkin, Ilya, 180
Templeton, Alan R., 171
Thomas, Northcote W., 157

Thompson, Charis, 178, 179
Thompson, E. A., 144, 152
Thorne, Alan G., 171
Timothy, Dallen J., 135
Tönnies, Ferdinand, 152
Trautmann, Thomas R., 28, 142
Triseliotis, John, 136
Tuniz, Claudio, 153, 171
Turner, A. J., 136
Tutton, Richard, 137
Twain, Mark, 64, 157
Twine, France W., 173
Tyler, Katharine, 137

Valentine, James W., 143, 147
van den Berghe, Pierre L., 148, 149, 150, 151, 158, 159, 175
van Mulken, Margot, 180
van Reenen, Pieter, 180
van Winkle, Barrik, 135, 154, 157
van Wyhe, John, 181
Verdery, Katherine, 150, 151, 157, 158, 161
Vogt, Carl, 172
Vryonis, Speros Jr., 166

Wachter, Kenneth W., 140, 157
Wade, Nicholas, 148, 149
Wade, Peter, 165
Wagner, Anthony, 141
Waldinger, Roger, 153
Waldman, Bruce, 144
Warner, W. Lloyd, 138
Washington, Booker T., 64, 157
Waters, Mary C., 153, 158, 161
Watson, Arthur, 139, 140, 144
Watson, Elizabeth E., 169
Watson, Julia, 139, 140
Weber, Max, 150, 179
Weidenreich, Franz, 171
Weinbaum, Alys E., 170
Weiss, Kenneth M., 160
Weiss, Mark, 168, 169
Wells, Rulon S., 146, 181
Wells, Spencer, 133, 134, 145, 148, 149, 177
Whaley, Diana, 162
Wildman, Derek E., 169

Wilkins, David E., 135

Wilkins, Ernest H., 139, 144

Williams, Brackette F., 157

Williams, Yaschica, 177

Williamson, Joel, 154, 156, 173, 175, 176

Wilson, Allan C., 149, 167, 169

Wilson, Margo I., 156

Wilson, Robert R., 141, 143, 151, 161, 164

Wilson, Terry P., 134

Wimmer, Andreas, 150, 153

Winston, Cynthia, 136, 137

Wipperman, Wolfgang, 175

Wittek, Paul, 163

Woese, Carl, 142, 145

Wolfe, Patrick, 157, 173

Wolpoff, Milford H., 143, 146, 151, 170, 171, 172

Wood, Bernard, 143, 145, 168

Wrangham, Richard W., 170

Zack, Naomi, 153, 154, 156, 157, 160, 173, 176

Zangwill, Israel, 108, 174

Zerubavel, Eviatar, 137, 138, 140, 143, 151, 152, 153, 155, 157, 159, 160, 161, 163, 164, 166, 168, 169, 170, 173, 174, 175, 176, 182

Zerubavel, Yael, 163, 164, 165, 179, 181

Zihlman, Adrienne, 167

Zimmer, Carl, 143

SUBJECT INDEX

Abraham, 78, 82, 87, 95
Adams, John Quincy, 115
admixture tests, 4–5, 74
adoption, 7, 55–56, 114, 118
anagenesis, 39
ancestor-centric genealogies, 33, 66
ancestor worship, 4, 34–35, 48
ancestral chains, 21–23, 25, 79, 82, 94, 125
ancestral depth, 16, 26–29, 34, 37, 39,
    46–47, 51, 65, 78, 87, 138n4
ancestral past, 6–7, 84
ancestral ties, 10, 17–18, 26, 53, 61, 67,
    80, 82–83
ancestry, 4–8, 11, 16–17, 24, 32, 35, 42, 55,
    58, 63, 68–71, 74, 103, 117–25, 129–30
anti-miscegenation laws, 112–13
apes, 3, 44, 82–83, 87–94, 98, 101, 117
assimilation, ethnic, 108–10
Australopithecus, 89, 94, 96

belongingness, 9–10, 56, 84
biblical genealogies, 4, 15, 26, 32, 45, 62,
    80–82, 86–87, 100
bilateral descent, 67, 84, 158n86
blended families, 116
blood, 5, 7, 9, 20, 55–58, 60, 62–64, 67, 72,
    88, 99, 102–03, 110–11, 113–14, 118;

"communities of," 55–56; ties, 31, 55–58,
    60, 88, 118
bloodlines, 20, 55, 120
blood quantum, 5, 58
bonobos, 88–92, 94, 168n90
braiding, 84–86, 102, 108, 115
branches, 34, 40–41, 49–50, 95, 97–98,
    101–03, 127, 129–30
branching, 40–41
Buffon, Georges, 27, 29, 40, 87

children, 6–7, 16–18, 25, 32, 42, 54, 61–62,
    64, 68, 84, 86–87, 105–07, 110–11, 114,
    116–17
chimpanzees, 3, 88–94, 101, 168n90
citizenship, 47, 56
cladistics, 39–41, 48–49, 122
cladograms, 41, 50
clans, 47–48, 54, 86, 112
clipping, 82–84, 101, 124
cloning, 117
co-ancestry, 106–07
co-descendants, 10, 34, 36–37, 48, 83, 86,
    98–99, 106
co-descent, 9, 12, 34–35, 46–48, 51, 87,
    122
co-ethnics, 12

common ancestors, 9–10, 34, 36–39, 41–47, 49–51, 59–60, 86, 91, 94, 96–98, 106, 122; recency of, 9, 36–38, 41–44, 49–50, 91, 98, 122, 124

common descendants, sharing, 10, 106, 112

compounding, lexical, 84, 94

co-nationals, 60

consanguinity, 55–56, 60, 118, 121–22, 130; tables, 36

construction: of genealogical communities, 11, 46; of genealogies, 4, 9–10, 36, 77–78, 81–82, 117; of pedigrees, 9, 26, 77, 80–81, 122

contemporaries, 11, 16, 27, 32, 88

cousinhood, 3, 35–39, 49

cousins, 8, 12, 32, 34, 36–39, 43, 45, 59, 71, 87, 89, 91, 112, 121–22, 127; second, 11, 36–37, 39, 43, 46, 60, 112; third, 36–37, 43, 60, 65

Darwin, Charles, 9, 39–42, 48–50, 87

degrees of genealogical separation, 21–22, 36

descendant-centric genealogies, 66

descendants, 4, 6, 10, 16, 19–20, 23, 25–26, 34–36, 42, 48–51, 55, 57, 59–60, 62, 69, 78–82, 95–96, 99, 105

descent, 4, 11, 16–17, 19, 24–25, 39, 42, 47–48, 51, 56, 59, 61, 64, 68, 80, 84, 100, 114, 117–18, 120, 122, 130; common, 39, 47, 60; paths of, 55, 65–67, 71; reckoning, 23, 61–64, 102; tracing, 10, 26, 37–38, 65, 67–68, 71

discontinuity, historical, 27, 78, 124, 164n37

distant ancestors, 19, 37, 51

distant relatives, 4, 36–37, 45, 50, 71–72, 89, 97, 127

DNA, 5, 42, 44, 54, 59, 62, 69–71, 74, 88; mitochondrial, 42, 69–71; Y-chromosomal, 42, 69–71

dummy ancestors, 82

dynasties, 19, 22, 32–33, 119, 125

endogamy, 112

essentialism, 55–60, 70–72, 101, 118, 129

ethnic groups, 3, 9, 47, 56, 73, 110

ethnicity, 9, 47, 56–57, 60, 83, 108, 110, 112, 118

ethno-nations, 12, 47–48, 56–57, 60, 72–73, 86

ethnoracial "essence," 55, 57–58, 70, 73–74, 99

ethnoracial identity, 58, 63, 84

eugenics, 105–06, 114

evolution, 9, 29–30, 32, 39–41, 44–45, 49–50, 88–89, 99, 101, 113, 122

evolutionary trees, 12, 40, 48

exogamy, 106, 112

extinction, 75, 89, 94, 113–14

family, 3, 9, 11–12, 34, 46, 48, 51, 55–56, 67, 72, 75, 83–84, 106–08, 114, 116, 118, 122; extended, 46–47, 56; reunions, 34, 46, 72; taxonomic, 48, 50–51, 89–92, 94; trees, 4, 12, 20, 33–34, 39–42, 48, 77, 103, 117, 127–28, 130

filiation, 16–17, 32, 46, 117–18, 120

forgetting, 9–10, 65, 67–70, 72–73, 78, 83, 95, 101, 157n77

founding ancestors, 24, 34–35, 47, 86, 120, 127

full-bloods, 5

genealogical affinity, 40–41, 43, 54, 88, 93

genealogical amnesia, 68

genealogical anchors, 78

genealogical apartheid, 99

genealogical appropriation, 78, 161

genealogical asymmetry, 61–64, 110–11

genealogical awareness, 11, 16, 19, 66, 78, 130

genealogical bewilderment, 7

genealogical capital, 24, 120

genealogical charts, 24, 34

genealogical claims, 4, 25–26, 47, 51, 60, 62–63, 78–80, 84–85

genealogical communities, 9–10, 46–52, 55, 57, 67, 72, 75, 87, 106, 110, 114, 116

genealogical complexity, 36, 68–69, 84, 102, 116

genealogical connectedness, 8–9, 20, 29, 34, 39, 46

genealogical contamination, 25, 64, 98–99, 111

genealogical continuity, 19–20, 23, 61, 78, 81–83, 124–26, 164n30

genealogical conventions, 9–10, 33, 60, 62, 64–65, 71–72, 77
genealogical credentials, 25
genealogical denial, 68–69, 81, 98, 102
genealogical departure, point of, 79
genealogical distance, 9, 36–39, 43, 49–50, 59–60, 93, 97, 112, 124; measuring, 21–23, 36–37, 42–44
genealogical divergence, 12, 40, 40–45, 51, 88, 91, 98, 101, 113, 122
genealogical embeddedness, 7, 30, 136n34
genealogical engineering, 11, 105–14
genealogical epiphanies, 8
genealogical exclusiveness, 68, 78, 95, 98–99, 101, 103
genealogical fantasies, 7–8, 53–54, 60, 78
genealogical fractions, 4–5, 58, 84, 116
genealogical horizons, 28
genealogical identity, 5–8, 23–25, 47, 51–52, 56, 58, 60–63, 67, 69, 72, 77, 83–84, 108–09, 115–16, 130; multiple, 84, 116
genealogical imagination, 11, 16, 60, 75, 105, 117, 130–31
genealogical inclusiveness, 10, 30, 50–52, 72, 78, 86–87, 92, 94–95, 98
genealogical information, 6, 70, 82
genealogical integration, 88, 106–10, 112, 114
genealogical landscape, 9, 32, 59, 115–16
genealogical memory, 19, 26, 52, 82, 101
genealogical metaphors, 20, 33–34, 41, 47, 108–09, 122, 136n34
genealogical myopia, 83
genealogical narratives, 10, 25, 32–33, 41, 45, 61, 64, 68, 77–78, 81–82, 84, 87, 101–02, 122
genealogical others, 8
genealogical paradoxes, 116–17
genealogical "passports," 25
genealogical proximity, 3–4, 9, 36–37, 41–43, 49, 59, 72, 88, 91–92, 107, 112, 117, 168n90
genealogical purity, 11, 74, 81–82, 99, 102–03, 110–12
genealogical relatedness, 3–4, 8–11, 31–34, 36, 38, 41, 43, 46, 49–50, 54–55, 62, 64, 67–68, 86–87, 105–06, 115–18, 122, 124,

130; measuring, 9, 58; reckoning, 8–10, 59–60, 65, 95, 116
genealogical segregation, 11, 100, 109–14
genealogical stains, 25, 63, 99
genealogical systems, 34, 37, 68
genealogical tactics, 10, 78, 106, 122; prospective, 106–14; retrospective, 79–103
genealogical tents, 87, 98
genealogical topology, 36
genealogical tourism, 6, 117
genealogical tunnel vision, 32, 69
genera, 48, 50–51, 92–93
genes, 42–43, 45, 57, 59–60, 73
genetic ancestry testing, 4, 6, 8, 43, 62, 70, 74, 117
genetic distance, 42–44, 60, 93
genetic makeup, 42–45, 74, 130
genetic markers, 42–44, 73, 115
genetic proximity, 43, 59
Goodman, Morris, 88–92
gorillas, 3, 88–93, 101, 168n90
grandchildren, 66, 86, 105, 107, 117
grandparenthood, 16–19, 26, 32, 35
grandparents, 8, 16–19, 26, 32, 36–37, 39, 57, 65–66, 68, 73, 78, 84, 105
Great Chain of Being, The, 29, 40
great-grandchildren, 105
great-grandparents, 19, 22–23, 26, 36–37, 39, 57, 65, 68, 78, 84
great-great-grandparents, 19, 26, 36–37, 63, 65, 68–69, 97
group-centered conception of genealogy, 33, 66

Haeckel, Ernst, 40, 88, 94
half-breeds, 5
half-siblings, 35, 61, 116
haplogroups, 44, 148n64
heirs, 95, 129
Herder, Johann Gottfried von, 56
hereditary organizations, 25, 80
heredity, 31, 41–42, 57, 59, 73, 111
Hesiod, 4
Hitler, Adolf, 111
hominids, 90–92
hominins, 91–92
hominoids, 89

Homo erectus, 94, 100
homology, 41–42
Homo sapiens, 28, 96, 99
human distinctness, 27, 75, 82, 90, 92–93, 95–98
Huxley, Thomas, 28, 88
hybridity, 85
hyperdescent, 102
hyphenation, 84, 94, 103
hypodescent, 102

inbreeding, 65, 106, 112
incest, 36, 60, 68, 107, 112
indigenousness, 57, 80
in-laws, 11, 55, 106, 116
interbreeding, 40, 74, 113–14
intergenerational contact, 22–23
intergenerational succession, 67
intergenerational transmission, 24–25, 55, 57, 61, 121
intermarriage, 3, 105–06, 108–12, 115
intermediate species, 75, 94

Jacob, 22, 47, 60, 86, 95
Jesus, 15, 25–26, 78, 80–82, 118
jus sanguinis, 47, 56

kin, 47, 106, 112, 118
kin recognition, 37, 72
kinship, 9, 34, 36, 43, 47, 54–56, 59–60, 86–87, 127

Lamarck, Jean-Baptiste, 29–30, 39–40
language, 19, 93
limpieza de sangre, 25, 99, 103
lineage, 19–21, 23–26, 29, 33, 40, 42, 48, 55, 61, 66, 70, 78–79, 81, 98, 120, 124
lines, 20, 29, 33; ancestral, 6, 20, 42, 65, 70, 78, 98–99; maternal, 68, 70, 77; of descent, 20, 67–68, 77, 82, 84, 95, 118, 120–21; of inheritance, 20, 60; of succession, 20; paternal, 23, 61, 68, 77
Linnaeus, Carolus, 50, 87, 92–93
LUCA (Last Universal Common Ancestor), 39

lumping, 86–95, 98, 106, 108, 126, 166n60
Lyell, Charles, 28

maiden name, 67
marginalization, 95–98, 101, 127, 129–31
mathematization, 5, 57–59, 84
matrilineality, 67–68, 116
melting-pot, 108–10, 115
"milk kinship," 60
mixed-bloods, 5, 63
mixophobia, 111
mnemonic dead-ends, 68
Mohammed, 5, 25, 78–79, 81, 120
molecular clock, 44
monogenism, 45, 87
monophyly, 39, 49–50
multiculturalism, 85, 108
multilinearity, 32–33, 39, 41, 78, 84–85, 101, 143n6
multiregionalism, 99–100
mutations, 42–43, 74

names, first, 19, 125. *See also* surnames
naming, 47, 75, 93–94, 118, 124
nations, genealogical foundations of, 11, 47–48, 56–57, 110, 127
nativism, 80, 110
naturalness, 7, 9, 53–56, 59, 74
Neanderthals, 3, 89, 95–99
nephews and nieces, 32
Noah, 79–80, 82, 87
norms of classifying, 9–10, 72, 77
norms of remembrance, 9–10, 65, 67, 77

offshoots, 95, 127, 130
offspring, 8, 43, 63, 67
one-drop rule, 61–64, 69–70, 102–03
order, zoological, 48, 50, 87
organicism, 9–10, 55–57
origins, 8, 28, 39, 47, 49, 65, 67–68, 70–71, 78, 82, 84–85, 98–101, 108; common, 34, 45, 47, 86–87, 98, 126; contaminative, 25, 98, 99; multiple, 65–66, 84–85, 102; separate, 99

outbreeding, 106, 108, 112
out-pasting, 80

"padding" pedigrees, 82
parallel ancestral lines, 99–100
parenthood, 16–17, 26, 35–36, 46, 115, 118
parentlessness, 83, 117
parents, 7–8, 16–19, 24, 32, 35–37, 39, 43, 54–57, 61, 63, 65, 67–68, 78, 83–84, 116
parthenogenesis, 117
passing, 102
pasting, 81–82, 84, 124–25
paternity, 4, 62, 111
patrilineality, 23, 61–62, 67–68, 80–81, 114
patronymics, 23–24
pedigrees, 25–26, 61–62, 68, 77–83, 102, 124; braided, 85–86; deep, 26, 61, 78–80; negative, 25; pure, 82, 99; unilineal, 68
peoplehood, 47, 56–57
person-centered conception of genealogy, 66–67
Perthes, Jacques Boucher de, 27
phenotypic features, 41, 45, 48, 70, 73
phylogenetic trees, 40–41, 50
phylogeny, 40–41, 43–44, 49
polygenism, 99–101, 103
pre-Adamites, 100
primordialism, 56–57
proto-humans, 88, 91
pruning, 101–06, 114
purebloods, 5
purebreds, 79, 85

quasi-ancestral ties, 118–21
quasi-consanguineal ties, 121–22
quasi-familial ties, 55, 117–18

"races," 11, 45, 74–75, 99–101, 111–13
"racial" divisions, 99–101
"racial" purity, 102–03
rape, 8, 102, 111, 114
reification, 54–56, 60, 73, 118
reproductive isolation, 47, 113, 176n43

reproductive technologies, new, 116–17
rootlessness, 83
roots, 54, 56, 80, 83; common, 126; multiple, 66, 84, 86, 103
Roots, 79

Sarich, Vincent, 88, 98
Scriptural chronology, 27–29
siblinghood, 35–36, 46, 116; extensions of, 35–36
siblings, 8, 12, 32, 36–37, 39, 43, 46, 54–56, 59–60, 67, 91–92, 116–17, 122
side branches, 95–97, 127–30
sidelining, 95–97, 101, 127
speciation, 40, 113, 176n43
sperm-bank siblings, 117
sperm donors, 6–7, 116
splitting, 98–101, 106, 114
step-parenthood, 116
stretching, 79–80, 82, 84, 87
subfamily, taxonomic, 91–92, 168n90
succession, 20, 67, 95–96, 118–19, 126, 129
surnames, 19, 23–24, 51, 61, 67, 83–84, 93
surrogacy, 116–17
symbolic ancestry, 117–25, 129
symbolic consanguinity, 121–23
symbolic descent, 118–21; intellectual, 120–21; spiritual, 118, 120, 126
symbolic genealogical communities, 126–27
symbolic heirs, 124–30
symbolic kinship, 118, 121–22, 127
symbolic lineages, 118–21, 124–25

taxa, 48, 50
taxonomy, biological, 48–50, 75, 87, 89–93, 101
traditions of classifying, 9–10, 72, 75, 77
traditions of forgetting, 9, 65, 68–69
traditions of reckoning relatedness, 10
traditions of remembering, 9, 65, 67, 77
transmutation, 29–30, 39
trees, 34, 36, 40–41, 54, 121–22, 129. See also evolutionary trees, family trees, phylogenetic trees

tribalism, 25, 47, 86, 115
tribes, 47, 110; taxonomic, 92
trunk, 34–35, 54, 95, 98, 127, 129–30

uncles and aunts, 32–33, 39, 55, 86,
    95, 97
undesirable ancestors, 82

undesirable relatives, 83, 98–99
unilinearity, 32, 39–40, 68, 78, 84, 88,
    102, 143n6

Vogt, Karl, 101

Wilson, Allan, 88